The Fanfiction Reader

The Fanfiction Reader

Folk Tales for the Digital Age

Francesca Coppa

University of Michigan Press
Ann Arbor

Published in the United States of America by the
University of Michigan Press
Printed and bound by CPI Group (UK) Ltd, Croydon, CR0 4YY

2020   2019   2018   2017   4   3   2   1

A CIP catalog record for this book is available from the British Library.

Library of Congress Cataloging-in-Publication data has been applied for.

ISBN 978-0-472-07348-1 (hardcover : alk. paper)
ISBN 978-0-472-05348-3 (paper : alk. paper)
ISBN 978-0-472-12278-3 (e-book)

Spydere man spydere man
Doth al things a spydere kan
Sondry webbes he kan weaven
Thieves lyke flyes he kan cacchen
Lo anon comth spydere man
    —Chaucer Doth Tweet @LeVostre GC (July 12, 2015)

Preface

One Pringle, One Dorito, One Oreo

So there are about a thousand ways in which a book like this is a crazy idea.

Story selection, I can tell you, was unbelievably difficult: not only is there no way to comprehensively survey the field (who can read literally millions of stories?), but fanfiction has, among its many other merits, a freewheeling and fabulous disregard for traditional story lengths. I can point you to wonderful stories that are one hundred words long (drabbles, we call them) and great stories of over a million words. And in fact, some of the best fanfiction stories out there are on the longer side: stories that do considerable world building, or shift the terms of the source universe in some profound way.

But I couldn't include these stories[1] if I wanted this book to have any breadth: unlike fanfiction writers, I *am* bound by traditional publishing categories, and so I only have a certain number of words to play with. So I've looked for stories of about five thousand words, and while length is not necessarily an indicator of complexity, I have to admit that I have fantasized about doing a volume that contains three thirty-thousand- or two forty-five-thousand-word stories: such a volume would necessarily be a very different beast.

Then there's the question of what fandoms to include. Most people prefer to read fanfiction featuring characters they recognize, but a lot of fanfiction is written about stories, movies, and TV shows that are a bit off the beaten track. Fans love the cult, the obscure, the canceled, the foreign; fans are often motivated to transform the mediocre, the *really-nearly-almost great,* into the marvelous by loving it into being with our brains: we tell it the way it should have happened. So a lot of fanfiction has been written about TV shows and characters that a nonfan might not have heard of: *The Professionals, Highlander, Blake's 7, Due South, Stargate SG1, Quantum Leap, Forever Knight, The Sentinel, Sports Night, Xena: Warrior Princess, Stargate: Atlantis, Hercules, Firefly.* That's not even to go into the question of Western versus Eastern media (fanfiction about anime and manga are extremely popular, and there are thousands of individual sources for fic) and different genres: fanfiction about video games, or radio plays, or Korean pop stars, or, most obviously, books: obviously there is a very long tradition of literary fanfiction and pastiche, and one could do a whole reader just on that; in fact, one could argue that a good chunk of the mainstream literary tradition already *is* that.

But a line has to be drawn somewhere, so this book is not only limited to Western media fandoms, but to some of the biggest and best-known examples: *Batman, Star Trek, Buffy the Vampire Slayer, Doctor Who, Sherlock Holmes, Harry Potter.* But even as I've chosen these fandoms specifically to appeal to a broad range of readers—and I have been lucky enough to have been able to test-drive various iterations of this book with my students at Muhlenberg College as well as with students at the University of Pennsylvania—I can't help but regret the missed opportunities: for example, to introduce you to characters like Benton Fraser or Aeryn Sun, if you don't already know them; or to bring you to Atlantis or Twin Peaks or Babylon 5 or the Redverse of *Fringe.*

I've also tried to choose stories that are comprehensible. That may sound like an obvious criterion, but a lot of the best works of fanfiction are not comprehensible to a general reader, just as a lot of the best poetry depends on you having a fairly deep knowledge of the traditions and history of poetry, and the better you know Homer's *Odyssey,* the better you'll understand Joyce's *Ulysses.* A lot of terrific fanfiction stories are not only immersed in the specific details that comprise the canon of a particular world—requiring you to know more about the history of Vulcan or the origins of the First Slayer or the various and contradictory backstories of Bucky Barnes than you might—but in the traditions of fandom and fanfiction writing itself.

Like other art forms, fanfiction has its own genres and tropes, its own preoccupations and obsessions, and its own ways of demonstrating literary competence and mastery. While some fans do stay in a single fandom for their entire lives, devoted to *Star Trek* or *The Man from U.N.C.L.E.* or *The*

West Wing, others migrate from story world to story world, taking their practices and traditions with them. Henry Jenkins used Michel de Certeau's term *nomads* to describe fans who are "constantly advancing upon another text, appropriating new materials, making new meanings."[2] Fans have described this movement across fandoms (positively) as being like a "fannish butterfly" or (more controversially) as "migratory slash fandom," the latter phrase sometimes being used to critique other fans as too dedicated to the erotic tropes of slash fiction and insufficiently dedicated to the particular characters or stories to which they're applying them.

But whether we see fans as flying or flighty, it's hard to deny that the movement of fanfiction fans across story worlds has resulted in a series of literary practices and conceits that make perfect sense if you're a part of the culture—and may be incomprehensible to those outside of it. That said, I have tried in the introductions to these stories to make those practices, tropes, and conceits visible when present. A culturally attuned fan would know what to make of a *Five Things* story or a *Mary Sue*, a *genderswap* or a *racebending* story. They'd have no problem parsing an *mpreg* story or an *alpha-beta-omega* universe. They'd rate a successful *casefic*, appreciate the attempt at *kidfic*, and give points for the clever use of vampires, soulbonding, wings, or tentacles.

How would fannish readers know these things? They'd have seen them before; over and over, in fact. A fanfiction-reading fan would come to see how one fanfiction story was reacting to another, how one narrative idea was building upon another. They'd know what was *canon* (that is, a fact or piece of information from the original source) and what was *fanon* (a fan-authored idea or interpretation that is so perfect, so convincing or fun that other fan-authors simply adopt it wholesale) in the story; what was innovative and what was the creative application of a well-loved trope. A fan would likely be immersed in a whole universe of fanfiction—not just within the fandom of the story, but across a whole series of fandoms stretching back through her life as a fan of fanworks.

This leads me to the most perverse thing about this book: that I am giving you one Pringle, one Dorito, and one Oreo. A single nacho, one pretzel nugget. A tiny little tester teaspoon of ice cream. One pita triangle's worth of hummus. Now, as I really hope I don't have to explain to you, it's unnatural to eat a single Pringle or one Oreo. Oreos are meant to be eaten in sleeves, with a giant glass of milk.[3] The experience of fandom, especially in the age of the internet, is one of binge reading: most new fans, upon discovering fanfic, gobble it down. The first story you read is usually an eyebrow raiser; shocking, maybe a bit embarrassing. "What is this craziness? Do people really do this? I don't think I like it. Are they all like this? Let me just look at one more . . ." And then the next thing you know, it's four in the morning, it's three days later, it's ten years on. You are at your friend's house, and the floor around you is covered with zines. You are on the internet, and you haven't showered in days. Your browser history is a dreadful embarrassment. You've read roughly forty-five thousand stories, some of them amazing, many of them terrible, and you now have all sorts of opinions about tropes and genres. You have developed a particular taste in fanworks. You really like *femslash*, or *hurt/comfort*, or *cavefic*, or long, plotty *gen*. But I guarantee you this: no matter what you like, and no matter how much there is of it—*there isn't enough of it.*

And so some readers (and some of you) will start to write. You'll write the thing you want to read, because how hard can it be? You can do better than that story you read last night. And that other story you read was okay—except, you know what would have been *really* good? You know what would have been *great? This. This is gonna be great.*

That is the experience of fanfiction, and it's an experience I can't create for you in this book. Moreover, it's often—as I think my metaphor makes clear—a gendered experience. The advent of Netflix and on-demand services notwithstanding, the experience of binge watching, binge reading, binge eating, has historically been cast as female, and as indubitably bad (although not all forms of passionate engagement are; it seems to be fine to be glued to the sports channel, and you're not a freak if you finish a video game that takes sixty-five or seventy hours of gametime). One of the most derided figures in Western culture is the woman in sweatpants watching television and eating ice cream out of the carton,[4] and I've often thought about why that woman is so detested. I think it's because she is not objectified at that moment. She is not dressed to please. That woman is enjoying herself—she is feasting her eyes, she is eating something delicious, she is wearing comfortable clothes. She is feeling pleasure. She is enjoying a story. If this woman has had or is maybe about to have an orgasm,[5] everything would be perfect.

What I am describing characterizes an experience of art that certainly predates media fandom: it is the experience of early nineteenth-century novel reading[6] that Jane Austen describes in *Northanger Abbey*, when devoted reader Catherine Moreland falls for Henry Tilney, a fellow fan who has gobbled "hundreds and hundreds" of novels and is willing to engage with Catherine "in the never-ceasing inquiry of 'Have you read this?' and

'Have you read that?'"[7] It is the experience of late nineteenth-century theatergoing described by critic A. B. Walkley when he sneers at young women at the matinees who are watching the play while eating chocolates, then the latest theatrical refreshment. "To see scores of women simultaneously eating chocolate at the theatre is an uncanny thing. They do it in unison, and they do it with an air of furtive enjoyment, as though it were some secret vice and all the better for being sinful."[8] It is the experience of going to the movies once a week, eating popcorn and watching the A picture, the B movie, the newsreel, and a couple of cartoons; it's the experience of eating hotdogs and watching baseball all season long.

It is the experience of fandom. So if you like these stories—or if you're a bit freaked out by them, and want to see if they're all like this (or maybe you want to read just one more, just to be sure you don't like it)—then take yourself to the Archive of Our Own, or to Fanfiction.net, or to Wattpad, or maybe even take yourself to the library at the University of Iowa or the University of California at Riverside or Texas A&M (all of which have large fanfiction zine collections) and check out how fans used to do it in the predigital age.

There's lots more where this came from, is what I'm saying. Read your heart out.

Contents

Acknowledgments

This book came out of a postpanel discussion with Kristina Busse at Media in Transition 5: wouldn't it be great, I asked her, if we could put out a collection of fanfiction modeled on the *Canterbury Tales*? Kristina, who loves fan tropes, immediately began to brainstorm with me; I still have my hastily typed notes from that day, and I am grateful to her both for her encouragement and for her brainwork in support of this book.

Peter Decherney and the Department of Cinema Studies at the University of Pennsylvania graciously offered me the opportunity to teach fan studies as the Wolf Professor of Television Studies: many thanks to the students of Television and Fan Culture and Sherlock, James, and Harry: Transmedia Characters. I want to thank Rebecca Tushnet, Phil Malone, and the team at Stanford's Juelsgaard Intellectual Property and Innovation Clinic (Bethany Bengfort, Eric Dunn, Jef Pearlman) for reviewing the manuscript; their support and guidance was invaluable. Rebecca Tushnet and Jessica Litman helped this book find a supportive home at the University of Michigan Press, and brought me to my fantastic editor, Mary Francis.

Last but not least I have to thank my academic home, Muhlenberg College, for its enthusiastic support of my scholarship. This book was partly written with the support of Muhlenberg's Class of '32 Research Professorship, as well as other research funds and travel support provided by the Provost. These stories were read and analyzed by my Muhlenberg students year after year; they were my best readers. This book is for them.

(This book is not, per se, for fandom: fandom doesn't need this book, though I hope all fans of fanfiction enjoy it. But you don't need one Pringle, one Dorito, and one Oreo, guys. You have the banquet; you can have anything and everything on the menu.)

Introduction

Five Things That Fanfiction Is, and One Thing It Isn't

Fanfiction, and the broader culture of fandom within which fanfiction is written and read, seems to keep being discovered, and rediscovered, and re-rediscovered. Hardly a day goes by without some media outlet or other "discovering" fanfiction, though thankfully the tone of these articles is starting to change: fanfiction is no longer presented as a wacky thing that only strange people do, as if writing fiction was any weirder a hobby than gardening or painting or being in a garage band. In fact, fanfiction has become an increasingly mainstream art form, and fandom itself is moving fast from subculture to culture. More people than ever participate in some form of organized fan activity like reading or writing fanfiction, creating fan art, making fan films or vids, organizing wikis, collecting merchandise, writing meta, doing cosplay—or if they don't do these things themselves, they likely know someone who does.

Far from being a new phenomenon, fanfiction has a critical literature over forty years old. In 1975, in their famous last chapter of *Star Trek Lives* entitled "Do-It-Yourself Star Trek—the Fan Fiction," Jacqueline Lichtenberg, Sondra Marshak, and Joan Winston describe the same kinds of stories that you can find today at Fanfiction.net or the Archive of Our Own, everything "from outright sexual fantasies . . . to straight adventure, to tender love stories, to hilarious parodies, to provocative, voluminous, long-running series fiction."[1] Lichtenberg, Marshak, and Winston not only described and celebrated fanfiction (and wrote it themselves; Lichtenberg was nominated for a Hugo for her *Star Trek* fanfiction in 1974), but they also expanded the audience for it. "Do-It-Yourself Star Trek—the Fan Fiction" was many people's first exposure to the idea of fanfiction, and after reading about the wonderful range of stories described, many were moved to seek fanfiction out.

But what exactly is fanfiction? There are various ways to define it, each slightly different and none of them correct or exclusive. In fanfiction, fans have a genre called the "Five Things" story: a classic Five Things offers a reader five (often contradictory) scenarios featuring the same characters. In the spirit of a Five Things story, I hereby offer you five definitions of fanfiction, each with its own distinct emphasis; in fact, I'll give you what fans call a "5 + 1," or "Five Things That Fanfiction Is, and One That It Isn't."

1. Fanfiction is fiction created outside of the literary marketplace

> A lot of fanfic authors go on to become professional authors, and keep on writing fanfic in whatever spare time they have. I am not a special snowflake in this regard. I belong to a blizzard.
> —Seanan McGuire[2]

The term "fanfiction" comes out of science fiction fandom, where *fan* fiction was defined against *professional* fiction, and originally meant nothing more than original science fiction stories written in a nonprofessional or semiprofessional context, like a low-budget periodical or a zine. Many fanfiction writers aspire to be professional writers, and so write for practice and experience. But also, in the science fiction community, most if not all professional writers still identify as science fiction fans (even as poets must be poetry fans, and musicians music fans, though they might not take on a "fan" identity as such), and so may also write for low or no pay in certain contexts: this work is still commonly described as "fan" work, as opposed to normal paid, professional work. The World Science Fiction Society continues to give a Hugo Award for Best Fan Writer, and there is no rule that says that the award can't be won by someone who also publishes professionally. The award is given for fiction or nonfiction that appears in a semiprozine or fanzine, and now, increasingly, on a website or blog.

In the late 1960s, a group of mostly female science fiction fans—who would later reimagine themselves as "media" fans—began producing fanfiction that was even further outside of the literary marketplace in that it didn't even aspire to be "original"—and thus potentially publishable—fiction. Rather, as Camille Bacon-Smith has noted, it was created "for an insider audience trained to share in the conventions of the literature."[3] The fanfiction produced by media fans thus began to move "in a very different direction"[4] than the protoprofessional fanfiction produced in the science fiction community, with very different results; as Catherine Tosenberger has argued, writing fiction outside of the marketplace

> allows people to stake claims over texts that they wouldn't normally be allowed to if they wanted to publish, and frees them to tell the stories they want to tell. You can do things in fanfiction that would be difficult or impossible to do in fiction intended for commercial publication, such as experiments with form and subject matter that don't fit with prevailing tastes.[5]

One could argue that, today, media fanfiction is starting to function more like amateur science fiction does: that is, as direct preparation for a professional writing career. Some media fanfiction is finding a place in the market through old vehicles like tie-in novels and new vehicles like Kindle Worlds, and some fans are being solicited by literary agents and being offered publishing contracts on the strength of their fanfiction. Work created outside of the literary marketplace thus can be seen as a calling card or portfolio. But fanfiction is rarely a mere entry point to the market, instrumental: most fan-turned-professional writers continue to write fanfiction for fun (and for free) even as they write other stories for money, showing that fanfiction is its own thing with its own intrinsic value, and continues to be "outside the market" in important ways, routinely defying commercial norms in terms of theme, length, genre, and style.

What's important is that "fan" in this context indicates nothing about either the *originality* of the story elements or a story's *quality*; rather, it simply distinguishes work done for love (the original meaning of *amateur*) from work done for money. And one can argue that this definition is still the essential one. Fans do creative work that one could get paid for in the marketplace—if one were willing to accept the limitations and restrictions that make it more like work and less like self-expression. But most fanfiction writers write for love rather than for money, and to their own specifications rather than the market's.

2. Fanfiction is fiction that rewrites and transforms other stories

What doesn't change, or rather, what never disappears, is the writerly habit of writing from sources.
—Anne Jamison[6]

Discussions of fanfiction tend to focus more on its appropriative aspects than its noncommercial ones. The definition of fanfiction that most people think of today is more like Lev Grossman's: "stories and novels that make use of the characters and settings from other people's professional creative work."[7] Grossman puts emphasis on fanfiction's engagement with other texts, and he therefore connects fanfiction to more mainstream literary works like Tom Stoppard's *Rosencrantz and Guildenstern Are Dead* (which rewrites *Hamlet*) and Jean Rhys's *Wide Sargasso Sea* (which retells *Jane Eyre*). Grossman asserts that all these works have the same goals: to assert "the rights of storytellers to take possession of characters and settings of other people's narratives and tell their own tales about them—to expand and build upon the original, and, when they deem it necessary, to tweak it and optimize it for their own purposes."[8]

This move connects fanfiction to the broader literary tradition; in her book *Fic*, Anne Jamison connects fanfiction to Shakespeare's *Hamlet* (the qualifier is necessary because, as Jamison explains, "Shakespeare [himself] wrote fic for the Ur-Hamlet," and that fic was "more compelling than its source")[9] and to the Arthurian tales, wryly framing Chrétien de Troyes's "Lancelot: The Knight of The Cart" as a threesome written for a long-ago Arthurian fanfiction challenge: "a request for Arthur/Lancelot/Guinevere with a cart (the exact wording of the request has been lost)."[10] Fans often construct this sort of literary lineage for themselves, arguing—only partly tongue in cheek—that Dante was not only writing Virgil fanfic in the *Inferno*, but a "Gary Stu" (a self-insert of the author) to boot.

This idea is also behind my organization of this book as a modern *Canterbury Tales*. Then as now, we pass the time by telling stories to each other; fanfiction reminds us that storytelling isn't a professional activity, but a human one in which originality and publishability is rarely the point. As in the *Canterbury Tales*, storytelling in fandom is social, communal, responsive; a game of sorts. The *Tales* is organized as a storytelling challenge ("That each of you, beguiling the long day / Shall tell two stories as you wend your way / To Canterbury town; and each of you / On coming home shall tell another two") of a kind familiar to any fanfiction writer. Fandom loves story challenges—ficathons and fests, Secret Santas and Big Bangs, porn battles, flash fiction, bingo challenges, Yuletide[11]—which encourage and organize creativity for the general pleasure of the group; just as the pilgrims get to hear all the tales, challenge participants get to read the glut of stories produced. And as the Host notes, this storytelling game shall "give you joy, and it shall cost you nought."

Moreover, as in Chaucer, not only are the framework and the tropes not original (others had used the pilgrimage to structure stories; others had told of the "loathly lady" and of patient Griselda) but the characters aren't the social-realistic individuals of the modern novel, but familiar types: the Knight, the Squire, the Merchant, the Clerk. The characters that fandom loves are similarly archetypical: the Starship Captain, the Spy, the Wizard, the Detective. And that might be James Kirk, James Bond, Harry Potter, and Sherlock Holmes—or it might be Mal Reynolds, Jason Bourne, Gandalf, and Veronica Mars—but the stories keep circulating. Our cultural myths, the stories that tie us together, are not about knights but about Jedi Knights, not lords but Time Lords. We love scientists, pilots, warriors and kings, gods and aliens; Prometheus and Icarus, Hercules and Arthur, Thor and Superman. Fanfiction is an essential part of the process by which these characters are expanded and made epic, loved by their fans into greatness.

Books become important when their interpretations are contested, when new readings of them are developed. Plays become important when they enter the repertory: as the theater scholar Alan Sinfield has noted, Shakespeare remains relevant because he is constantly interfered with:[12] Shakespeare has an army of fans—actors, directors, designers, critics—interpreting his characters, adding meanings that he never intended and making the stories relevant to new and different audiences. *Richard III* isn't about fascism; *Othello* isn't about race in America; *The Merchant of Venice* was not originally in conversation with the Holocaust. *Hamlet* is not about a graduate student who doesn't get along with his family. Except of course it is; of course they are. And, in literature as in fanfiction, some interpretations or elaborations of the source are so great they become what fans call "fanon," that is, a take on canon so convincing or fun that it's adopted by other fans wholesale. For instance, nearly everyone seems to agree, in the wake of Ernest Jones's study *Hamlet and Oedipus*, that Hamlet has an Oedipus complex; the Arthur/Lancelot/Guinevere triangle is now a permanent part of the mythos; and Sherlock Holmes now says "Elementary!" and wears a deerstalker cap.

Holmes has not been harmed or made less valuable by the thousands of interpretations of him across literature, radio, television, film, video games, and other media; in fact, one could argue that the free hand that Arthur Conan Doyle gave his collaborators in interpreting Holmes—he told playwright William Gillette, "You may marry him, murder him, or do anything you like to him"—is largely responsible for the great detective's great success. Far from harming literary characters, appropriation and re-writing are the making of them. We care about Rosencrantz and Guildenstern because of Stoppard; nobody cares about Reynaldo. (Yet.)

3. Fanfiction is fiction that rewrites and transforms stories currently owned by others

Fan fiction is a way of the culture repairing the damage done in a system where contemporary myths are owned by corporations instead of owned by the folk.
—Henry Jenkins[13]

A definition of fanfiction that only emphasizes its continuities with the literary tradition does not explain why *Rosencrantz and Guildenstern Are Dead* launched Stoppard's theatrical career and *Pride and Prejudice and Zombies* was a huge publishing success while most fanfiction has had to fight for its right to exist, let alone be recognized as valuable. While in my heart—and in my organization of this book—I agree with the idea that fanfiction is no different than other literary retellings or reimaginings, and that in fact retelling and reimagining—*revision*—is at the very heart of all creativity, full stop—I have often found it useful to define fanfiction more narrowly as "creative material featuring characters that have previously appeared in works whose copyright is held by others."[14]

The legal distinction is not meaningless—far from it; it has marginalized a group of (mostly female) writers and their literary practices. The definition of fanfiction as applying only to works currently covered by copyright, trademark, or some other intellectual property scheme serves to emphasize the (very odd) fact that stories can be *owned*. This is a relatively recent phenomenon, and one can argue, in Kristina Busse's formulation, that "copyright *embraced* and in a way *needed* an aesthetic theory that emphasized the original creation"[15] of an individual genius author, and furthermore that fans still embrace that formulation to the extent to which we sign our names—or our pen names, which are as reputation-bearing in fandom as legal names are in the regular world—to our fanfiction stories. But increasingly, the stories that we share on a national or even global level—the mass-media stories that Henry Jenkins refers to as "contemporary myths"—aren't even owned by individual auteurs, but by huge corporate conglomerates: that is, movie studios, television networks, production companies, and, increasingly, online behemoths like Apple, Netflix, Amazon, and Google. The average person is—in the Marxist sense—alienated from the process of storytelling.

It is only in such a system—where storytelling has been industrialized to the point that our shared culture is owned by others—that a category like "fanfiction" makes sense. Everyone's always surprised by how huge the world of fanfiction is; I'm not. Fanfiction is what happened to folk culture: to the appropriation of fables and the retellings of local legends, to the elaborations of tall tales and drinking songs and ghost stories told round the campfire. Fanfiction is the bastard child; the disavowed heir; outlawed.

4. Fanfiction is fiction written within and to the standards of a particular fannish community

> It starts like this. Somewhere, in cyberspace, someone complains: "I had a lousy day! Need some cheering up." Soon after, a friend posts a story dedicating the piece: "This is for you, hon—your favorite pairing and lots of schmoopy sex. Hope it'll cheer you up!"
> —Kristina Busse and Karen Hellekson[16]

If you only define fanfiction in terms of its engagement with other stories, copyrighted or not, there's no distinction between fanfiction and, say, Gregory McGuire's novel *Wicked* (which retells *The Wizard of Oz* from the Wicked Witch of the West's point of view), or Michael Chabon's *The Final Solution* (which features a beekeeping detective uncannily like Sherlock Holmes). But it seems that there ought to be a distinction. Sure, unlike fanfiction, these books were produced for the market, but fanfiction isn't simply fiction created *outside* the market; it's also fiction produced *inside* the community and within the culture of fandom. One could argue that every girl to some degree invents fanfiction for herself: alone in her bedroom, she wonders "what if" and changes the story in her head. She may even write it down. But it's when she begins to share her work and to read and write with other fans that her stories become fanfiction per se, and begin to be shaped to community norms and expectations. Fans often experience the finding of fan community as a kind of homecoming: "I didn't know other people did this, too."

Fanfiction is a case study in community production and reception; what fanfiction writer, *New York Times* best-selling author, and Archive of Our Own founder Naomi Novik calls "the network." "Fanfiction," she notes, "is not just written from one single person, speaking to an audience"; rather, the stories are written within, from, and for a community, and these stories "communicate with one another, and they communicate with what's in canon at that particular time."[17] We can therefore define fanfiction as *networked creative work produced within and for a community of fans*; in particular, the (largely female) media fans who split from science fiction fandom in the late 1960s and early 1970s, and their exponentially multiplying descendants, who have communicated and organized over the years via BBS, Usenet, mailing lists, blogging and journaling platforms, Twitter, and Tumblr.[18] This community, as Mel Stanfill has noted, "isn't really just one community, but people who have been in fandom for a while, and in several fandoms over time, have been exposed to and/or acculturated into a set of practices and values that has had some continuity."[19]

In their introduction to *The Fan Fiction Studies Reader*, Kristina Busse and Karen Hellekson note that some from this group became fans of fanfiction itself:

> Fan fiction began to create its own fandom with its own infrastructure. Zines might include fan fiction from a variety of shows and cons, such as Media*West, held in Lansing, Michigan, which even today brings together media fans from multiple film and TV texts to celebrate and share fan creations, including fan fiction, filk, cosplay, vids, art, and crafts. Although there are many different forms of derivative and transformative fiction based on other media texts, the term fan fiction as the majority of fan scholars use it mostly tends to adhere to this tradition. As a result, other developing traditions, such as yaoi, boys' love, Sherlockian published pastiches, fantasies depicting fan relationships with their favorite movie stars, or even fan-written soap opera scripts often do not fit the generalizations put forth about fan fiction and media fandom.[20]

By this definition, engagement with the community is crucial; fanfiction is not just any continuation or interpretation of a story, but one that happens within, because of, and for a particular community.

This isn't a simple matter of fandom being the audience or the marketplace for the work; rather, the key point is that fanfiction is shaped to the literary conventions, expectations, and desires of that community, and is written in genres developed by and in community—for example, in media fandom, *slash*, *het*, and *gen*, *first-time* stories and *alternate universe* stories and *sex pollen* stories and *cavefic* stories and *mpreg* stories. *Bodyswap*, *hurt/comfort*, *kidfic*, *hookerfic*, PWP (plot what plot?), *epilogue tags*, *fix its*, *teamfic*, *slavefic*, *undercover in a gay bar*—these[21] and literally hundreds more are as familiar to fans as the bildungsroman, lyric, tragedy, elegy, and epic are to literary scholars. They are labels indicating a set of narrative and thematic expectations. Anime and manga fandom has its own artistic styles, language, and forms that have now crossed into other communities: for example, *lemon* or *lime* for designating the intensity of erotic content; *yaoi* and *yuri* and *boys' love* and *magical girls*. More recent fans talk of *one shots* (vs. serials) and have developed genres like the *alpha/beta/omega* (A/B/O) universe, where sexual roles have a biological basis and are adopted from the study of animal behaviors, or *imagines*, self-insert teen fantasies ("Imagine being friends with Catwoman and your father, Bruce Wayne, catches you while stealing jewels from a rich family," "Imagine passing notes to Harry in class"). The point here is not to catalog all the various tropes and genres, which I couldn't possibly do anyway, but to argue that fanfiction is written within and for particular communities that have highly specific expectations for fiction, which can be seen in their elaborate vocabulary and critical literature, which fans call *meta*. Fans have never had any trouble explaining themselves to themselves, or their work to each other, in essays written for zines or on websites like The Fanfic Symposium, or Metafandom, or Fanhackers, or Fanlore.

The fiction that is written in and for fandom is not only written to community specifications; it is also typically written as a gift. This means more than that the work is written outside the marketplace; rather, it implies a whole social structure around gift giving and receiving. Fanfiction reading and writing tends to create social obligations: many people write their first story to say thank you for all the stories they read previously, to give something back to the community that's fed them, narratively speaking.

In her famous 1999 essay, "Slash Fiction Is Like a Banquet" (sometimes known as "the hummus essay" for its central metaphor), Arduinna compares the slash fanfiction community to a big, pot-luck banquet, but complains that lately everyone's bringing the same thing to the table: lemon-garlic hummus.

> And for a long time, this banquet was sort of hidden away. People came, and enjoyed. Those who decided to contribute maybe started out on appetizers, but soon moved on to bringing other dishes as well. So the table kept expanding, as people kept adding more dishes. Some of the earlier dishes got pushed back into the shadows, but people remembered them, and talked about them, and newcomers eventually found their way back there to try them.
>
> Then a while ago, the doors to the banquet hall were thrown open, and people at the banquet looked out and smiled and said, "hey, come on in and enjoy! And if any of you can cook, great! Bring your favorite dish, we'd love to try it. If not, feel free to just eat whatever you want—we love having diners as well as cooks." And people came to the banquet and enjoyed. And a lot of them wanted to contribute, because they were having such a wonderful time. So they decided on an appetizer, but because they weren't really sure of their cooking ability yet, they went out and got a tub of store-bought lemon-garlic hummus and some pita bread, and that's what they brought. People were pleased; hummus is good! So there were all these little bowls of hummus, all with the exact same ingredients mixed in the exact same way, taking up more and more of the banquet table. And every time new people walked into the banquet hall, they'd see a table full of bowls of lemon-garlic hummus, and think "oh, it's a lemon-garlic hummus banquet! I can do that!" and they'd go buy the same hummus and put it in a bowl and put it on the table.[22]

Arduinna's essay is a critique of what she sees as the homogenization of stories by the sudden influx of new fans in the late 1990s, but it's her metaphor that's striking: fanfiction is a banquet that fans make together, with everyone cooking and diners prized as much as cooks. (There's a reason I use a food metaphor in the preface, "One Pringle, One Dorito, one Oreo"; the fan community I come from values communal eating.) It also values the gift: Karen Hellekson talks about the importance of gift culture to fandom in her essay "A Fannish Field of Value: Online Fan Gift Culture." She points out that fanworks—fanfiction, as well as vids, art, archives, meta, wikis, and so on—are given by fans to each other to create solidarity, a social structure. These gifts "are incorporated into a multivocal dialogue that creates a metatext, the continual composition of which creates a community. . . . The individuality of that piece is lost; it becomes a part of something greater."[23] This is another of the underlying assumptions of the preface: that there's something perverse about looking at a single fanfiction story in isolation, apart from the community that produced it.

There has lately been some pressure on the idea of fanworks as a gift. Fans themselves have questioned what's at stake in keeping fanfiction, a female-dominated art form, out of the marketplace. In her 2007 essay "How Fanfiction Keeps Us Poor," Cupidsbow notes, "A friend of mine who works in the publishing industry has two major objections to fanfiction: it's derivative and it keeps women poor. I think the 'derivative' argument has been well answered within the fanfic community, so I won't rehash it here. But the 'keeps women poor' comment made me pause." Does fanfiction's commitment to gift culture keep a huge swath of women's writing "in the unpaid ghetto along with other women's crafts"?[24] In a 2009 article, "Should Fanfiction Be Free?" Abigail DeKosnik claimed that fanfiction was fast approaching its "Sugarhill moment," that is, "the moment when an outsider takes up a subculture's invention and commodifies it for the mainstream before insiders do."[25] DeKosnik argued that female fans should commodify fanfiction themselves, both to do it right (that is, before the outsiders) and so that women could begin to profit from this female-dominated literary form instead of "giving our talents away as gifts."[26]

In 2012 that more or less happened: E. L. James published *Fifty Shades of Grey*, a version of her *Twilight* fanfiction "Master of the Universe," and made an enormous amount of money. In 2015, DeKosnik wrote a follow-up article, "Fifty Shades and the Archive of Women's Culture," in which she argued that *Fifty Shades* should not be equated with fanfiction because it was published "as a unique text rather than as a text embedded in a larger archive of fictions produced by a particular community of predominantly women writers and readers," James having disavowed the community within which *Fifty Shades of Grey* was created. DeKosnik was not the only one to disqualify *Fifty Shades* as fanfiction once it was removed from its community and context: Sarah Wanenchak noted in "*Fifty Shades of Grey* and the Ethics of Fannish Prosumption" that "fandom is intensely collaborative in nature, with inspiration for a work often hard to trace to a single source, and with many potential participants in the creation of a work, even though it may technically have only one listed author."[27] So James sold something created in, by, and for a network as a single, commodifiable object; a book. In "Fifty Shades of Exploitation: Fan Labor and *Fifty Shades of Grey*," Bethan Jones cites a fan who expresses her disappointment with James in terms that evoke gift culture and the banquet: "As much as she fed us [with her weekly installments of "Master of the Universe"], we fed her with our comments AND suggestions in how far she could or couldn't take the story."[28]

5. Fanfiction is speculative fiction about character rather than about the world

> Fanfic is speculative fiction where the speculation is centered on a story or person thought of as a character. SF is speculative fiction where the center is the nature of the world.
> —Mary Ellen Curtin[29]

Having rehearsed all these definitions—fanfiction as amateur work, as intertextual engagement, as transformation of copyrighted material, as a gift made within and for a community—I want to talk a little about the particular qualities of fanfiction as it is most typically recognized. We could argue about whether the *Aeneid* is fanfiction, or whether Pia Pera's *Lo's Diary* is, but there's no doubt that the hundreds of *Star Trek* zines and thousands of *X-Files* stories and hundreds of thousands of *Harry Potter* stories are, and these stories tend to have certain things in common.

Fanfiction tends to be deeply interested in character. Fan scholar Mary Ellen Curtin has gone so far as to define fanfiction as speculative fiction about character rather than the nature of the world. The phrase "speculative fiction," coined by Robert Heinlein in 1941, encompasses science fiction, fantasy, and horror, but also "Weird Tales, Amazing Stories, and Fantastic Fiction."[30] Speculative fiction is the genre of "What if?" and understanding that contemporary fanfiction spun out of the broader category of 1960s speculative fiction helps us understand the presence of genre elements like vampires, elves, time travel, aliens, and robots in universes where they don't originally appear. (Fans tend to think that few stories could not be improved by the addition of time travel or robots. I find myself thinking of Yahtzee's *Doctor Who* / *Sense and Sensibility* crossover, the charmingly titled "Relatives & Relativity,"[31] in which Elinor and Marianne

Dashwood meet the Ninth Doctor; a story, alas, too long to be included in this volume.)

As Curtin notes, in science fiction "What if?" is a question that tends to be asked about the world: What if the world were different? (What if we colonized Mars? What if people were telepathic? What if you could genetically customize your child? What happens when we run out of fossil fuels? What if Hitler had won the Second World War? What if dragons were real? What if humanity came to earth from outer space?) In contrast, fanfiction tends to ask, "What if?" about characters: what if a person were different? (What if Bruce Wayne had gone to boarding school with fellow genius-billionaire Tony Stark? Who might Harry Potter grow up to be, considering we leave him as an eighteen-year-old orphaned war veteran? What if a family other than the Kents of Kansas had found that alien baby: who might Superman have grown up to be?) Fans are interested in transformations of social identity (what if a character were female, black, Jewish, queer, disabled?), as well as class identity (what if a character were a barista? a CEO? a single father of three?), and then there are the more fantastical experiments: what if she were a werewolf, a vampire, an elf? These are questions of background, of psychology, intended to unearth notable people, relationships, events, and experiences that affect our understanding of who a character is.

Mainstream science fiction was historically criticized for not being interested enough in character; on the page, it is primarily a literature of ideas, and, as interpreted by the mass media of television and film, it is a genre of spectacle and action. Fanfiction changes this, allowing for smaller, more intimate stories; stories on a different scale entirely from those produced by the mass media. A movie like *The Avengers* has to be successful across the globe, with international audiences and translated into multiple languages; a fanfiction story might be written as a gift for just one other person. If mass media is an industrial and global product, fanfiction is the opposite: handmade—often custom made—and local.

Relatedly, fanfiction is interested in turning moving pictures into prose; in fact, fanfiction typically changes the medium of the original story universe, and thus represents what we today call transmedia. In saying this, I do not intend to discount the history or value of literary pastiche, past or present, and certainly fans do write enormous amounts of fanfiction about books and other literary works. That said, the biggest book fandoms tend to be for books that have already gone transmedia[32] in some way, and much of the fanfiction written about books applies the tropes and genres developed in mass-media fandom to prose work rather than being—strictly speaking—about imitating and extending a specific narrative voice the way pastiche does.

An awful lot of fanfiction turns film and television into words, and literature has different artistic values than film. Writing privileges interiority: it allows us to know a character's thoughts and feelings much more easily than film, which has to resort to clumsy techniques like the voice-over. Prose often focuses explicitly on narrative point of view; in fact, I'd argue that fanfiction writers are obsessed with point of view in a way that most professional writers are not.[33] Text represents sexuality and sex acts in ways importantly different from film: while evoking the bodies[34] of actors associated with particular characters, erotic fanfiction, unlike filmic pornography, does not require actors or any other real people to perform, and so readers don't have to worry about the objectification or exploitation of those people. And of course, words are cheap to work with and don't require the same social capital as filmmaking, painting, or symphony composing; consequently, they have been the medium of choice of marginalized storytellers in general and women in particular. Writers can focus on characterization, and they can also create fantastic worlds on a miniscule budget: rocket ships, a cast of thousands, seamless special effects. As Rebecca Tushnet has noted, it takes a big studio to make *The Avengers*, but it doesn't take a big studio to write *Avengers* fanfiction,[35] and fanfiction can take us into a character's mind and heart as easily as outer space.

+1: Fanfiction is made for free, but not "for nothing"

> I keep seeing people saying [about Amazon's Kindle Worlds] "you'll get 20% to 35% of the profit. And that's better than nothing!" (Well, sidebar: I don't get "nothing" from writing fanfic. If you're not a fanfic writer who shares their fic with a community of readers, it would take me another two thousand words to explain what you *do* get, but trust me. It isn't nothing.)
> —Livia Penn[36]

The world of fanfiction that I've been describing—an art world where fiction is written and read for free—is currently under scrutiny due to its enormous success. The internet has made fandom more visible, not only to potential new fans—who are coming to the banquet in droves—but also to commercial interests, who see fandom's gift culture as ripe for exploitation and monetization. But also, as fandom keeps growing and mainstreaming, its community standards change. Mainstream commercial values are encroaching: there can be an easy slippage between *valuing* fanwork and *appraising* it.

Companies like Wattpad and Amazon's Kindle Worlds have created business models explicitly built upon fanfiction, though right now the work that appears on those sites still seems different in its market orientation than that found, say, on the nonprofit, fan-built Archive of Our Own. (Disclaimer: I am one of the founders of the AO3.) Literary agents and publishers have always been interested in taking on successful fan writers as clients, but this is happening today to an almost unprecedented degree. (Many of the fanfiction writers in this book are also professional fiction writers.) Fans themselves are coming together to form small presses, and some are using Kickstarter and other online fund-raising platforms to bring the "zine" era of fanfiction into the twenty-first century. Others are exploring the possibilities of the digital "tip jar," which allows the audience to donate money if it likes your work. Even this book you're holding—university press notwithstanding—represents a new level of public visibility for fanfiction.

There are many good things about these changes—in particular, I value the opportunity for more women to become professional writers, if they want to be; fanfiction shouldn't make us poor!—but there are things to be valued in noncommerciality. As Rebecca Tushnet has argued, "People who create with no hope of monetary reward make different things than people who want to participate in the money economy, and both are valuable,"[37] although they may accomplish different things. Professional writing may make you money, but "the organic, noncommercial communities that create transformative remixes cannot be moved into the commercial sector without being fundamentally altered and diminished," because "the market changes what it swallows." [38] Anne Jamison agrees, noting that "all the major publishing contracts . . . have gone to heterosexual romances," citing as illustrative the case of a fan author who changed her *Sherlock* fic from a m/m to a heterosexual romance in order to reach "the largest audience possible."[39]

Beyond this, as John Scalzi has noted, "There's a difference between writing fan fiction because you love the world and the characters on a personal level, and Amazon and Alloy actively exploiting that love for their corporate gain and throwing you a few coins for your trouble."[40] Money matters—and especially for poor and pink-collar workers it matters!—but there's also something depressing about being offered money for a labor of love, partly because it can't possibly be enough. It's as if you knitted a blanket for a friend's baby and she offered you six dollars for it.[41] And if you decided to go into the baby-blanket business, let's face it: it wouldn't be the same blanket. It couldn't be.

So it bears saying: this book is a labor of love. None of the writers, myself included, were paid for their words or their work, aside from the old zine standard of "trib" (contributor's) copies. Any profits that this book generates will be donated to the Organization for Transformative Works, which built and maintains the Archive of Our Own. All of these stories were previously posted on the internet and, as far as I know, remain there, free to whoever wants to read them: a gift to the community. We all of us in this book put it together because we're proud of fanfiction writing and want to give "newbies"—teachers and students especially—a curated collection, a place to start. We did it for love, for free—a cynic would say "for nothing,"—but, to adopt Viviana Zelizer's terminology,[42] our work and our creativity aren't worthless. They're priceless.

Suggested Further Reading

The founding texts of fan studies in general and fanfiction in particular remain the big three from 1992: Henry Jenkins's *Textual Poachers* (Routledge, 1992), Camille Bacon-Smith's *Enterprising Women* (University of Pennsylvania Press, 1992), and Constance Penley's "Feminism, Psychoanalysis, and the Study of Popular Culture" (in *Cultural Studies*, ed. Grossberg et al. Routledge, 1992), which she later expanded in her book *NASA/Trek* (Verso, 1997). Jenkins's book, a real field-founder that lays out many of the theories and terms still in use today, was also the best-received among fans because, ironically, it was he who identified most strongly and directly as a fan himself. That said, it behooves us to consider what was at stake in that choice: I don't think it was an accident that the two women scholars were at that time less inclined to speak of themselves as fans when writing about this female-dominated fan subculture, nor that female fans responded with particular enthusiasm to the validation of a male scholar from MIT. But also, Jenkins's identificatory, materialist, and art-focused stance as an English professor was preferred to Camille Bacon-Smith's ethnographic one (Bacon-Smith is a folklorist and science fiction writer) or Penley's feminist psychoanalysis, which left some fans feeling "othered" as an object of academic study. Jenkins's contribution to the field of fan studies has been revisited in various ways, most recently with a twentieth-anniversary edition of *Textual Poachers* and a special issue of the *Journal of Fandom Studies* reconsidering Jenkins's impact, but Penley and Bacon-Smith are also overdue for critical reevaluations.

While there were several important articles on fanfiction in the following years (notably Rebecca Tushnet's 1997 "Legal Fictions: Copyright, Fan Fiction, and a New Common Law," and Sara Gwenllian Jones's 2002 article "The Sex Lives of Cult Television Characters," in *Screen*), as well as several monographs tracing fanfiction and particular communities of fanfiction writers (e.g., Sheenagh Pugh's *The Democratic Genre: Fan Fiction in a Literary Context*, 2005; Rhiannon Bury's 2005 *Cyberspaces of Their Own: Female Fandoms Online*), a second generation of fanfiction scholars came of age with the publication of Karen Hellekson and Kristina Busse's *Fan Fiction and Fan Communities in the Age of the Internet* (McFarland, 2006); this group, which includes Busse and Hellekson, Catherine Driscoll, Abigail DeKosnik, Louisa Stein, Deborah Kaplan, and others, including myself, was largely comprised of female scholars who were also active and self-identified fans. Many of us went on to found or publish in the open-access journal *Transformative Works and Cultures*, which is dedicated to the study of fanworks and fan culture, and which has nurtured a new wave of scholars, including Alexis Lothian, Anne Kustritz, Bethan Jones, Catherine Tosenberger, Mel Stanfill, Juli Parrish, and others. Fanfiction has also become a central case study in digital culture and the law; see, for instance, David Roh's book *Illegal Literature* (University of Minnesota Press, 2015) and Aaron Schwabach's *Fan Fiction and Copyright: Outsider Works and Intellectual Property Protection* (Ashgate, 2011).

It is important, however, to remember that these studies of fanfiction published by scholars with PhDs through academic or university presses came out after a series of important texts written by fans themselves a decade earlier: the real foremothers of fanfiction scholarship include Joanna Lichtenberg, Sondra Marshak, and Joan Winston, authors of the 1975 book *Star Trek Lives!* with its famous concluding chapter: "Do-It-Yourself Star Trek—the Fan Fiction," Patricia Frazer Lamb and Diane Veith, who wrote the 1985 essay "Romantic Myth, Transcendence, and Star Trek Zines," and Joanna Russ, whose "Pornography by Women, for Women, with Love," still inspires. *The Fan Fiction Studies Reader* (Iowa, 2014) brings together essays from across these phases of study.

The Communications Officer's Tale

Title: Lunch and Other Obscenities (2009)
Author: Rheanna
Fandom: *Star Trek* (2009)
Rating: General audiences
Additional tags: humor, female friendship, female protagonist,
  character of color, culture clash, women being awesome

Introduction

While there are other contenders for the title of "The Fandom That Started
It All" (both Arthur Conan Doyle's Sherlock Holmes stories and the 1960s
TV series *The Man from U.N.C.L.E.* make compelling cases), most fans
and fan scholars point to *Star Trek* as ground zero in the development of
modern media fandom.

Star Trek, the original series, which ran on NBC from 1966 to 1969, gal-
vanized its fans into organizing, first to save it from cancellation and then
to revive it into the transmedia juggernaut we know today (twelve movies,
five distinct television series, and an animated series, not to mention un-
countable tie-in novels, comic books, video games, etc.). *Star Trek* was also
the fandom that caused what came to be called "media" fandom to split off
from science fiction fandom, commonly considered the granddaddy of all
other fandoms; until recently, to be "in fandom" was to announce yourself
as a reader of science fiction and fantasy. *Star Trek* fans—who, despite the
mainstream caricature of "Trekkies" as guys who live in their parents' base-
ments,[1] tend to be female—began to organize their own conventions and
zines, eventually expanding to include a variety of popular mass-media

fandoms including *Star Wars*, *Starsky and Hutch*, *The Professionals*, *Blake's 7*, and *Doctor Who*.

Perhaps most importantly, the original *Star Trek* is the source of many of the most beloved tropes in fanfiction—*Star Trek* canon gives us pon farr (i.e., mate or die), body- and genderswap, alternate universes, time travel, crossovers, rapid aging, sex pollen, AMTDI (Aliens Made Them Do It), amnesia, and much more.[2] *Star Trek* is the big bang as far as fandom is concerned; if you wanted to start fandom on another planet, you could do worse than drop off the *Star Trek* box set and wait.[3] And while both Sherlock Holmes and *The Man from U.N.C.L.E.* have "buddy" as well as homoerotic dynamics, it was *Star Trek* that really codified "slash" fiction as a genre: stories in which Kirk and Spock were friends were called "K&S" stories, while stories in which their relationship was erotically charged were labeled "K/S" stories. The diagonal punctuation mark—a slash or virgule—came to define the genre, and gave its name to early slash fandom infrastructure like the Virgule-L mailing list and the Virgule slash convention of the early 1990s.

While Kirk/Spock slash is probably the most famous kind of fanfiction—almost paradigmatic fanfiction, shocking to outsiders and so featured in the first paragraph of most journalistic introductions to fandom—it is certainly not the only kind to have come out of *Star Trek*. In their famous conclusion to *Star Trek Lives!* (1975), "Do-It-Yourself Star Trek—the Fan Fiction," authors Jacqueline Lichtenberg, Sondra Marshak, and Joan Watson discuss a variety of *Star Trek* fanfiction, much of it fleshing out Vulcan history and culture[4] from the clues given us on the show. In *Boldly Writing: A Trekker Fan and Zine History, 1967—1987*, Joan Verba describes a staggering variety of zine fiction, including Mindy Glazer's *Tales of Feldman*, a comic novel about Jewish crewmember Ensign Fiona Feldman and the cultural clash that results when she accidentally marries Mr. Spock.[5] And in *Textual Poachers* (1992), Henry Jenkins discusses stories like Jane Land's *Demeter*,[6] in which Lieutenant Uhura and Nurse Chapel lead an all-female landing party to a lesbian separatist space colony; Jenkins notes that the story "not only provides these characters with a chance to demonstrate their professional competencies, but also to question the patriarchal focus and attitudes of the original series and its male protagonists."[7]

The story I have included here, Rheanna's "Lunch and Other Obscenities" (2009), shares characteristics with all of the above stories: it's a story about two professional women and also features a culture clash. A *Star Trek* reboot story (that is, a story from the 2009 *Star Trek* film directed by J. J.

Abrams), it tells the story of Uhura's first days at Starfleet Academy, and in particular, of the culture clash she experiences with her roommate, Gaila, who hails from the planet Orion.

You might not think you know Gaila, but you probably noticed her if you saw the 2009 *Star Trek* movie: she is the green-skinned alien woman having sex with Kirk when her roommate Uhura inadvertently interrupts. Sexy, green-skinned aliens (originally called "Orion slave girls") date from the very beginning of *Star Trek*, and an image of one appeared in the closing credits of every episode, signaling the show's science fiction "otherness." An Orion slave girl appears in the original pilot, dancing seductively for an all-male audience in a harem-like tavern; we are told that these slaves girls are "like animals: vicious, seductive. They say no human male can resist them."[8] While the captain *is* ultimately able to resist, the show fails to imagine even the *language* of female sexual desire: we are told not that Orion women enjoy sex but that they "like being taken advantage of." While green-skinned seductresses have appeared on other episodes of the original series, as well as *The Next Generation*, it wasn't until forty years later, on *Star Trek: Enterprise*, that the writers tried to mitigate some of the obvious sexist and racist implications of their intergalactic geishas, postulating that Orion women emit pheromones that turn men lustful (so it's not the men's fault, you see) and that they only *pretend* to be slaves; in reality, Orion women enslave their men. Most fans disliked the episode and were disappointed by the continuing misogyny and heterosexism of the conceit. The 2009 film didn't do much better: reboot Kirk is seen trying to bed the green-skinned Gaila.

Fanfiction author Rheanna imagines Orion society differently: as a sex- and body-positive culture. In "Lunch and Other Obscenities," Uhura walks in on Gaila while she's having sex. Gaila is unembarrassed by this and doesn't understand why Uhura is angry. "Are you annoyed we didn't ask you to join us?" Gaila asks afterward, and Uhura explains through gritted teeth that Earth people have strong taboos about sex and consider it a private act. Uhura soon discovers, to her vast irritation, that while Orions have no hang-ups about sex ("It's fun and it feels good and I just don't get why it's such a big deal for your species"), they have *huge* hang-ups about food. "Chew!" rather than "Fuck!" is Gaila's swearword of choice; "masticator," not "fucker," is her insult.

Uhura asks for a room transfer, but is told that "in the course of your career, Starfleet will expect you to be able to live and work successfully with a lot of intelligent beings, all of whom will come from different cultures than yours. In short: if you don't want to have to deal with people who aren't exactly like you, you're in the wrong job." This is the kind of Starfleet that fans like: one that respects cultural differences and supports diplomatic modes of engagement. Uhura comes to realize that life at the Academy (which is located on Earth, in San Francisco) is much harder for Gaila than for her: most Academy socializing takes place while eating and drinking, which to Gaila is the equivalent of a giant public orgy. Uhura also comes to think about her own culture differently: as Spock (who is also the only one of his race at the Academy, and so also an outsider) points out, there are a lot of similarities between eating and sexual activity: "Both are necessary biological functions. Both are a source of physical pleasure." But in our culture, it's acceptable to pleasurably stimulate one of our orifices in public, but not the others. Uhura and Gaila eventually become friends, and what Uhura learns from that friendship helps her become a better communications officer—and also to save Spock's life.

While *Star Trek* is beloved by fans for its attempts to be racially and sexually progressive—the original series featured television's first interracial kiss, for example, and many *Trek* story lines are thinly disguised allegories of racial difference—it hasn't always hit the mark, particularly in terms of gender and sexuality.[9] "Lunch and Other Obscenities" treats its themes of sexual and racial difference with intelligence and sensitivity, putting the Nairobi-born, Swahili-speaking Uhura at the center of the story and making its central relationship that of two female friends. Virginia Woolf once suggested that it would be radical to read a book in which "Chloe liked Olivia. They shared a laboratory together . . ."—that is, a book in which women are friends (rather than rivals or mere vehicles for exposition) and engaged in meaningful work. More recently, Alison Bechdel articulated what has come to be called the Bechdel test: does a story feature two women who talk to each other about something other than a man? "Lunch and Other Obscenities" succeeds on these terms: it's a story in which Uhura likes Gaila, and Gaila likes Uhura, and they share a Starfleet Academy dorm room together.

It is also a story that might make you question your own attitudes about sex. Many people, encountering fanfiction for the first time, wonder why so much of it is erotic.[10] Anne Jamison, in *Fic*, gives a pretty good answer: a lot of fanfiction questions mainstream assumptions about gender, sexuality, and desire. But writing erotic fanfiction is also a wonderful game. The fanfiction community might be the first place where a woman is encouraged to enjoy her sexual fantasies and praised for the dirtiness of her imagination. Writing and reading fanfiction is a social, communal activity, and considering how much shame is still attached to the expression of female sexual desire (what's so funny about it?) the creation of shared erotic fantasies is still radical. We lose our shame together. We enter a sex-positive culture together. Many of us were a little shocked when we first encountered sexually explicit fanfiction, just like Uhura was a little shocked to stumble on Gaila enjoying herself so unapologetically. But we're not shocked any more.

Suggested Further Reading

Much if not most of the earliest and best writing about fanfiction and fan culture is also about *Star Trek*: Joanna Russ, Camille Bacon-Smith, Constance Penley, Lamb and Veith, Joan Marie Verba, Lichtenberg, Marshak, and Winston, Henry Jenkins, and John Tulloch, among others (including me) have written on the phenomenon of *Trek* and its fan culture. Lincoln Geraghty's 2002 bibliography captures much of this scholarly work. But *Star Trek* is not a thing of the past: new critical work on the show and fandom continues to be produced, including Nancy Reagin's *Star Trek and History* (Wiley, 2013) and Roberta Pearson and Máire Messinger Davies's *Star Trek and American Television* (University of California Press, 2014).

Lunch and Other Obscenities

Rheanna

Nyota liked her roommate just fine until she met her.

She'd been at Starfleet Academy for less than a day: just long enough to enroll, collect her brand-new cadet reds, download a vast amount of orientation material to her personal data pad, and then wander around the campus for most of the afternoon, experiencing a tiny thrill every time her freshly issued ID gave her access to a new building, library, or lab. Exploring turned out to be so much fun that it wasn't until the crowds had thinned out and the sun was dipping below the Golden Gate Bridge that Nyota realized the only place she hadn't been yet was her dorm room.

She sat down on the steps of Ji Hall and thumbed on her data pad, scrolling through pages of documentation to find her room assignment. Starfleet Academy had adopted the practice of naming its student residences after great individuals in the histories of the Federation's founding members, and so Nyota was going to spend the next four years living in Surak with a cadet called Gaila Uhu from Orion.

The last detail made Nyota blink. Orion wasn't a member of the Federation; although officially neutral, its continued practice of slavery and sentient-trafficking meant that political relations were cool at best. Growing up in Nairobi, one of the largest centers of population on the African continent, Nyota had interacted with, or at least seen, representatives of literally hundreds of different species. But she couldn't remember ever meeting . . . her train of thought stuttered to a halt as she realized she didn't even know the right word to use for an Orion native. An Orionite? Orioner?

Well, she decided, that could be the first thing she asked to break the ice. And later, when they'd gotten to know each other a little better, Gaila would tell Nyota why she'd chosen Starfleet instead of whatever the Orion equivalent organization was, and soon it'd feel like they'd known each other forever. It was going to be weird, Nyota thought, sharing a room with someone for the first time in her life, but she was sure she'd get used to it, and already she could picture the two of them borrowing each other's clothes and supporting each other through exam crises. She smiled at the idea, then stood up, dusted herself down, and set off briskly across the campus.

The dorm, when she got there, was quiet; most of the students had moved in earlier in the day, and had already left for parties and mixers organized by their departments. But the indicator panel next to the door of room 364.3 was glowing green, which meant—according to the Academy Student Guide—that there was someone inside, but visitors were free to enter. Maybe, Nyota thought, Gaila had decided to wait until she met her roommate before heading out to whatever social event the Engineering faculty was hosting that night. It was a friendly gesture, and Nyota decided they were going to get along just fine.

Then she walked into the room.

Two naked people—one male and pink, one female and green—were enthusiastically having sex on one of the two beds.

For a second, Nyota just stared. It was hard to do anything except stare; the tiny portion of her brain still functioning seemed to have determined that the aspect of the situation most urgently requiring analysis was how exactly Gaila (it had to be—who else could the naked green woman *be?*) had gotten her legs to bend like that. Because, wow, that was one hell of an obtuse angle.

"*Fuck*," Nyota said at last. She didn't swear often, but this instance hardly counted, she supposed, since technically it was a statement of fact.

Gaila turned her head, and saw Nyota for the first time. Instead of looking embarrassed or even faintly perturbed, she smiled brightly. "Oh," she said, between short, shallow gasps, "You must—*uh*—be Nyota—*oh*— we'll be done—ah, *ah*—in a second, oh, oh, *oh!*"

With that, she tipped her head back and arched her spine and came with noisy abandonment. Her partner made a couple more thrusts before he, too, gave a shudder and a satisfied grunt and then slumped against Gaila's chest, his head pillowed on one of her round, perfect breasts.

"Oh, hey, what time is it?" Gaila asked.

Nyota answered, a distant and slightly hysterical part of her mind noting that she was the only one in the room wearing a watch. "It's twenty hundred hours."

Gaila frowned and said something that sounded like "Chew!" and slapped her partner lightly on the buttocks. "I have to get ready to go out. Come on, move."

The guy made grumbling noises, but then Gaila started to wriggle out from under him, making it impossible for him to stay where he was. He got up and stretched, wearing a dopey, contented smile. "Can I use your bathroom?"

At that, something in Nyota snapped. "No! No, you can't use her bathroom, because it's my bathroom, too, and *I* haven't used it yet! Just—go!"

"Touchy," the guy said, looking as if he might have been annoyed if he hadn't been too high on postsex pleasure endorphins to care. He was still smiling as he ambled past Nyota to leave. Lowering his voice, he confided in a tone of utter sincerity, "I *love* being in Starfleet."

"*Out*," Nyota ordered.

The door closed behind him, and Nyota looked back to Gaila, who, still naked, was pinning her fire-colored curls into a tight knot at the back of her head. "Do you mind if I shower first? I have to be somewhere in twenty minutes."

"The light was *green*," Nyota said, aware that was a conversational non sequitur, but past the point of caring.

Gaila's hands went still as she seemed to realize, for the first time, that all was not completely well. "Well . . . yes."

"Green," Nyota repeated. "Did you *want* me to walk in on you having sex?"

"Not especially," Gaila said, sounding puzzled. She frowned. "Are you annoyed we didn't ask you to join us? You know, I would have, except I'm a little pushed for time tonight."

Deep breaths, Nyota thought. In and out. She wasn't some unsophisticated naïf from one of the remoter human colonies; there'd been three Andorians and a Tellarite in her kindergarten class, and she knew exactly how you were supposed to deal with an unexpected clash of social norms.

Very slowly, she said, "My culture has strong taboos about sexual intercourse. Most Earth humans consider it a private act, and if you and I are going to share a room, I need you to respect that."

"Sure, right," Gaila said, but Nyota could tell she wasn't really listening. Her attention was focused on the small bag of toiletries which she was rooting around in, presumably in search of more hair clips.

"Didn't you read any of the preattendance orientation material the Academy sent you?" Nyota asked. "There's a whole section for offworlders about Earth culture."

"I figured I'd work it out once I got here," Gaila said, working more clips into her hair. "And everyone's been really nice so far."

I just bet they have, Nyota thought sourly, thinking of the smirking male cadet. She dumped the duffel bag containing her belongings onto the floor and sat down on the bed that didn't have a damp patch.

Her stomach growled, and she remembered that she'd gotten so caught up in exploring the campus—and then rushing back to the dorm to meet her roommate—that she'd missed her first dinner in the Academy canteen. She unzipped her bag and took out the container her mother had packed for her before she left home. At the time, Nyota had felt embarrassed at the thought of arriving at Starfleet Academy with a packed lunch made by her mom, but right now she was deeply grateful for it. She peeled back the lid, unclipped the spoon, and scooped up a generous quantity of her mother's homemade *m'baazi*. The taste of it—the distinctive mix of sweet coconut milk and fiery chili—conjured vivid memories of home, and when she blinked the moisture from her eyes, it wasn't entirely due to the spiciness of the dish. For a second, she wanted nothing more than to open her eyes and find herself back having dinner with her parents instead of sitting in a dorm room in San Francisco with an alien sex maniac.

"What are you *doing*?"

Nyota snapped her eyes open. Gaila was staring at her with an expression which was equal parts horror and disgust.

"Eating dinner," Nyota said around a mouthful of *m'baazi*. It was ill-mannered to talk with her mouth full, but on the other hand, Gaila didn't seem to be big on personal boundaries, and a small and childish part of Nyota couldn't help thinking that if Gaila was a little offended, too bad.

Except that Gaila didn't look like someone who was a little offended. She looked like someone who was hugely offended.

She clapped her hand over in mouth in a gesture that seemed both emphatic and almost unconscious. Her eyes went comically wide and her cheeks flushed dark until they were the color of moss.

"That," she said from behind her hand, "is *disgusting*."

"That," Nyota said, swallowing, "is my mom's cooking." She held out the mostly full container. "Want some?"

"You—you—*masticator*!" Gaila shrieked, backing away in revulsion.

Which was how Nyota discovered that although Orion society had absolutely no taboos about sex, it had a *lot* of taboos about food and eating, and she'd just broken all of them.

When Starfleet Academy's Housing and Accommodation Officer—whose name, according to the sign next to her door, was Diane Maza—arrived at her office the next morning, Nyota was already there, waiting.

"My roommate's a sex-crazed exhibitionist with a food phobia," Nyota told her. "You have *got* to reassign me."

Maza didn't react. She regarded Nyota for a moment with a coolly appraising gaze that seemed designed to silently communicate that she hadn't just seen everything, she'd seen everything *plus* some other shit as well, and therefore any attempt to shock a reaction out of her was doomed at the outset.

"Why don't you come in and we'll talk about it," she said.

Ten minutes later, after Nyota had outlined the whole sorry story, Maza sat back in her chair and tipped her head to one side. "You know," she said, "Cadet Uhu is the only citizen of Orion currently enrolled at the Academy."

Attempting to sound conciliatory, Nyota said, "And I know that's got to make things tough for her—"

Maza interrupted, "There are eight billion humans on this planet with whom you share a core homeworld culture. I'm thinking that means you probably don't know."

"I had to eat dinner outside!"

"How tragic," Maza observed, her voice dry.

"Look, the only reason we're rooming together is because someone decided that the best phonetic rendering of her name in Standard is almost the same as mine. Can't you just decide to spell Uhu with two O's instead?" Nyota asked, desperate. "Listen: Oo-hoo. That works."

"Cadet Uhura," Maza said, "if we could unilaterally change other people to suit us better, the galaxy would be a more peaceful but very boring place." Maza's gaze flicked down to the screen in front of her, which was currently displaying Nyota's extremely brief Starfleet file. "I see you've chosen to specialize in communications."

"Yes."

"Then I suggest you consider this your first practical assignment."

"But—"

Maza held up a hand. "If you still want to move in a month's time, come back to see me and I'll do it. But before you do, consider that in the course of your career, Starfleet will expect you to be able to live and work successfully with a lot of intelligent beings, all of whom will come from different cultures than yours. In short: if you don't want to have to deal with people who aren't exactly like you, you're in the wrong job."

Nyota blinked, and said nothing. Starfleet's recruitment literature had had a lot to say about the role of the Communications Officer. It wasn't simply a matter of manning a glorified switchboard; the Comms Officer was also the ship's resident expert on non-Federation cultures, the person to whom the Captain turned for guidance in sensitive situations. On deep space missions, the Comms Officer was often the closest thing a starship had to a trained diplomat.

A communications specialist who ran away every time she came up against an unfamiliar culture wouldn't last very long.

Nyota nodded slowly, and stood up. "I understand. Thank you for your time."

"Glad to help," Maza said easily. "Oh, and Cadet Uhura? You might want to read some books about Orion history and culture. I believe the library has an excellent selection."

Yes, Nyota thought as she walked down the hall away from Maza's office, *but I bet it doesn't have any recipe books.*

The negotiations which followed were tough.

"You will not carry on any kind of sexual activity while I am here," Nyota said. "If you want to bring someone back to our quarters, you will let me know not less than twenty-four hours in advance, so I can plan to be somewhere else."

Gaila pouted, and jabbed a finger at Nyota. "Okay, but *you* have to agree not to eat or drink anything in the room."

"If you're not here—"

"I'd still be able to smell it when I came back," Gaila said, with clear distaste. "When I'm here, you can't put anything in your, you know"—she made vague gestures which seemed intended to indicate her mouth without actually naming it—"in front of me."

"I'm not going to step outside just to have a glass of water."

"You can go in the bathroom and close the door to do that," Gaila said, and then muttered under her breath, "like civilized people do."

"All right," Nyota conceded. A few seconds of frosty silence passed. "Do we have an agreement?"

"I guess," Gaila said reluctantly, scowling.

"Good," Nyota said. She smiled, brittle and false. "See? We're getting along better already."

The next month passed without major incident, and when it was over Nyota didn't go back to see Maza. It wasn't that she was getting on better with Gaila—the atmosphere in their room when they were both there was about as relaxed as the Federation/Romulan Neutral Zone—but they'd achieved a level of frosty mutual tolerance. If this was as good as it was going to get for the next four years, then Nyota figured she could manage. Once, coming back from the library late at night, she walked past the open door of one of the other dorm rooms, and glimpsed two female cadets, a human and an Andorian, sitting side by side on one of the beds, laughing together at something one of them had just said. Nyota's throat felt strangely tight for a second, but she walked on quickly, and tried not to think about it later.

The truth was, between attending classes, training with the track-and-field team, studying at the library, and rehearsing with the Academy Choral Society, Nyota was hardly ever in the dorm anyway. And that suited everyone just fine.

Things would have gone on like that indefinitely, if the approaching senior midterms hadn't meant that the library suddenly got a lot busier, and Nyota—a lowly freshman—was displaced from her preferred spot on the upper level by a stressed-looking cadet who was revising for a stellar cartography final. She had no option but to start studying in the dorm room, which quickly led her to realize that Gaila was there almost every night, not studying or having improbably athletic sex, but just . . . hanging about, lying on her bed and staring up at the ceiling. For the first week, Nyota just wished she'd find somewhere else to be, not least because it was annoying to have to get up and go into the bathroom every time she wanted to take a sip from her glass of water.

In the middle of the second week, Nyota was loitering in the entrance hall of Surak Residence, where she'd been banished with her cup of coffee, when a group of about twenty cadets went past, laughing and joking as they headed off campus together. Nyota recognized a couple of them from the cross-department mixers she'd gone to in the first weeks of the semester, and that, coupled with the snippets of conversation she could make out about dilithium conversion optimization and warp coefficients, led her to conclude the revelers were all engineering cadets.

"Looks like your department group's going off-campus for the night," she said when she got back to the room.

Gaila was lying on her side on her bed, facing toward the wall. She made a vague noise of acknowledgment, but didn't move. *Fine*, Nyota thought. *Be like that.*

"Aren't you going with them?" Nyota willed the answer to be yes. The idea of having their shared quarters to herself for an entire evening was deeply appealing. She could download a couple of movies from the entertainment server and then lie on her bed and eat popcorn and potato chips. She could get crumbs on the sheets if she wanted. It would be heaven.

"They asked," Gaila said after a second. "I said no."

Disappointment made Nyota's carefully cultivated veneer of politeness crack. "Why? Don't tell me it's because you have another hectic evening of lying around moping planned. If you broke up with someone, get over it already."

"I didn't break up with anyone."

"Then why don't you ever go out anywhere?" Nyota demanded, exasperated.

Gaila rolled over on to her back, and Nyota realized with a shock that there were wet stains on her cheeks; she'd been crying. "Because all you people ever do is *eat* and *drink*. The others are all going out to eat that round cheese-bread you all like so much—"

"Pizza," Nyota supplied automatically.

"—and after they're all going to go someplace to consume fermented beverages with hundreds of other people and, anyway, I don't even know the other engineering cadets that well because they all made friends doing that disgusting thing where you eat in front of each other—"

"We call that dinner," Nyota pointed out, but Gaila was still talking.

"—and I have to take this stupid pheromone suppression medication that gives me headaches all the time and I miss my clan-sisters and I was so happy when I got into Starfleet and it's nothing like I thought it would be and I can't—I just—it wasn't supposed to be like *this*."

There might have been more, but right then Gaila give a hiccupping sob and started to cry, curling up on her bed until she was a tight ball of misery bundled up in her cadet reds.

For a minute or more, Nyota just stood there, unsure what to do. She wondered if she should go and get one of Gaila's friends, before realizing she wasn't sure who they were—or even if Gaila had any. Eventually, she went over to Gaila's bed and sat down beside her. When Gaila didn't respond, Nyota reached out a hand and gently patted her shoulder.

"Hey, now. It's okay."

"No, it's not," Gaila said. She sounded resigned and defeated. "My clan matriarch was right: I should never have come here."

Nyota's parents had been thrilled and proud when she'd been accepted into Starfleet. Her choice had caused ripples of disapproval in some branches of the family: no one had expected the daughter of a sculptor and a composer to choose a career in the military. But Nyota's mother and father had supported her every step of the way, and Nyota suddenly wondered if she could have made it this far without their backing. She went and got a box of tissues and offered them to Gaila, who nodded her thanks and blew her nose noisily.

"Listen, have you visited the de Young yet?" Nyota asked her.

Gaila sniffled, and then blinked at the apparent change of subject. "The art museum? No."

"Then let's go together. You and me. Right now. My semantics paper can wait until tomorrow."

"I don't know," Gaila said uncertainly. "I'm not really into art."

"Honestly, neither am I," Nyota told her. "But if I know one thing about art museums, it's that they don't let you eat or drink in the galleries."

"All right," Nyota said, "your turn."

Gaila studied the canvas hanging on the wall in front of them. "Okay, I'm seeing a rock. A rock surrounded by giant floating triangles. They're probably *symbolic* floating triangles."

Nyota put her head to one side and tried to make sense of the riot of colors and shapes in the picture. "What do you think they're symbolic of?"

"I don't know. The artist's antagonistic relationship with geometric shapes, I guess. Maybe he was savaged by a rogue hexagon as a child."

Nyota burst out laughing; the sound echoed loudly in the cavernous exhibition space, and she quickly stifled herself. She needn't have worried; it was late in the evening, and there were few other visitors for her and Gaila to disturb. Their visit to the de Young, San Francisco's foremost art museum for more than three hundred years, was turning out much better than she could have hoped. It had become very clear to Nyota, very quickly, that neither she nor Gaila knew the first thing about art, and their stilted attempts to have sensible conversations about the works had swiftly degenerated into a kind of game where they tried to come up with ever more outrageous interpretations. Gaila was better at it than Nyota; she had a gleeful, absurd sense of humor, and Nyota had spent more time laughing in the past few hours than she had since—well, since she started at the Academy.

"It's embarrassing that I know so little about this," Nyota remarked as they made their way on to the next section of the exhibition. "My dad's a sculptor," she added in explanation.

"What about the rest of your clan? Are any of them in Starfleet?"

"One of my mom's cousins is, but I've never met him."

"It's weird . . ." Gaila started, then broke off, probably worried that whatever she'd been planning to say would cause fresh offense.

"What's weird?" Nyota prompted.

Gaila hesitated, then said, "You have clan you've never even *met*. At home, to live apart from your clan would be . . . well, you wouldn't do it unless you had no choice."

Nyota thought about that. Gaila had applied for Starfleet knowing that it would mean leaving her extended family for years at a time. No wonder there were so few Orions in the service. It couldn't have been an easy decision to make. "How big is a typical clan? How many people in yours?"

"Mine is pretty small," Gaila said. "Only 253."

"There are four of us at home," Nyota said. "Well, three, now. My sister moved out when she got married. I miss having her around." Holomessages and visits were nice, but it wasn't the same as having Elinah in the room down the hall. The house had felt a little bit empty without her.

"Yes," Gaila said wistfully, "I miss my first-circle and second-circle siblings." Nyota wanted to ask more about how Orion clans worked, but before she could, Gaila said, "Okay, I don't get this."

Nyota followed Gaila's gaze and found herself looking at a painting of a man and woman locked in a passionate embrace. Only the couple's heads and parts of their arms were visible; the rest of their bodies were swaddled by a richly patterned cloth which enveloped them in sensuous folds. One of the woman's hands was placed on top of the hand of the man which cupped her cheek, and her other hand was just visible curling around the back of his neck, drawing him closer as she turned her face up, eyes closed, to allow his mouth to meet hers.

"That's a pretty famous painting," Nyota said. "It's by a twentieth-century artist, Gustav Klimt. It's called *The Kiss*."

"I don't understand how you can have so many taboos about sex but still put pictures like this in a museum and encourage people to come and look at them," Gaila said. Her brow was furrowed in frustration. "If your society just didn't talk about sex, well, it'd be weird, but at least it'd be *simple*. But you don't. Why is it okay to put pictures like this on display and make holovid stories which are all about people having sex then arguing about having sex and then having more sex, but it's not okay to walk up to someone and ask them if they want to have sex?"

Nyota couldn't help wincing. "You did that?"

Gaila sighed in a way that Nyota figured meant the answer was probably yes. "I don't get it," she said again. "It's just sex. It's fun and it feels good and I just don't get why it's such a big deal for your species."

Nyota opened her mouth to offer an explanation, and abruptly realized she didn't have one.

"It's like there's a whole set of rules everyone here knows," Gaila concluded, "and every time I think I've got them worked out, something else happens and I realize I don't."

Nyota was quiet for a moment, thinking about what it would have been like if she'd had to go to Orion to join Starfleet Academy; what it would be like to be the only human on an entire planet. Maybe people would have been friendly to her at first, and invited her along to their getting-to-know-you orgies, but she would have had to say no, because it would've been too strange and uncomfortable to abandon the beliefs and social norms she'd grown up with. Eventually, Nyota supposed, people would have stopped asking, and just left her alone.

"You know," she said slowly, "if there are things you want to ask about, you can ask me."

Gaila looked away, and her expression became shuttered. "Yeah, well, I wouldn't want to accidentally offend you."

Nyota shifted uncomfortably. "I guess I kind of . . . overreacted that first day."

"I guess I did, too," Gaila said.

They were both quiet for a second. Then Nyota said, "Don't look now, but there's a still life with fruit on the wall behind you."

Gaila made a face. "At home, you'd have to get written permission from the Minister of Culture to look at that kind of thing."

"Come on," Nyota said, "let's go find where they keep the nudes."

"Kissing in public?" Gaila asked.

Nyota thought for a second. "Okay. Usually. Kissing on cheeks and hands and closed mouths is fine. Kissing with open mouths might attract some attention."

Gaila nodded and used her stylus to scribble something on her data pad, the tip of her tongue poking out from between her lips in concentration.

"And public sex?"

"No. No, no, and definitely no."

Gaila's hand paused. "Oops."

Nyota winced. "Where?"

"Um. We might need to study in another library for a while."

Nyota grabbed the pillow from her bed and threw it across the room. "I liked the anthropology library!"

Gaila caught the pillow and slipped it neatly behind her head as she flopped back on her bed. "And it wouldn't be a bad idea to avoid the planetary sciences labs, too."

In retaliation, Nyota opened the drawer of her bedside locker and took out the apple she kept there for just these situations. She bit into it, crunching loudly.

Gaila made retching noises. "Ewww! That's revolting! I feel sick!"

Nyota grinned and took another bite.

Gaila, of course, didn't eat meals in the Academy mess. She had alternative arrangements which Nyota, wisely, hadn't enquired about. She suspected to do so would be roughly equivalent to asking someone their favorite masturbation techniques.

But even though Gaila wasn't there to express her disgust at the custom of communal eating, Nyota must have been starting to empathize with her, just a little bit, because somehow mealtimes just weren't the same anymore.

It was little things, really: tiny details that would have slipped by her a few months ago. Like the command-track cadet who always sat at the table by the window and talked with his mouth full, so that Nyota could see tiny flecks of spit and food flying from between his lips, glinting in the bright shafts of sunshine. Or the bearded cadet who invariably got morsels of his lunch trapped in the cleft between his nose and upper lip. Even the neat eaters somehow unsettled her: the Aurelian female, for example, who spent twice as much time cleaning her mandibles after a meal as she did actually eating it.

These days, Nyota was a lot more choosy about who she sat with at lunch.

"Do you mind if I join you, Commander Spock?"

He was sitting at a table by himself at the most distant end of the mess hall. She would have expected the Academy's sole Vulcan instructor to stand out from the crowd, both for his heritage and the fact that in a sea of red-uniformed cadets, he was wearing the uniform of a commissioned officer. Yet Spock, self-controlled and self-contained, seemed to melt into the background; if he hadn't been the instructor of the senior phonology class (which Nyota had already decided was on her list of must-take courses) she wouldn't have glanced twice in his direction. She wondered if he was eating alone by choice or because most people found making small talk with a Vulcan hard work. But the only other free seat Nyota could find was at a table where a Borellian was eating live slimeworms by sucking them out of their skins, and Nyota felt that if there wasn't a taboo about doing *that* in public, there damn well should be.

Spock looked at her, his expression mild. "There is no reserved seating; you may eat wherever you wish. It would not be logical for me to raise an objection."

Nyota decided to take that as a yes. She sat down opposite him; the other four seats at the table were empty. She started to eat her salad, noting with relief that the Vulcan was just as tidy an eater as she'd thought he would be, using his knife to neatly dissect the selection of lightly grilled vegetables on his plate, before putting them in his mouth with the precision of a military operation.

"Is something wrong, Cadet?"

Uh-oh. Nyota realized she'd been staring. "I'm sorry," she said. "My roommate's Orion. They have some weird social taboos about eating, and I think it's rubbing off on me."

"Your use of the word 'weird' implies a value judgment on your roommate's culture which is inappropriate. I understand Orion society does not share the sexual taboos exhibited in the majority of galactic cultures. Doubtless there are aspects of human society which appear strange to an Orion."

"You can say that again," Nyota said.

Spock arched one eyebrow. "Was my phrasing unclear?"

"No, it's a—" Nyota broke off. "It's just an expression. I was agreeing with you."

"Ah. I see." Spock continued to talk, while deftly slicing the larger pieces of vegetable on his plate into evenly shaped and sized chunks. "Consider, for a moment, the similarities between the consumption of food and sexual activity. Both are necessary biological functions. Both are a source of physical pleasure."

"And both are kind of gross if you really stop to think about what they actually involve."

Spock paused. If Nyota hadn't known better, she could almost have classed the look on his face as one of amusement. "There is . . . certainly some merit in that proposition."

"So you're saying that either all cultural taboos are weird, or none are."

"I am saying that it is difficult to conduct successful diplomatic relations with other species if you consider their cultural norms so ridiculous as to be unworthy of consideration."

Nyota nodded slowly, thinking that through. "You have to understand the culture, not just the language. The universal translator makes it easy to translate the literal meaning of words in one language into another, but it doesn't tell you anything about the cultural context behind them."

"Correct. And the universal translator is by no means complete or infallible. It will often give a single translation in Standard to a group of words which have differently nuanced meanings in the original language. For example, this dish of *vekh* I am eating." He gestured at the plate in front of him. "On Vulcan, it would be made with six different types of root. The recipe used by the Academy kitchens substitutes a single one, as the names of all six varieties are translated into Standard with the same term. The result is . . ." He paused, then concluded, ". . . somewhat unsatisfactory."

"I hear there's a great Vulcan restaurant in the Haight," Nyota said, and instantly regretted it, because that had sounded like she was flirting with him. And, yes, underneath that severe haircut and those sharply angled eyebrows, he *was* an attractive man, but he was also an officer and a *Vulcan*. What was she thinking? Quickly, she said, "Uh, I'm sorry, Commander, I didn't mean to give offense."

But Spock just looked faintly puzzled. "Why would I be offended by your recommendation of a restaurant?"

Nyota exhaled in relief. "No reason." Apparently, what most people took to be Vulcan superciliousness was actually just a certain unfamiliarity with Earth social norms. Maybe Spock, in his way, was as baffled by human customs as Gaila was.

His meal finished, Spock stood up, lifting his tray to return it to the bussing station. "I have an appointment at 1400 hours. I must take my leave."

"Of course," Nyota said. And then she added, "I hope I didn't disturb your lunch."

"On the contrary," Spock said. "I found our discussion most stimulating. Thank you for your company."

"Ooooh," Gaila said, "he thinks you're *stimulating*."

She was lying next to Nyota on the towels they'd laid out on the roof of

Surak Residence. Strictly speaking, the roof was off-limits, but there were no active security feeds up here. Nyota was propped up on one elbow, going through the notes she'd taken on her electronic data pad that day, adding tags and categories for ease of reference later. Gaila, just back from swim team practice, was painting her toenails a bright shade of blue. Her damp red hair fell in loose twists on to her bare shoulders; she'd taken off her swimsuit to let it dry in the sun and hadn't bothered putting anything else on instead. No sexual taboos seemed to mean no taboos about nudity either; it had been a little disconcerting at first, but after a while, Nyota had found she'd almost stopped noticing. The same couldn't be said of most of the Academy's other cadets—males and a significant proportion of females—and so, outside of their shared room, Gaila had reluctantly restricted her naturist tendencies to the dorm roof.

Gaila was smirking knowingly; Nyota flicked her bare leg with the corner of her towel. "Shut up."

But Gaila wasn't going to be put off that easily. "Do you want to have sex with him?"

"No!" Nyota said at once. Gaila gave her a look. Nyota sighed: she was fast learning that Gaila had an infallible bullshit detector when it came to all aspects of sexual attraction. It was probably the result of not having to think through the obfuscating layers of human social influence. "Okay, yes, maybe a little. But it doesn't usually work like that in my culture. We'd have to at least have dinner first. Uh, sorry," she added, as Gaila winced and Nyota realized what she'd said. In an attempt to change the subject, she asked, "Shouldn't you be using sun block?"

"No way," Gaila said. "I'm trying to get more exposure to sunlight, not less. I'm not photosynthesizing enough as it is."

Nyota opened her mouth to reply, then stopped, and mentally rewound that sentence and replayed it in her head. "You . . . photosynthesize?"

"What did you think this was, green paint?" Gaila asked, slapping her thigh.

"It's—chlorophyll?" Nyota said, incredulous. "Wait a second. I thought Orions were mammalian."

"We are. It's a symbiotic relationship. I'm part moss at the cellular level. I get about a quarter of my energy needs directly from sunlight."

"That's why you spend so much time naked," Nyota realized.

"That, and I happen to like it." Gaila stretched out a little more, so that every possible part of her skin was bathed in the rich late-afternoon sunshine. She looked drowsy and content, the way humans might after a good meal, and Nyota wondered what it felt like to draw the sun's energy directly into your body, through your skin. No wonder Orions had taboos about eating; it must seem so messy and inefficient compared to this. Gaila rolled on to her front and started to paint her fingernails, humming happily to herself as the sun warmed the small of her back. "So, you want to have sex with the cute Vulcan. That only leaves one other relevant question: Does he want to have sex with you?"

"I don't know. I've only talked to him once."

"You could just ask him."

"He's a Vulcan," Nyota said. "They're even weirder about sex than humans are. Do you know Starfleet Medical doesn't teach Vulcan reproductive biology? Vulcan High Command won't let them. *Vulcans* probably don't even know where baby Vulcans come from."

"Why does everyone in this corner of the galaxy have so many hangups about sex?" Gaila waved the nail varnish brush in hand to emphasize her point. "You'd all be a lot happier if you just got over yourselves. Oh, *chew* it," she swore, as a glob of blue polish dropped off the end of the brush and landed on the towel.

"Says the woman who thinks lunch is obscene," Nyota said.

"Two words: macaroni cheese," Gaila replied. "I rest my case."

But having sex with Spock—or having dinner with him, or even just getting to know him a little better—was a theoretical problem rather than a practical one, because right after that, he vanished.

He disappeared from his regular spot in the mess hall, and after a week, a group of noisy Tellarites claimed it. Nyota didn't give it a lot of thought until she discovered, by way of an overheard conversation between two fourth-year phonology students, that he hadn't turned up to teach his classes for several weeks, and another instructor had taken over. She made some discreet enquiries, but no one seemed to know what had happened.

When three weeks had gone by, and Nyota still hadn't seen Spock or found out what the problem was, she decided to take matters into her own hands.

She waited outside the lecture hall where the Senior Phonology class took place and watched the final-year cadets file out past her. When the last of them had gone, she went in.

The substitute professor, a blue-skinned, bald-headed Bolian, was tidying away his teaching materials. "First-year linguistics is in the other lecture hall," he said as Nyota approached him.

"I know," Nyota said. "Actually, I wanted to ask about Commander

Spock. I heard he handed over his classes, and I was wondering—" She hesitated. *I was wondering if he was okay* felt like too personal an inquiry to make about someone she barely knew. "I'm hoping to take his phonology course next semester, and I wanted to know if he's still going to be teaching it."

"If I knew, I'd tell you," the professor said, his attention mostly on the electronic planner he was holding in his hand. "Mr. Spock is unwell, and has been for several weeks."

That was a surprise. Nyota couldn't imagine a Vulcan laid up with the flu or its equivalent. "Is he getting treatment?"

"Oh, yes." Nyota felt a weird little jump of relief, which immediately went away when he went on, "The doctors on his home planet will know what to do, I'm sure."

"He has to go back to Vulcan?"

The response was a shrug. "You know Vulcans—they've got a secretive streak a mile wide about their biology. And while your concern is touching, Cadet, I suggest it would be better directed toward your studies." And with that he hurried out of the room, frowning at his scheduler.

Nyota had only been in Starfleet Academy's teaching hospital once, when she'd had her preenrollment medical exam, and she had to stop several times to ask the medcenter computer for directions, which it gave her in its calm, emotionless female voice. When Nyota finally located the right room, she stopped at the nurses' station before going in. "I'm here to see Commander Spock."

"Well, you're the first," the nurse said. "Go on in; he's awake."

Spock was sitting up in bed when Nyota came into his room. He didn't look surprised—surprise, Nyota was sure, was on the Vulcan emotional no-no list—but he did raise an eyebrow. "Cadet. This is . . . unexpected. Please, take a seat."

He gestured at the seat next to the bed; the movement was weirdly clumsy and uncoordinated. He really was sick, Nyota realized. She sat down, noticing how bare the room seemed without any of the get-well cards or small gifts which would have been normal in a hospital room occupied by a sick human. "How are you?"

"This is the first time I have been ill since infancy, and I confess I am not finding the experience pleasant," Spock said.

He sounded so peevish that Nyota had to smile. "No one likes being sick."

"Indeed."

"I heard you're going back to Vulcan," Nyota said. "Will you be back next semester?"

"I do not know. If I am successfully diagnosed and cured, I shall certainly return. However, my physiology is . . . unique, and presents certain complexities not found in other Vulcans. My illness has coincided with my first lengthy period of absence from Vulcan. Logic suggests that is not by chance."

"You think something in the environment on Earth is making you unwell? An allergen?"

"Or the lack of something, perhaps," Spock said. "If either scenario is true, I may have to reconsider my future career. It will be difficult to serve in Starfleet if I cannot leave Vulcan for any length of time. There would be . . . a certain irony inherent in that outcome." He half-closed his eyes as he spoke; he looked, she thought, as though he had hardly any strength, and his face was slack and expressionless. His tone, though, was one of weary resignation tinged with bitterness, and it told her everything she needed to know. Spock must have realized it, too, because he said, "You must forgive me, Cadet. I am finding emotional discipline somewhat difficult to achieve at the moment."

Privately, Nyota thought it was okay to lose some emotional discipline when you were facing the possible end of your career for medical reasons.

"I must ask you to leave now so that I can rest," Spock said. "My stamina is greatly reduced."

"Of course," Nyota said, and stood up to leave. At the door, she paused. "I enjoyed having lunch with you. When you come back next semester, maybe we could do it again."

"That would be acceptable," Spock said. He opened his eyes. "I do not believe you have yet told me your name."

"Nyota Uhura."

"Your visit was not required, Cadet Uhura. However it was . . . welcome."

Nyota smiled. "I'm happy to know that, Mr. Spock."

Nyota stopped walking and scanned the landscape ahead of them, feeling tiny and insignificant under the vast sky. "Are you sure this is the right way?"

Gaila peered at the map she was holding. "Um. Maybe?"

"Let me see that." Nyota took the map and studied it, then pulled her compass out of the pocket of her field jacket and checked the direction they were heading. "We should be going that way," she said, pointing.

"Oh, great. Up another hill," Gaila said with a sigh. "Be honest, aren't you just a little bit tempted to use your communicator to call base camp and tell them we're lost and need a transport back?"

"That's an automatic fail," Nyota pointed out.

"You know, I think I could live with that."

"They'd make you do it again. You can't pass first year without being able to navigate unfamiliar terrain unassisted. What would you do if you were assigned to a landing party on your first posting?"

"Follow someone who knew where they were going," Gaila said, and Nyota laughed.

"Come on. We'll take a break at the top."

Gaila grumbled, but followed, and another half-hour's hiking brought them to the top of the ridge. From here, the view was superlative; Earth was a crowded planet, but right here, in the middle of Yellowstone Park, it was easy to believe that they were explorers on a new and pristine world. Nyota shivered at the thought, and wondered how much more powerful that feeling must be when you knew it was the truth and not pretense for the purpose of a training exercise.

While Gaila sat down on a flat-topped rock to rest, Nyota pulled out her water bottle and took a drink, taking care to turn away so Gaila couldn't see her. Her stomach growled; they'd been hiking and climbing since early in the morning, and they still had a distance to cover. "This is a great spot for a picnic," she said without thinking.

"Picnic?"

Of course Gaila wouldn't know the term. Nyota winced a little as she realized she'd have to explain it. "It means eating a meal outdoors."

Gaila shook her head. "That's *depraved*," she said, but she sounded more amused than disgusted. That gave Nyota enough confidence to bring up the awkward subject of lunch.

She shrugged off her backpack, opened it and pulled out foil-wrapped field rations. "Speaking of depraved . . ."

"Yeah," Gaila said, "me too," which Nyota had learned was as close as she'd get to admitting to feeling hungry. Gaila opened her own backpack and took out an identical packet of foil-wrapped rations, handling it with the kind of discomfort more usually associated with armed sonic grenades. She turned it over a couple of times without opening it.

That was her cue to go somewhere else, Nyota thought. She looked around and saw a boulder a short distance away; it was large enough that she'd be hidden if she sat on its other side, and it had the added advantages of providing shade from the sun and shelter from the breeze. "I'll be back in ten minutes," she said as she stood up.

From behind her, Gaila said, "You don't have to go."

Nyota stopped and turned around, thinking she must have somehow misheard that. But Gaila was still holding her foil-wrapped rations, and although her expression was uncomfortable and uncertain, Nyota knew she hadn't misunderstood.

"The day we went to the art museum," Gaila said softly, "I'd decided to quit and go home. My clan-mother didn't want me to join Starfleet. Before I left, she gave me a big lecture. She told me that humans were all wicked masticators, that they'd make me take drugs to alter my body chemistry, that they thought all Orions were slaves or slave-traders and hated us for it." Gaila gave a half-shrug and a rueful smile. "I thought she was trying to scare me, but then I got here and found she was pretty much right about all of it. The part she didn't tell me . . . is that clan is whoever you decide it is. And it's okay to eat with clan. So . . . eat with me."

Nyota couldn't answer for a second as she took in what it was that Gaila was offering her. Then, slowly, she said, "If you're okay with it."

"I'm okay with it," Gaila said.

Nyota nodded, and came back to sit next to Gaila on the flat-topped rock. She waited until, slowly and with great care, Gaila started to unwrap her field rations, and only then unwrapped her own, following the label's instructions to activate the self-heat function. The tub hummed in her hands, and when she unclipped the lid a minute later, the savory smell that wafted up to greet her made her mouth water. It wasn't restaurant quality but, after a morning's physical exertion, it didn't need to be.

It was hard to resist the temptation to dig in right away, but Nyota made herself wait until she saw Gaila using a slim implement to spear something in her own ration tub. She started to lift it out, and Nyota watched just long enough to glimpse a small, white cube that looked a little like tofu. She looked away before Gaila put it in her mouth, and didn't look again.

She was ravenously hungry, but she made herself eat in small mouthfuls, chewing and swallowing as quietly as possible. They sat side by side and ate their meals in silence, sitting under the sun in a wilderness on the most densely populated planet in the Federation, and Nyota thought it was both the strangest and the most normal thing she'd ever done.

After she'd finished eating, Nyota packed away her empty ration tub. When she looked up again, Gaila was settling back on to the rock, tilting her face up to the open sky. "How much further do we have to go?"

Nyota consulted the map. "Another twenty klicks."

"Better keep my energy levels up," Gaila said. She started to take off her jacket and then said, "Mind if I . . . ?"

Nyota waved a hand. "Sure."

Less than a minute later, Gaila was basking in the sun, every inch of her chlorophyll-tinged skin exposed from the roots of her hair to the soles of her feet. "Oooooh," she said happily. "That's *nice*. I swear the quality of light's better out here." She wiggled her toes. "Will you see Spock again before he leaves?"

"I doubt it. The *Carolina* leaves for Vulcan today. He's probably going to be on it."

"Well, that *sucks*," Gaila said, with feeling. It was a Standard colloquialism she'd adopted with enthusiasm, although Nyota suspected that it had slightly different connotations when Gaila used it.

"Yes," Nyota agreed. She felt a stab of something like regret at the thought that she probably wouldn't see Spock again, which was weird, considering she really didn't know him. But even in their brief conversations, she'd found herself warming to him, and she was sorry she wasn't going to get a chance to know him better. It was weird how things worked out sometimes: tiny twists of chance that sent lives spinning in new directions. If Gaila's name had been spelled differently in Standard, if Maza had agreed to assign Nyota a different room when she'd asked, if Spock didn't have to give up his career before it had even started because there was something about Earth that made him ill . . . *or the lack of something, perhaps.*

Nyota froze. She stared at Gaila, long enough and hard enough to make even an Orion self-conscious. "Nyota? Is something wrong?"

Nyota raised a finger and pointed it at Gaila. "If you didn't get enough exposure to sunlight, you'd get sick."

"Well, yes," Gaila said. "Light deficiency's pretty common. You get tired and moody, and you have to increase your exposure until you start to get better."

Nyota stood up. "I know what's wrong with Spock," she said excitedly. "Come on, we have get back, right now. I'm going to call in and request an immediate beam-out." She took out her communicator.

"Wait, wait!" Gaila scrambled to her feet. "We'll have to do this *again*!"

"You said you didn't mind."

"That was before I thought I was actually going to have to do it!"

"Gaila—" Nyota broke off. "Think how you would've felt if you'd had to give up Starfleet."

For a second, Gaila looked torn. Then she nodded. "Fine. I can cope with one failed class, I guess. But you're going to explain this to me, right?"

"Later, there's no time," Nyota said, flicking her communicator on to the emergency channel, the one they'd been instructed only to use if they needed to abort the field exercise. "The *Carolina* could be leaving orbit right now."

"Okay, but you *seriously* owe me for this," Gaila said, crossing her arms resolutely. She frowned. "What are you waiting for? You just said there's no time."

"There's always time to put on clothes, Gaila."

"Oh," Gaila said. "Right."

One Week Later

"May I join you, Cadet Uhura?"

Nyota looked up from her meal and saw Spock standing on the other side of the table in the Academy mess. "It wouldn't be logical for me to object," she said. Spock looked at her, and for a second Nyota wondered if she was going to have to explain friendly teasing to him. But then he nodded, set his tray down, and took a seat opposite her.

"You're looking a lot better than when I last saw you," she told him, and it was true: a week ago, he'd been lying in a hover-bed, about to be transported to the *Carolina* and off Earth.

"I am still feeling somewhat lethargic," Spock said, "but my condition is improving daily." He produced a small bottle, which he unscrewed. He tipped it up and poured a small measure of the contents—a viscous, green fluid—into a spoon, and then swallowed it down. Nyota was sure that the faint grimace he wore as he did so wasn't just her imagination. Even Vulcans didn't like taking their medicine.

She pushed her untouched glass of fruit juice across the table, offering it to him. "Here. Drink something to take the taste away."

He accepted the glass and took a drink from it. "It is remarkable that the lack of a single amino acid should have such a profound effect on the health of the body." He paused for a second. "I might add that I am greatly impressed that a cadet majoring in communications was able to reach a correct diagnosis where qualified physicians had failed."

"I got lucky," Nyota said. "And, anyway, I didn't reach a medical diagnosis—I just figured out that you had . . . a translation problem."

Spock arched an eyebrow. "That is one way of describing it. If I had realized that the lack of accurate translations of specific ingredients in Vulcan dishes was causing the Academy kitchens to prepare food lacking in one of the compounds essential to my health, I would have perhaps lodged more vigorous complaints regarding the quality of the food."

Nyota looked at him for a second, trying to decide if that really was what it sounded like: a joke. Spock's face was perfectly impassive; then again, she thought, who else could play the perfect straight man but a Vulcan?

"Then again," Spock continued, "a full Vulcan would not have suffered the same extreme effects of the deficiency that I did. And while the doctors were diligent, they cannot be faulted for not having access to full information regarding Vulcan physiology. Perhaps the lesson to take from the experience is that more communication between different cultures is always desirable."

"Yes," Nyota agreed. "So I've discovered."

"Which brings to me to the purpose of this conversation," Spock went on. "Cadet Uhura, I owe you a great debt of gratitude."

Nyota shook her head. "The doctors on Vulcan would have figured out what was wrong with you pretty quickly, once you were back there."

"But not before I would have been forced to give up my post at the Academy, at least for the remainder of this academic year. I am, as I say, most grateful." He paused. "I have been speaking to your roommate, Cadet Uhu."

Uh-oh, Nyota thought. She tried to imagine an encounter between Spock and Gaila, and failed to come up with any scenario that didn't end in toe-curling embarrassment for all concerned. "You have?" she asked finally, in as neutral a tone as she could manage.

"I asked her what she thought an appropriate gesture of thanks might be."

Oh, *no*. Nyota tried not to wince. She took a breath. "You know, in Orion culture, it's very normal to express emotions through, uh, physical relations."

Spock said, "She suggested I should ask you out to dinner."

Nyota stopped. "Dinner?"

"I am reliably informed that there is an excellent Vulcan restaurant in the city." Spock's face was grave, but there were tiny creases at the corners of his eyes. He was amused, Nyota thought. He was *totally* laughing at her. "It is called the Yem-tukh Nar-tor'i. In Standard, it means—"

"Acceptable Food," Nyota translated. Of course it was called that. What else would a Vulcan restaurant be called?

All at once, it was too much. She giggled, and when she put a hand to her mouth to stifle the sound, she only succeeded in turning it into a half-snort. "I'm—oh, I'm sorry, Commander Spock," she said once she could speak without laughing. He was looking at her quizzically; a fit of the giggles was probably no more strange to him than any of the other displays of emotion he was forced to contend with on a daily basis. "We're all weird, aren't we? Humans, Vulcans, Orions, all of us, with our strange customs we can't explain, even to ourselves. But we keep trying to understand each other anyway. Isn't that strange? Isn't it . . ." She broke off, unable to think of the right word.

"Personally," Spock said, "I have always found it quite marvelous."

"Marvelous," Nyota agreed. She leaned forward and put her elbows on the table, resting her chin on her hands. "Mr. Spock: let's do lunch."

The FBI Agent's Tale

Title: The Sad Ballad of Mary Sue's Blues (1998)
Author: Pares
Fandom: *The X-Files*
Rating: General audiences

Introduction

Oh, *Mary Sue*. The term, which originally delineated a self-insert character who is young, female, and utterly perfect, was introduced into the fannish vernacular by Paula Smith,[1] author of "A Trekkie's Tale" (1973).[2] Smith's parody fanfiction stars Lt. Mary Sue, "the youngest lieutenant in the fleet—only fifteen and a half years old." Over the course of the story, Mary Sue saves everybody multiple times, earning Kirk's love and Spock's admiration, before falling fatally ill; she dies "surrounded by Captain Kirk, Mr. Spock, Dr. McCoy, and Mr. Scott, all weeping unashamedly." This kind of obvious wish-fulfillment was mocked as poorly written and embarrassing, and as Camille Bacon-Smith notes in *Enterprising Women* (1991), Mary Sue stories soon "developed strong negative connotations"[3] within the fanfiction community.

While Mary Sue started out narrowly defined—Bacon-Smith describes her as "a very young heroine, often in her teens and possessing genius, intelligence, great beauty, and a charmingly impish personality"[4]—some people have applied the term to any character that resembles the author or, worse yet, to any original female character at all.[5] This has led fandom to ask whether the use of "Mary Sue" is self-policingly sexist; after all, mainstream genre stories *regularly* feature special teenage boys who save

47

the world. While fandom has back-formed the labels "Gary Stu" or "Marty Stu" to describe a male self-insert, these terms haven't had the same chilling effect. Even today, some fans worry about having their original female characters labeled as Mary Sues, which is to say as unrealistic, poorly characterized fantasy figures.

In the *X-Files* story "The Sad Ballad of Mary Sue's Blues," Pares gives us a Mary Sue very different from this fan archetype: who is, in fact, an *anti*-archetype. At the start of the story, Pares teases us—and also teases Agent Fox Mulder, the handsome hero of *The X-Files*—with a Mary Sue who conforms to expectations: the bartender Naja, an attractive Asian girl with "a plum shine" to her hair and a silver hoop in her eyebrow. Then Pares's real Mary Sue arrives with a thunderclap. She is Hortense Wahlberg, and she is God.

She is also a fanfiction writer of the 1990s, "one of many," and so she is

> twenty-five or forty, fat, not very fair. I'm still in school, or I work at one, or I haven't worked in years, and I have three or more cats and a forest of overwatered ferns. I drink too much coffee. I may or may not smoke, I may or may not have a husband, and I often have a surprising number of outside interests.

While some aspects of Pares's portrait may be more typical of the 1990s (when internet access correlated more strongly with a university affiliation and people were more likely to smoke), many aspects still ring true today. Fandom still seems to have a high proportion of students and teachers (not to mention librarians.) Fanfiction writers, like most writers, tend to drink a lot of coffee. Fans—like most denizens of today's internet (witness the devotion to MoneyCat and Maru)—still really like cats. Fans may or may not have husbands; today, many female fans also have wives.

Most importantly, however, most women, fanfiction writers or not—still don't look like the women we see on TV and in movies. In fact, the picture of Mary Sue that Pares draws for us is of a kind of woman who rarely achieves representation. Hortense Wahlberg—the name is deliberately unmusical—is plain, overweight, and sallow from not spending time in the sun. She has a roll of belly fat and her jeans are too tight. She also has fingers "like sausages," dull hair, and blackheads—though Hortense, who is of course the story's writer, and so the author of her own unflattering portrait, admits that she's being a bit hard on herself to make the point:

in fact, she's "not actually all that bad looking." But she certainly does not look like a TV or movie star, let alone like a fantasy-self insert. She's not the kind of woman who usually gets to kiss Fox Mulder, but Pares allows her to do exactly that: Hortense asks Mulder for a kiss, and gets one, though the moment isn't the typical idealized kiss between Mary Sue and her hero.

Pares also gives us her opinions on Mary Sue's psychological state: Hortense claims that many fanfiction writers are working through "some kind of emotional trauma" and that writing fanfiction gives them what they want: control. This argument has been made in various forms and with varying intensity over the years. For instance, Camille Bacon-Smith controversially argued that hurt/comfort stories lie at "the heart of the community" and function as a way for women to transform their pain[6]; Bacon-Smith talks persuasively about rape, for example, as a kind of physical and psychological terrorism that female fanwriters transform in fanfiction. There is also the more generalized and less disputable claim that fanfiction represents a female (if not always feminist) rewriting of pop culture texts and sexual/erotic tropes for the pleasure of a female audience (or, to put it in Joanna Russ's famous formulation, that fanfiction is "Pornography by Women for Women, with Love"). Whether you think fan writers are transforming their trauma or playfully reimagining mass media for other women, it's hard to say they aren't taking control of the text.

In "The Sad Ballad of Mary Sue's Blues," Hortense Wahlberg controls the whole universe: she is literally God. While Mary Sue has always been defined as an authorial self-insert, she normally lives (and dies) within the storyverse. But Pares makes Hortense a true authorial avatar, and thus a person of immense (and supernatural) power even as she's portrayed as flawed and imperfect—as all gods are. This actually makes "The Sad Ballad of Mary Sue's Blues" a perfect *X-Files* story: here, as on the television series, it is FBI agent Fox Mulder's role to search for truth (*The Truth Is Out There!*) and to encounter the strange and unnatural (his partner Scully is the skeptic.) And if, as Mikel Koven has argued, *The X-Files* was a show defined by its "writerliness"—that is, by its high- and low-culture references, by its auteur, Chris Carter, and by its experimentations in narrative form and perspective—who *else* could God be but a writer? In "The Sad Ballad of Mary Sue's Blues," Mulder has a miraculous encounter with a divine power: he meets his maker. It turns out there *is* a secret force controlling his life, but it isn't an alien conspiracy. It's a fanfiction writer.

Mary Sue, in all her mysterious glory, turns out to be the ultimate X-File.

Suggested Further Reading

When I first started putting together this collection, *The X-Files* was a foundational text though a relatively distant one, the second of the two feature films having been released in 2008. But the fandom never went away, and like most huge fandoms, it came roaring back when a new season of *The X-Files* debuted in 2016.

Because it was the first mainstream internet fandom, *The X-Files* is an important media studies text as well as the subject of some of the earliest aca-fannish work. *The X-Files* is central not only to collections like David Lavery, Angela Hague, and Marla Cartwright's 1996 *Deny All Knowledge: Reading the X-Files* but to studies of cult TV (e.g., Sara Gwenllian Jones and Roberta Pearson's 2004 *Cult Television*; David Lavery's 2010 collection *The Essential Cult TV Reader*) and of television noir and conspiracy narratives (e.g., *Conspiracy Culture: From Kennedy to the X-Files*, 2013). As the first born-digital fandom, X-philes were specifically examined in works like Christine Scodari's 2000 article, "Creating a Pocket Universe: 'Shippers,' Fan Fiction, and *The X-Files* Online" and Rhiannon Bury's 2005 *Cyberspaces of Their Own: Female Fandoms Online*. But *X-Files* fandom continues to be a subject of interest, with more recent articles like Bethan Jones's "The Fandom Is Out There: Social Media and *The X-Files* Online" and Emily Regan Wills's "Fannish Discourse Communities and the Construction of Gender in *The X-Files*" (both published in 2013).

The idea of the "Mary Sue" also continues to be debated inside and beyond fandom. *Transformative Works and Cultures* published an interview with Paula Smith, who coined the phrase, to talk about its meaning, but feminist criticism has, more broadly, done battle with the idea that female self-insert characters are somehow any worse than male ones; there is a vast literature celebrating girls and girl culture. Pat Flieger gave a paper called "'Too Good to Be True': 150 Years of Mary Sue" at the 1999 American Culture Association, connecting the figure of Mary Sue to the protagonists of nineteenth-century fiction, and Julia Beck and Frauke Herrling have tried to reimagine what being Mary Sue might mean in terms of video gaming and role-playing games. Kristina Busse's 2016 essay "Beyond Mary Sue: Fan Representation and the Complex Negotiations of Identity," in *Seeing Fans: Representations of Fandom in Media and Popular Culture*, thoroughly grounds and complicates the conceit.

The Sad Ballad of Mary Sue's Blues

Pares

> Mary Sues, of course, are those original female (sometimes male)
> characters written into fanfic whose resemblance to the author in
> question is surely more than co-incidence. You know them by the
> way Duncan and Methos fall at their feet and by the way that Jim
> and Blair hang on their every word. You know them by their selfless
> endeavours to get our boys together where they belong—in each
> other's arms. And of course there's the whole kill the bad guys/save the
> universe thing they've got going . . . but I digress.
> —Wombat, "Mary Sue Drinking Game"

The bar was nearly empty. Trying not to glance at his watch again, Mulder
loosened his tie and tapped the gleaming teak to catch the server's attention. It didn't look like his informant was going to show.

"Another."

The smirking barkeep tilted her head and said, "You sure you'll be okay
to drive?"

He made a small attempt at a smile and she shrugged.

"We ran out of lemon," she informed him.

"Lemon's overrated," he replied, as he took a sip of the unsweetened
iced tea. He studied her for a moment before she padded down the bar to
serve another whatever it was to the woman at the far end. Round face,
almond eyes, curly eyelashes. Asian, mixed maybe, definitely cute. And
she had been flirting, after all. He liked the plum shine to her hair, even
the glint of the silver hoop in her eyebrow.

"I've never paired you with an Asian girl. Her name's Naja. Short for
Natalie Jane. She was one of those Goth girls at Boston Latin; I based her
on a friend of mine from middle school."

Startled, Mulder swung around to face the speaker.

"What?"

"She's a little young for you, don't you think?"

"I—What—I don't understand. Who are you?"

The woman from the end of the bar was now sitting beside him.

"You really don't know me, do you?" She sounded unsurprised, and vaguely bored.

"Should I?"

"And after all we've meant to one another." The woman snorted, and the plosive sounded less like humor than congestion.

She looked like someone who had very little to laugh about.

A pie-faced woman with small smudgy eyes, dulled behind glasses thicker even than Frohike's, she swelled, wide and vast, in his vision.

"You should know me. It's unfair, really, for me to expect it, but I want you to remember me anyway."

"Who are you?" His whisper was rusted with the terrible thought that he should know her.

"Hortense Wahlberg," she said, and offered him her hand.

He took it, and shook it firmly, but her hand was rough, and unpleasantly moist.

"That's not always my name. In fact, it's never my name," she explained. "I'm kind of an antiarchetype."

Squinting, Mulder tried to make some sense of her. Her skin looked ashy . . . there was something that suggested promise, a warmth to it, had she ever gotten sun, but as it was, she was pallid and yellowed as old paper. She couldn't have been more than forty.

Ms. Wahlberg had the strangely youthful face of the very overweight, but the dull hair and closed expression of someone who spent a large amount of time alone.

"Ms. Wahlberg—"

"I'm being self-indulgent," she intoned, and she patted her hand on the bar. Her knuckles were thick; her fingers were like sausages. "I'm not actually all that bad looking. Trust me, Mulder, I clean up real nice."

Naja appeared with another drink. Hortense smiled at her, showing off a mouthful of small, crowded teeth. Naja smiled at her dishrag as she swabbed the bar.

"Bartenders always love me. Pets and kids do, too."

"What is this about, ma'am?"

"Have you ever read the Tale of the Green Knight? The knight goes out in search of what it is women really want, and he finds an old crone who promises to tell him if he'll marry her?"

Mulder nodded.

"The answer. Do you remember the answer?"

He opened his mouth to speak, but she robbed him of it.

"Control," she said, and it was a word as thick and sweet as taffy in her mouth. "We want control. We want our lives to be orderly. We want to avoid tax audits and rabid dogs and runaway buses and lives of toil, empty of meaning. We want to live in perfect contentment, and we are sure that if everyone merely does our bidding, we can be happy."

"Look, Ms. Wahlberg, I'm sure you—"

She gave him a sour glance.

"Play along, here. You can do that much at least of your own free will. I thought you had a certain empathy for victims?"

"Victims . . . ?"

The woman's second chin jiggled as she nodded. Her bra didn't fit well, and Mulder was distracted by the odd impression that Hortense Wahlberg had four breasts.

"We're usually poor," Hortense confided, as if she'd answered him. "Often, there's some kind of emotional trauma we're trying to shake off, and I would have to guess that most of us are fat." She gestured at the roll of belly that strained the faded pink T-shirt above where her too-tight jeans buttoned.

"Us?" Mulder wondered if he'd fallen asleep at the bar. His dreams were not unlike the conversation he was having with Ms. Wahlberg; although they usually involved someone he'd failed directly and then resolved themselves later with the not-unpleasant sensation of many groping hands caressing him as he was passed around the crowd at Carnegie Hall.

"That's not one of mine. You seldom dream coherently or pleasantly when I write you."

"Who are you? How did you know my name?"

"I'm not your contact, Mulder. And I'm Hortense Wahlberg, twenty-five or forty, fat, not very fair. I'm still in school, or I work at one, or I haven't worked in years, and I have three or more cats and a forest of over-watered ferns. I drink too much coffee. I may or may not smoke, I may or may not have a husband, and I often have a surprising number of outside interests. I'm also God. And only one of many."

Mulder tipped his iced tea with his elbow when he got to his feet. There was something pitiable and unnerving about Hortense Wahlberg.

"Don't be afraid," she whispered kindly.

"Who are you?"

"I am me, and you, and many. Not a spilt personality, but a compound identity. We are Mary Sue. Kind of like the Borg collective, only we tend to be less subtle and much more interested in sex."

There was a headache building behind his eyes; now it was only a tap, but soon it would bloom into an impatient banging on the pipes. He had to get out of here.

"I can make you stay. I'd rather not, but I can."

Shaking his head slightly, Mulder frowned. "Look, lady, I don't need this. I'm sure that you have every reason to be upset, but I can't help you. I just want to go home and get some sleep."

"He married the crone."

"Who? Oh. Gawain? Or was it Gareth?"

She smiled at him, a real smile, her mouth strangely prim.

"I can't remember. That's probably why you can't."

"Please," Mulder entreated. "I'm tired."

"I know you are. That's what we like about you." She touched his shoulder gently. "I don't think people tell you this enough, Mulder. You're very beautiful. And I happen to like the nose."

Mulder couldn't decide if the lump in his throat was tears or a bubble of incredulous laughter.

The homeliest woman he could remember seeing outside of Home, PA, and she was telling him he was beautiful.

Her smile was genuine, pleased, and it nearly made her pretty.

"You're beautiful when you suffer. You don't know how we appreciate that. When I cry I get blotchy, and my eyes swell. No one wants to come anywhere near me. But you . . . you sorrow. And it's very affecting. It doesn't hurt that most of us can't decide whether we like you best in those suits or out of them entirely." She chewed her lip thoughtfully. "I think your own lack of love life appeals, too. Every one of us is a yenta of some sort."

Mulder's headache had already graduated to the polite but firm knock of a visiting Jehovah's Witness. Soon enough it would metamorphose into—

Hortense Wahlberg's fingertip, complete with chewed cuticles and torn nail, tapped him lightly between the eyes.

And his headache disappeared.

"You know how I did it. I'm God, here. Goddess of the pure white page. I'll tell you something, I'll tell you a secret, Mulder, you've never really done exactly as I say. I've always liked that about you. All of you have a willful streak, and that can make the pen skid, or the train jump the tracks. You've talked yourself out of the best-laid plans, Mulder. I can't count the number of times you've balked at the bed scene, or refused to soften up when I wished you would."

Delusional. Jesus. The poor woman.

She smiled again.

"And the empathy. Self-pitying or not, Mulder, there's always room at your Inn. For the victims. You do know me, don't you?"

He shrugged. "Not you. I've never spoken to you. I think I've dreamt of—I think I've met some of the others. This is the most existentialist discussion I've had well, that I can remember. The others are . . ."

"Prettier than I am. Appealing in an undefinable way. Large eyed and engaging. Always thinner."

A wry smile curved his lips. He found himself feeling somehow proud of her. I'm proud of you, Mary Sue.

Nodding, her small eyes glinted behind the thick glass of her spectacles. She stood up and spread her arms, the biceps so soft they looked ready to drip from her bones and splatter the floor like batter slipping from a spoon.

"Kiss me, Mulder."

Closing his eyes, Mulder nodded. She'd been brave. He could do brave.

"Pity will do. Just this once."

I don't want it to be pity, he thought.

"It's nice that you think so. I appreciate it."

He stood up and stepped close to her. Her deodorant had faded, and the faint stale odor of her breath made him want to breathe through his mouth.

"Kiss the crone," she commanded. "Warts and all."

Warts!?

She actually chuckled, a rich, if wheezy sound.

"That one, at least, is a figure of speech. But you may want to close your eyes anyway. My skin's not very good. There's nothing lovely about blackheads."

I like that you're smart.

"And I like that you're charitable. Let's go."

Mulder felt his hands sink into the soft flesh of her shoulders, and he let go, lest he be stuck to her like the fool's goose. He bent his head, screwed his eyes shut, and pecked her narrow, chapped lips.

"Mulder?"

When he opened his eyes, Scully was peering at him in alarm.

"Are you all right? The bartender said you'd fainted; she found your phone and hit redial. Mulder?"

"I'm fine. Sorry. Fine. I'm really fine," he managed, but not before hugging his partner to him, cherishing the scent of her clean scalp, enjoying the neat way she fit against him.

She shrugged him away and gave him a look that was half glare, half concern.

"Mulder, what is going on?"

He cupped her face in his long hands, thumbs tracing the fine arch of her brow. Her skin was smooth and fine, nearly poreless. He let his hands fall away, only to stroke the unutterable softness of her lower lip with one forefinger. Rich pigment colored his fingertip, and he smiled at it.

"Scully. You're beautiful. I'm sure people don't say that enough."

She shook her head, and he squeezed her shoulder.

"I've had a weird night, Scully. Could you drive me home?"

Nodding warily, Scully helped him find his coat and followed him outside.

She unlocked the door for him, and he eased back against the car seat. Before she closed the door, Scully leaned in and rested one small, square hand on his shoulder.

"Mulder? Has anyone told you that? That you're beautiful?"

He gave her his warmest crooked grin.

"You just did."

> "If you do not tell the truth about yourself, you cannot tell it about other people."
> —Virginia Woolf

The Slayer's Tale

Title: next (2004)
Author: Jennet Smith
Fandom: *Buffy the Vampire Slayer*
Rating: Mature, femslash (Buffy/Faith)

Introduction

Spoiler alert: The very last scene of *Buffy the Vampire Slayer* (1997–2003) finds Buffy standing triumphantly, breathless and beat-up, over the giant smoking hole that was Sunnydale, California. She and her gang have just won an apocalyptic battle to close the Hellmouth beneath their hometown, and now they're wondering what to do next. (The mall has, alas, been destroyed.) It is suggested to Buffy that, having totally saved the world, she might now finally get to live like a normal person. "How's that feel?" her fellow Slayer Faith asks her. Buffy's smile is beatific.

"What's next?" is a central question for fanfiction writers.[1] One of the best-known fannish genres is the "episode tag," a story set directly after a particular episode. Fans also love to write stories set after the end of a series, taking the characters in multiple new and different directions. (A note to creative professionals who want their stories to have an afterlife: fans really like open endings. A good example is *Due South* [1994–1999], a show whose famously open-ended finale, sending the protagonists off together on a dogsled, is still inspiring fanfiction fifteen years later; a good counterexample is *Stargate: Atlantis* [2004–2009], whose decision to bring its intergalactic voyagers home meant that stories set after the finale first had to do the boring work of sending them back into space. Elsewhere in this volume you can read about reactions to J. K. Rowling's epilogue, but let me go on record right now with the opinion that the fantastically successful Harry Potter series would have been even *more* fantastically successful, and much more likely to stand the test of time, if Rowling had resisted the urge to tie up every loose end in an epilogue.)

Jennet Smith's *Buffy the Vampire Slayer* story "next" is both an episode tag and postseries story, and takes Buffy from the iconic last moment of the series—that wonderful smile as she contemplates what's next—into her new life. In her author's note, Jennet Smith said she felt sorry for Buffy at the end of the series and "wanted to give her something nice to cheer her up."

That nice thing is a relationship with Faith Lehane, Buffy's fellow Slayer and sometimes antagonist. Faith, a working-class girl from Boston, was called to be a Slayer as a result of one of Buffy's (many) deaths. (She got better.) *Buffy the Vampire Slayer* is a show driven by characterological foils, and Buffy has no better foil than Faith, who is hip, street smart, and troubled where Buffy is earnest, well-meaning, and responsible. When Faith arrives in Sunnydale, she and Buffy become BFFs, and at first Buffy finds Faith's devil-may-care attitude refreshing. Faith likes clubbing and flirting and shoplifting and making trouble, all of which is new to Buffy, who is burdened with the obligations of being the Slayer. Faith's motto—which she teaches Buffy—is all id: "Want. Take. Have." But their friendship falls apart when Faith's free-spiritedness reveals itself to be a dangerous recklessness. Still, neither Buffy nor her fans ever quite got over her. Like the punk vampire Spike, who was also only supposed to have a brief arc, Faith became a fan favorite and continued on past her storyline, provoking and befriending Buffy by turns.

While *Buffy the Vampire Slayer* later introduced an important lesbian relationship into the show (Buffy's friend Willow came out as a witch and then got into an actual sexual relationship with a fellow witch, Tara), many fans thought there was more lesbian subtext in Buffy's relationship with Faith, and made Buffy/Faith one of the primary pairings of the fandom.[2] This is not surprising: Faith's attempts to get Buffy to see the "fun side" of slaying—the power, the weapons, the physical pleasure of the adrenaline high—are explicitly framed as seduction. Like a lover, Faith appears in the window of Buffy's classroom and lures her to come out and play. Faith breathes on the glass and draws a heart with an arrow stuck into it: *Come stab vampires*, she means, but that's hardly the only interpretation.

It's also Faith who reveals that killing vampires leaves Slayers "hungry and horny." Buffy denies this ("Well . . . sometimes I crave a nonfat yogurt afterwards," she explains weakly) but the first time they kill together, Faith turns to Buffy and asks, breathlessly, "Hungry?" "Starved," Buffy confesses, and even the most gen-oriented fan can see the subtext *there*.[3] So Faith has always been associated with various forms of desire, not the least of which was Buffy's desire to give up her enormous responsibilities and live like a "normal" teenaged girl.

That only becomes possible for Buffy after the show's final episode, and so it's not surprising that in "next," Buffy's final unburdening happens in the company of Faith. Jennet Smith's story is at least partly about the fantasy of giving up responsibilities—and not just the giant supernatural ones, but the more mundane ones, too. For instance, in "next," Buffy is relieved that she no longer has to "play mother" to her sister, that she doesn't have to "worry about whether Dawn was ditching school or kissing vampires." Buffy also doesn't have to be in charge of a gaggle of baby Slayers anymore. She can attend to her own life and pleasures—go shopping, go dancing, eat Snickers bars, and have sex—and of course Faith is there. Faith is the canonical symbol of self-indulgence, but now, it's a *good* thing.

So in fanfiction, at least, Buffy finally gets to enjoy the new life she's smiling about in the finale: "She's realizing you can do this, have no responsibilities, have fun." Part of that fun is a sexual relationship with Faith: many fans felt that the show had been on the verge of offering Buffy a lesbian or bisexual identity before foreclosing the possibility and shunting the "coming out" story onto the safer figure of Willow: not the heroine but the heroine's best friend. But fandom's argument that the lesbian story was really Buffy's must have been at least somewhat convincing, because in the comic book *Buffy the Vampire Slayer: Season Eight* (2008),[4] written by Joss Whedon himself, Buffy finally, canonically gets to explore her bisexuality—not with Faith, who was partnered in the finale with Robin Wood (a relationship that Jennet Smith hastily undoes in "next"), but with a Japanese Slayer named Satsu. But fanfiction had of course done it first.

Suggested Further Reading

Buffy the Vampire Slayer has been particularly blessed (or cursed) with scholarly attention; not for nothing do we talk of "Buffy studies." In addition to field-defining collections like Rhonda Wilcox and David Lavery's *Fighting the Forces: What's at Stake in "Buffy the Vampire Slayer"* and Roz Kaveney's *Reading the Vampire Slayer: An Unofficial Critical Companion to Buffy and*

Angel (both books, 2002), there is a vibrant ongoing journal called *Slayage: The Journal of the Whedon Studies Association* (http://slayageonline.com/) and several international academic conferences, including the ongoing "Slayage Conference on the Whedonverses," the seventh of which was held at Kingston University in London in 2016. Malik Isakkson's 2009 article "Buffy/Faith Adult Femslash: Queer Porn with a Plot," in *Slayage* 7, no. 4, is a good place to start with respect to Buffy/Faith fanfiction.

Isaksson is also one of a number of scholars working to organize scholarship on femslash, a somewhat neglected area of fan studies. Most of the classic slash pairings have been male/male, and so the scholarship has mostly focused on m/m slash. The big exception is *Xena: Warrior Princess*; Rosalind Hammer and Sara Gwenllian Jones among others have written about lesbian fan communities and Xena. Malik Isaksson has also written specifically about Buffy/Faith as well as Bella/Alice fiction from *Twilight*, and Julie Levin Russo has written of femslash pairings in *Battlestar Galactica*, *Law and Order: SVU*, and *The L-Word*; both Isaksson and Russo have full-length book projects on femslash in the works. Julie Levin Russo and Eve Ng, who has written about fanvids of lesbian couples, are coediting a special issue of *Transformative Works and Cultures* on queer female fandom that will generate new work on lesbian fandom and queer female characters and pairings, which is due out in 2017.

next

Jennet Smith

When Sunnydale crumbles into a huge hole in the ground, Buffy pauses to revel in the finality of it, letting time stop around her for a moment. This is her favorite part of apocalypses: the first minutes after, like the first minutes after the last Christmas present has been opened, when all the long hustle and drive is suddenly suspended, motor engaging no gears, and you have no idea what needs doing next, because there *is* nothing that needs doing next.

But when all their eyes turn to her and Xander says, "So what now, Buff?" she does not get to say, "I don't know." She glances over at the bus where Robin is bleeding and says, "We get our asses to the nearest hospital, pronto." But this is the last, the very last thing, she tells herself. Even though it has never been true before.

Of course once Robin is settled at Rodriguez Memorial, two towns over, somehow it is she who is flipping through the yellow pages and finding the cheapest motel and writing down directions and reading them off to Xander as he pilots their massive vehicle through strangely populated streets. Robin has left them his credit cards and they splurge: five rooms: one for Camp Slayer, one for Willow and Kennedy to have post-I-became-a-goddess sex in, one for Giles and Xander (Giles is remarkably sanguine about this), and one for Buffy and Dawn—and theoretically Faith, if she doesn't end up spending the night at the hospital, which Buffy doesn't figure she will, Florence Nightingaling not being Faith's strong suit.

Buffy is still wandering around the room trying to do that unpacking/

nesting thing you do to a rented room to make it a little bit yours, but finding the process to be hampered by a lack of things to unpack, when there is a knock at the door and Giles pokes his head in and smiles at her hopefully. Buffy waves him in. Dawn slips out the door behind him before he gets a chance to close it, saying something about checking in on the kids. Buffy finds this suspicious but tries to test out her theoretical new not-in-chargeness by not quizzing Giles about it. Instead she sits cross-legged on the bed and asks, "What's up?" and tries to make it sound perky while all she really wants to do is figure out how to get hold of some clean clothes in the next twenty minutes so she can shower (which she's really really looking forward to doing) and not have to put these dirty ones back on again.

Giles hems a little bit, takes off his glasses, and polishes them. Buffy is patient. Eventually he looks up at her and says: "I suppose you realize, Buffy, that it's urgent I return to England to try to salvage what's left of the Watchers."

Buffy hadn't realized, on account of not having had time during the last weeks to give it much thought.

"You couldn't just look the other way and then oops, it'll be too late?" she asks hopefully, but mostly because she knows he expects it of her: she'd known he'd leave soon after the apocalypse was over, and anyways she's not particularly eager to have Giles around while she grieves for Spike. That's going to be a complicated enough process as it is.

"You know I can't, Buffy," he says. "But—there's something else. Dawn and I were talking, a few days ago, and she's agreed to come back with me."

Buffy feels silence settling into her bones as she parses this. She watches Giles, waiting for more. Her gaze is making him squirm a bit and that's okay by her.

"I'd been hoping for a while to have the chance to train her as a Watcher," he says, miserably. "And now—and with your present situation—"

"You mean my complete lack of any kind of housing structure to keep her in?" Buffy asks.

"Something like that, yes," Giles says.

The feeling which is slowly creeping through Buffy is familiar. She felt it when she realized that her house was in little pieces a mile below the surface of the earth. It was a good part regret—the house was her mother's house, was filled with memories—but it was also, overwhelmingly, relief. To not have to play mother, to not have to worry about whether Dawn was ditching school or kissing vampires, to hand her over to the man who was in a very real sense Buffy's father-god. Even just for a little while.

She looks up to see Giles still desperately uncomfortable, and she smiles. "Thank you, Giles," she says. "I think that would be a great idea."

The next to go, two days later, are Kennedy and the kids, of course. They are bursting with the awe of being slayers and they have no desire to stick around some sleepy California town when there's another Hellmouth just a few thousand miles away in Cleveland. They are very hopeful that it will produce lots of things with asses they can kick. They seem to expect Buffy to come with them as camp counselor, but when she shrugs they are just as happy to follow Kennedy. What Buffy hadn't thought through was that, of course, Willow is going to follow Kennedy—and Xander is going to follow Willow. (On the up side, Andrew is going to follow Xander.) It is harder than losing Dawn. There are tears.

"I'll be there soon," Buffy promises. "A few months maybe. But I can't right now, guys. I can't be in charge. I need a vacation."

"But what are you going to *do?*" asks Xander, maybe remembering his abortive road trip a few years ago.

Buffy shrugs and tries to smile. "Maybe I'll go to Disneyland," she says.

She sees them off the next morning in the yellow monstrosity and when she comes back to her room, Faith is there.

"Oh," says Buffy. "Hi. Um, how's Robin?"

"Things are growing back where they should be," Faith says. "Just said goodbye to the gang, huh?"

Buffy shrugs.

"But you're staying here," Faith says. Buffy looks at her: they'd discussed this at the hospital the night before. "I mean, I wanted to ask," Faith says, edging around her point as she usually does when she's about to ask for something, "you're going to hang out with me, then? And Robin."

"He gets out tomorrow, right?" says Buffy.

"Yeah," Faith says. "And after that?"

Buffy shrugs. She feels empty. She feels unable to make a decision.

"Hey," Faith says. "I got an idea. How about we go shopping? Buy, you know, girly things."

Buffy starts, "I don't have any—" but Faith holds up Robin's Master-Card, grinning. "We got plastic, baby," she says.

Buffy is pretty sure the only kind of shopping Faith enjoys is for weapons, but somehow they end up in an actual mall at a store which does indeed have girly things. To Faith's credit she pretty much leaves Buffy alone to take in the wonder that is capitalism. It's been awhile since Buffy's indulged like this and she takes a few minutes to just wander. It's a little overwhelming at first but then the old instincts kick in and she begins loading up.

In the dressing room she finds she's dropped a size or two and most of the clothes she's brought in don't fit all that well. But there's a little black dress which is about perfect, low scoop neck, cute spaghetti straps, nice cling around the hips; it almost makes her look curvy. She twists in front of the mirror a few times, then goes out into the main dressing area to check herself out in the bigger mirror out there.

She's only been admiring herself for a few seconds when another dressing room door opens and Faith emerges. Wearing the exact same dress.

Faith's face visibly falls. "Hey," she says. "That looks great on you. I don't think this one really fits me anyway."

She's lying. It might look great on Buffy but it looks fantastic on Faith. She's put on the curves Buffy's lost. Maybe the scoop neck shows off Buffy's collarbone but it shows some really delicious cleavage on Faith and it clings along the curve of Faith's hip in a truly sweet line. Buffy suddenly remembers Faith saying: "It feels like it's mine . . . Guess that means it's yours."

"No, that's all right," Buffy says, and the smile, when it comes, doesn't feel forced. "You should get it."

Faith meets her eyes and smiles hesitantly, and Buffy finds herself imagining what it would be like to slip that strap off Faith's shoulder with one finger.

In the end, Buffy gets a pair of silk slacks and a tiny halter top that ties behind her neck and under her shoulder blades and shows almost her entire back and all of her tummy. It's a little terrifying but she reminds herself that in high school she would have pulled it off without a second thought. Faith's reaction: "I guess you'll go braless then. Me, I've had to wear the damn things every day since I grew these huge boobs in prison."

Now, Buffy says wistfully, holding her shopping bag, "Too bad we don't have anywhere to wear them."

"Hey," Faith says, "who's in charge here?"

Buffy thinks: you are. It's not as bad a thing as she'd have once thought.

The last time Buffy was at a club with Faith, Faith killed a man after. Buffy's not thinking about that. She's thinking how long it's been since she's been at any club but the Bronze, and how this place with its punks and goths and drinks that burn your throat on the way down and women in skimpy dresses dancing on platforms feels less safe than the Bronze, and she's wondering why anyone would ever want to go to a club that felt safe.

And she's thinking about how long it's been since she danced with someone who really knows how to dance, and she's enjoying how many sets of eyes are on her and Faith.

Instead of remembering all the bad parts about those days she played at being like Faith, senior year, she's remembering how good it felt. She's realizing you can do this, have no responsibilities, have fun, you can do this for a little while, sometimes, and you don't have to let it eat you up.

They aren't playing the sort of hip indie bands Buffy learned to love at the Bronze, but the beat is good and she can feel her entire body responding. It's the same kind of completely physical activity as finally getting to grips with a vampire after the long stalk through a graveyard, and she and Faith work as well in this context as they do in their best moments of slaying together, their movements relaxed and synchronized. For the first time in a long time, Buffy feels beautiful.

So it's a little jarring when Faith says, "I'm going to the little girl's room—I'll be back," and moves off through the crowd with that loose-limbed walk which Buffy finds so compelling and so annoying. The beat's still there but Buffy doesn't feel any longer as though the music is moving her through a force of its own. This aggravates her. So she can't just relax and have fun all on her own, she needs to feed off Faith to do it? Automatically she turns to watch Faith making even going to pee into something cool and slightly dangerous, and sees her ducking out of the bathroom—that was quick—and sliding along a wall and out the club's back exit through a cloud of cigarette smoke.

Buffy finds that following though the writhing crowd isn't a quick process. The temptation to just toss a few bodies out of the way is overwhelming. When she finally reaches the exit and looks out it takes a minute to see what's going on. She worries she was too slow getting here. The door opens on a little alleyway lined with people who have ostensibly stepped out to smoke, but since smoking is if anything encouraged inside the club, have mostly come out for some more nefarious purpose. Buffy smells pot right off and imagines that there are plenty of real drugs out here too. But what concerns her is the sight of Faith holding a man up against a wall by his throat. They're in a corner and being sort of quiet about the whole thing and anyways the druggies don't much care so there is not the general sense of alarm that you might expect a scene like this to engender. Then Buffy sees the young woman cowering against a wall and begging Faith not to hurt him and things begin to resolve. Faith yanks out a stake and uses it efficiently, and the man in her grip becomes dust and the young woman gapes. Faith says brusquely, "Next time, pick one that just wants to fuck you and leave you," and turns to stalk back inside. Buffy has to scramble to keep ahead of her, and as it is she doesn't manage to get back to the same spot in the shifting crowd before Faith catches up to her.

Faith looks at her curiously, but says nothing, and they drop easily back into the rhythm. Buffy feels oddly . . . protected: assured that she isn't going to have to be constantly alert, that maybe they can actually trade that job off. It's an odd feeling, and she figures she's going to have to live with it for a while before she decides if it's a gift she's comfortable accepting.

As they get back to the motel room Buffy is really looking forward to sliding into the lumpy bed and sleeping. She has a premonition that tonight she's going to sleep through the night and of all of the many premonitions she's had she thinks she likes this one the best. Usually her nights go something like this: she wakes up at four worrying that Giles is in the basement staking Spike. She gives herself a firm talking-to about the limits of Giles' stupidity and starts to relax again and then ten minutes later is wide awake: what if she should *let* Giles stake Spike? What if that commotion in the next room is Spike biting the neck of the Japanese girl whose name Buffy can never pronounce right? Or what if he's seducing her? Is she a horrible person for worrying more about that possibility? She rolls over and looks at her clock and realizes that it's 6:45 and the commotion was the normal early-morning scramble for first shower rights, before the hot water's all gone, which normally happens by 7:50 (showers, however, continuing cold until 9:00 or 10:00).

Tonight, though, she doesn't have to worry about slayerettes—not even to wonder whether they're out late experimenting with their new powers and getting into Situations with vampires which Buffy really should have taught them about so when they get their necks snapped it'll be all her fault—tonight she is alone. Except for Faith. She doesn't have to take care of Faith; Faith can take care of herself. And the only decision Buffy has to make is whether to let *Faith* try to take care of *her*. Which is a decision she doesn't need to make tonight. Tonight, she can just sleep.

First, though, she really wants to shower, and Faith wins the coin toss for first rights. All the other times she'd saved the world, Buffy didn't really think she should have gotten paid for it. At least, not as more than a wistfully passing thought. But after this time, after giving up her house, it just seems hard that she has to share a grimy hotel bathroom with Faith.

Buffy becomes engrossed in channel surfing while she waits, and by the time Faith comes out of the bathroom door toweling her hair, accompanied by clouds of steam, Buffy is watching *Pretty in Pink*.

"Holy shit," Faith says.

"What?" Buffy says. "Oh. We can watch something else."

"That's okay," Faith says, sitting down next to Buffy on her bed. "You actually like this shit?"

"It's the only thing on," Buffy says, but truthfully she has a soft spot for any story about the way her life should have been. Not with the bad fashion sense, but with the not having to worry about whether your boyfriend was going to wake up evil. Just worrying about whether he was ever going to want to be your boyfriend. And inevitably finding out that he did. "You know what we need?" says Buffy. "We need popcorn."

Faith rolls her eyes over at Buffy and says, "Fat chance. We don't even have a microwave."

"No, but you know what we need," says Buffy, knowing that there is a candy machine down the hall, "we need some Snickers."

"Done," says Faith, swinging her legs off the bed and ambling into the hall wearing I swear to god just a towel. It's like sending your boyfriend out in the middle of the night for cookies, Buffy thinks. She is asleep by the time Faith gets back.

Buffy wakes up in gray predawn light. She thinks: oh god I never showered, I never brushed my teeth. She should feel disgusting. Instead she feels warm, snuggled in her bed. There is a blanket tucked over her. Faith must have done that. Looking across the room at Faith's sleeping form, Buffy has a realization. Faith will never say it. Faith believes Buffy doesn't want it and that it is now her role to be the friend. That asking for more would return them to their relationship of four years ago.

Buffy makes a decision.

If she thinks about it, she won't do it. She is almost unable to breathe, and she can feel every heartbeat unnaturally loud. She's afraid the sound is going to wake Faith even before she starts to slide out of bed. She's afraid her two steps across the small space between the beds is going to wake Faith. She's afraid her awkward scramble into Faith's bed is going to wake Faith. But as she eases herself into the bed (with her back to Faith, not quite daring to face her yet), feeling all elbows and knees, Buffy notices Faith's shallow breathing and realizes she's been awake this whole time. If it is possible, this makes Buffy panic even more, as if realizing that they are going to actually have to interact now comes as a surprise. She's dithering about what exactly she should do next when Faith slowly slides one leg between hers and an arm over her hip. They lie still like that for a long minute, and then Buffy turns over.

The kiss starts slow. Buffy's not really sure what to *do* at first, and Faith seems unwilling to call the shots. But then it comes as a sudden revelation: kissing a girl requires exactly the same skill set as kissing a boy. And Buffy's actually not bad at that. And when she stops worrying so much about whether she's doing it right, she's able to start to notice just how right Faith's doing it. She can feel it down to her toes. And then suddenly Faith is rolling her over to lie on top of her and she's winding her hands into Buffy's hair and kissing her like she wants to eat her up, like their faces could melt together, like Buffy's the best thing she's tasted in her life. And Buffy realizes she's actually making little moaning noises. The kiss seems to last for hours and then Buffy finally pulls back a little and opens her eyes, and Faith's eyes are open too, and they look at each other. Buffy's thinking: Oh god, now she's going to be Faith, she's going to say something offhand and cool and I'm going to feel like an idiot.

But what Faith says is: "Are you sure?"

And Buffy says, "Oh, yeah."

They sleep late. They wake up slowly. They cuddle. It occurs to Buffy that she never thought of Faith as the cuddling type, but she does a pretty good job of it. They lie quietly for a while, and then as she is running her hand up and down Faith's side, slowly, enjoying how soft her skin is, Buffy says: "It was also my first time, you know, cheating." She hadn't thought about Robin until now, and she doesn't feel too much guilt about it: this thing between her and Faith, it's much older than Faith's relationship with Robin, which might anyways be too young to really be called a relationship.

Faith says, "I guess we'll straighten that out when we check him out of the hospital in a few hours."

Buffy, who had forgotten, says: "Oh god."

Buffy had envisioned holding hands with Faith on the way to the hospital and then having to deal with awkwardly letting go outside Robin's room. She had forgotten that Faith does not go in for sappy things like hand-holding. So she does not get to make her great lesbian statement in the lobby. This is, she admits to herself, a relief.

When they open the door to Robin's room he is just finishing tying his laces and looks up eagerly: he is glad to see them, and he is gladder to be escaping from this prison. But then his expression changes and Buffy realizes that the hand-holding was irrelevant. They are standing too close together or they have a happy postcoital glow or something. It doesn't matter. He knows. She says brightly: "Well, um, good morning, Robin! So are you ready to go?"

There is a pause in which Robin and Faith both simultaneously turn to stare at her. Then Faith says "*God*, Buffy." Her tone says both "You are such a boob" and "I can't believe I'm in love with a boob." Except that Faith would never say "boob," but without access to her cool Boston vocabulary that's the best Buffy can come up with.

"You lied to me," Robin says to Faith. They are both ignoring Buffy now.

"I didn't lie," Faith says reasonably. "I told you nothing was going on. Nothing was going on. Then."

"Fine," Robin says. "I'll take a cab. If you'll just give me my credit card back, I'll be going."

Buffy is bemused: in her experience breakups involve a lot more tears and a lot less icy disdain.

Faith digs Robin's credit card out of her pocket and hands it to him. As Buffy starts to do the same with his other card, Faith puts her hand on Buffy's wrist, pulls Buffy's hand out of her pocket, and wraps their fingers together: suddenly they are holding hands. How sweet. Buffy is momentarily distracted from the immorality of basically stealing Robin's credit card by the fact that she is holding hands with a girl, in public.

"Look, Robin," Faith says, "let's not part on bad terms, okay? I had fun. I bet you did too. And I learned something. So no hard feelings, okay?"

Robin considers this for a second. Then something inside him visibly relaxes and he says, "Okay. No hard feelings. But that doesn't mean I'm going to be a third wheel with you and your girlfriend while you go kill vampires in wherever it is you're going. Where are you going?"

Faith turns to look at Buffy, grins, and says, "So what's next, B?"

And Buffy says, "I don't know."

The Super Man's Tale

Title: Three Fairy Tales of Smallville (2003)
Author: Koi
Fandom: *Smallville*
Rating: Mature (slash, Clark/Lex)

Introduction

Superman. Cultural icon, defender of Truth, Justice, and the American Way. There has been a fandom around Superman since his 1938 debut in *Action Comics* number 1, and the character has appeared in comics, books, radio, television, animation, movies, video games—you name it. George Reeves and Christopher Reeve both played popular incarnations, but it was the television series *Lois and Clark* (1993–1997) that coincided with the explosion of internet fandom in the mid-1990s. *Lois and Clark* was a very popular fandom (fans called themselves "FoLC" —pronounced "folk"— for "fans of Lois & Clark")[1] that produced lots of Clark/Lois fanfic (some of it *nfic*, or "naughty fiction"), and it probably would have been the "big" Superman fandom had there not come along a little show called *Smallville*.

Smallville, which debuted in 2001 and ran for ten years (*ten years!*), tells the story of Clark Kent's life before he became Superman. Clark grows up in a small town with his loving parents Jonathan and Martha. Alas, Kryptonite meteors give the local inhabitants strange powers and sometimes create weird and terrible monsters that have to be stopped, and on top of that, Clark has to negotiate a complex friendship with Lex Luthor, who's been sent to Smallville to run one of his cruel father's many factories. If *Lois and Clark* was successful because of the show's focus on Teri Hatcher's

Lois Lane, then *Smallville* was successful because of Michael Rosenbaum's Lex Luthor, who was seen as "charmingly bruised, emotionally vulnerable, and very attractive to his fans."[2] Clark and Lex meet in a pivotal scene in the pilot, where Lex, driving his Porsche much too fast, loses control, hits Clark, and goes careening off a bridge into the river. Clark, being an invincible alien, saves Lex from drowning, pulling him out of the wrecked car and giving him mouth-to-mouth resuscitation. This is the start of a long, complicated, and profoundly homoerotic friendship.

Clark/Lex—known as Clex—instantly became a *colossally* popular slash pairing, and calling out *Smallville*'s obvious "HoYay" (homoeroticism, yay!) became one of the chief activities of the internet forum that became Television Without Pity, even (or maybe especially) among the show's official recappers. (Consider this sample from longtime recapper Omar: "[Lex and Clark] stare at each other for what seems like hours, earning themselves the coveted Gayest Look of the Episode[3] award. Clark gives a tiny smirk and then says he has some more deliveries to make. I start hearing '70s porn 'Bonk, shuka, bonk, bonk' music in my head.")[4] He wasn't the only one.

In addition to *Smallville*'s obvious HoYay, the complexity of Superman canon—which, like most comic book canon, is so crazy, contradictory, and convoluted that *anything* could happen—really: I mean *anything*[5]—meant that *Smallville* was ripe for fanfic AUs, or alternate universes. Anything could happen because anything had probably *already* happened, and no matter how weird your fanfiction idea, something weirder had happened in the comics. So while all fanfiction is based on a fan asking, "What if?" it is perhaps unsurprising that *Smallville* fandom developed its own unique genre of alternate universe fanfiction: the "Five Things" story.

Five Things stories have become so popular across fandom that most fans don't realize that they have a specific origin. But they do. In 2001, a fan named Basingstoke wrote a *Smallville* story, "Five Things That Aren't True,"[6] comprised of five scenes that were explicitly not in the same timeline, but gave glimpses of different crazy realities: for example, one in which Clark kills Lex by accident, and one in which a teenaged Lex runs into Bruce Wayne hanging upside down like a bat in the school gymnasium. As Jayne noted in her DVD commentary to Basingstoke's story: "Individually, each snippet has its charm; together, under the umbrella of 'Things That Aren't True,' they make the reader think about *why* none of these scenarios have been found in canon, and why they could—or couldn't—reasonably show up in canon before the end of the series."[7] Many fans were eager to try

Basingstoke's formula for themselves, and arguably her assertion that these snapshots were "not true" gave fans even more permission to be creative: in fanfiction, we not only write every version that could happen, but even the versions that *could never* happen. Fans began writing their own Five Things stories, which now include popular variations like "Five Things That Never Happened," or sometimes "Five Things That Never Happened and One That Did" (or, for the more mathematically inclined, "Four Things That Never Happened and One That Did"). The whole genre is known collectively as Five Things, or sometimes 5 + 1 or 4 + 1.

The following story, dedicated by the author to Basingstoke ("who started it all"), was meant to be a Five Things story, though the author, Koi, also known as Koimistress, only got to three out of five. "Three Fairy Tales of Smallville" is what it says on the tin, and as hard as it can be to explain fanfiction, it's even harder to explain what's so wonderful about an AU, because you have to know the source well enough to appreciate what's different: it's like listening to a mashup when you don't know any of the tunes. But I'll try, because these are three really terrific tales: "Julian," "Petrie Dish," and "Bleeding Kansas."

Julian

In season 1 of *Smallville*, we learn that Lex once had a brother, Julian, who died as an infant. Lex bitterly tells us that his father saw Julian as a chance "to have a son he could truly love." Later, in season 3 (after this story was written) we learned that Lex's unhinged mother actually smothered Julian in his crib because she was afraid that Lex's father Lionel was going to "pit the boys against each other," making them fight for his affection and turning them "into monsters."

In "Julian," Koi anticipates this development and puts a twist on it. In this alternate universe, Julian is alive (although a third brother, Napoleon, has died) and indeed, Lionel Luthor has pitted his surviving sons against each other. Lionel tests them and constantly forces them to compete, telling them brutally that one of them will be heir to the LexCorp fortune and the other will be cut off without a cent. But in "Julian," the boys eventually join forces to fight against their father's tyranny, and when Lionel Luthor's Porsche careens off a bridge and crashes into the river in Smallville (echoing Lex and Clark's first meeting), nobody saves him. And if the "exotic flowering weed" who is Lex's *adopted* brother Julian starts to seem a bit familiar to you—well, what if the Kents weren't the ones to find the crashed spaceship with the alien baby? And have Lex and Julian become monsters after all? You decide.

Petrie Dish

In Superman (and *Smallville*) canon, the alien baby who grew up to be Superman was found in a crashed spaceship by farmers Jonathan and Martha Kent, who raised him as their own, imbuing him with their own heartland values. But in "Petrie Dish," this turns out to be a lie: the alien was actually found by the U.S. government. Martha Clark—here an ex-army officer, CIA brat, and de facto expert on alien life—makes a proposal to a top-secret Senate subcommittee: "Why kill it," she asks, "when we can absorb it?" Her argument is that the alien baby is still more or less a primate, and will seek comfort from other primates. "If we bring it up as one of us, it will *be* one of us, loyal to our standards and morality." The government's solution: "A controlled environment. We call it Smallville." We know that, in canon, *Smallville*'s Martha had been desperate to have a baby: "I see a little face," she sighs in *Smallville*'s first episode. "It's all I ever wanted." Koi's version of Martha Kent is the same—and yet very, very different.

Bleeding Kansas

Pete Ross is Clark Kent's childhood best friend, and most of the time in canon, he's white. But *Smallville* made the bold move of casting Sam Jones III in the part, bringing some racial diversity to the show, at least for a while. Fans were disappointed, however, that the character was never given much to do, especially compared to Pete in the comics. To quote Pete's (bitter) Fanlore entry, "Unlike his DC Comics counterpart, who was white and would grow up to marry Lana Lang and become Vice President, *Smallville* Pete was black and would grow up to leave the show after only three seasons."[8] In stories like Yahtzee's pan-fandom classic "Them Mean Ol', Low-Down, Lando Calrissian Blues," Pete Ross unites with other "unfairly ignored black guys" on other shows to protest their token status: "We're tired of being the guys who stay behind to watch the car," Gunn from *Angel* says. "We're tired of being the guys sent to get help long before the interesting stuff actually happens."[9]

In "Bleeding Kansas," Koi makes Pete central to the story in a different way: by giving Kansas itself an alternate, and terrifyingly plausible, history. *Smallville*'s writers were given the dictum, "No flights, no tights," meaning no stories in which Clark flies or wears a costume. But in this story, it's Pete who is desperate to fly —and can't.

Suggested Further Reading

There's no shortage of critical material on Superman in general or *Smallville* in particular. Cory Barker, Chris Ryan, and Myc Wiatrowski's 2014 collection *Mapping "Smallville": Critical Essays on the Series and Its Characters* (McFarland, 2014) and Lincoln Geraghty's *The "Smallville" Chronicles: Critical Essays on the Television Series* (Scarecrow, 2011) are good places to start for studies of the television show. Slash fandom is also well represented in the literature with articles like Melanie Kohnen's "The Adventures of a Repressed Farm Boy and the Billionaire Who Loved Him: Queer Spectatorship in *Smallville* Fandom," in *Teen Television* (McFarland, 2008) and Michaela Meyer's "Slashing Smallville: The Interplay of Text, Audience, and Production on Viewer Interpretations of Homoeroticism," in *Sexuality and Culture* 17 (2013).

It remains to be seen if fanfic-writing fandom will embrace Superman in his most recent incarnation, as portrayed by Henry Cavill in the Zack Snyder movies *Man of Steel* (2013) and *Batman vs. Superman* (2016). It hasn't quite yet, but then again, the new DC-film-verse hasn't quite jelled yet. Fandom, which likes to write about relationships, partnerships, and teams (see "The Billionaire Superhero's Tale," later in this volume), might well be waiting for the formation of the Justice League.

For now, though, *Smallville* is still the Superman fandom to beat.

Three Fairy Tales of Smallville

Koi

Julian

His father had long had a list of names for his potential sons—*Alexander, Julian, Napoleon, Xerxes*. Because he possessed a fiery and imaginative ambition, the names gave no quarter where fashion was concerned; because he was exacting and analytical, they would be bestowed in alphabetical order.

It was probably just as well that only two Luthor sons took these names to the school playground, and that the alphabet had been kind to them.

Lex remembered when Julian was a toddler—the wary eyes that followed Lionel's big adult hand as it swung down to stroke his cheek, as though even then Julian were not sure of his welcome in this house. No more than Lex was, for the Metropolis mansion was the civilized equivalent of some minefield in a country where wars never truly ended, and to survive and thrive you learned to watch every signal. Julian had copied Lex in those days, and Lex had taken him aside, behind closed doors when the nannies and tutors were gone, to coach him in what to say and do.

He'd loved Julian then, in an uncomplicated way. When had that changed? When had the Lionel voice in his head gone from saying, "Take care of Julian, Alexander," to "Watch out for Julian, Alexander"?

Maybe it was when those dinners at home had gone from lessons in deportment to cockfights over the white linen tablecloth. Red wine in Dad's glass like spilled blood, and Julian, opposite, older now, beautiful and composed as he answered Lionel's test questions—with a gentle, infuriating smile on the ones that Lex had just blown. Lex had been spoiled, he knew; unused to real competition. Lionel had been thrilled to throw his brilliant younger son against the older.

"Explain entailments to me," Lionel said one evening over his glass of blood.

"Property is limited to a specified selection of heirs," Lex said. "It's an old enough concept; fairy tales are full of younger sons who don't inherit and have to go out into the forest to seek their fortune." He didn't look at Julian.

"Indeed. And what about the French?"

Lex was silent. He hated these pop quizzes. What the hell did real families talk about, anyway?

After waiting a discreet moment, Julian said, "The tradition in France was to share property equally among sons, as opposed to England, where estates were entailed on a line of succession through the oldest."

Lionel gave one of those approving looks he never seemed able to call up for Lex. "Correct as usual, Julian."

Julian smiled unreadably at Lex, who imagined plunging a fork through his brother's throat. Lex didn't mean anything by it; he'd been imagining the same thing about Lionel for years. It kept him from going crazy at the dinner table.

"And the result?"

"Sons in France were happier, I assume," Lex told his father. Even at the age of sixteen he knew he could pack more sarcasm into a single look than most people could spell.

"And what happened to the property?"

"Logically, it would be broken into smaller pieces with each generation, until there was none left. Really, Dad, if you're going to go from this to the split of the Roman Empire into east and west—"

"Someone must always be disappointed if empires are to remain intact." He gave them a heartily cheerful look, like a TV father proposing a fishing trip. "How do you suppose we should solve this?" He tipped back the wine glass for the last drop. "Eh? There's always the Borgia way . . . or perhaps a nice game of *Parcheesi* . . ."

Julian was a precocious sociopath, anyway. He was good company when he chose to be, even though Lex hadn't been able to tell what he was thinking since he was six. It was those private sessions with Lionel that really galled, though. The study door would close behind them, and Lionel would be all smiles when they emerged, his hand on Julian's shoulder in a proprietary way.

No such personal attention for Lex, the hothouse flower, the freak, the boy who rubbed sunblock into his head every morning. In contrast, Julian was a weed—some exotic, flowering weed of the Amazon, with roots you couldn't get at. Strong and perfect. Just what you'd want in a son.

Lex was nineteen. Two days after his birthday, he was in his bedroom, packing his own bags. Julian walked in, in the quiet, catlike Luthor way, wearing a black turtleneck. He sat on the bed, cross-legged, and watched.

"Can I have your comic collection?"

"I'm transferring to Princeton, I'm not making out my will."

"Why?"

Lex glanced at the beautiful, opaque face. *Why* was not a question that was thrown around much in their world. He dropped a few CDs in the suitcase, thought a moment, and said, "Julian? What do you and Dad talk about in the study?"

"The future," said Julian.

"Your future? My future? The future of the human race?"

Julian was silent. He said, "Are you transferring to get away from me?"

Christ. It was odd what a shock the question was. Lex had relied on the fact that Luthors communicated with each other in subtext; this was completely against etiquette.

He turned to get another sweater, keeping his face away from Julian's line of sight. "The world doesn't revolve around you, little brother." When he turned back, he was confident that he showed nothing. "You can *read* the comics. Don't touch the ones in plastic."

Sometimes Lex thought his father had it all wrong. He clearly wanted to use Julian as a goad for Lex, a mechanical rabbit to keep him running fast and strong. His father's psychology was brutal, but Lex wondered if it were accurate. Maybe if Julian weren't there, Lex would have been less awkward, less self-conscious, more bold; maybe he would have finished college early and been eager to take on the world.

Finishing college, however, only meant a return to Metropolis, and to his brother. No point in hurrying that along. There was plenty to learn at Princeton. And then, Yale had a good graduate program . . .

Twenty-three years old. He felt like Michael Corleone when he got the call. "This is ridiculous, Lex," his father said. "I've been patient."

"I have a degree to complete," Lex replied, as if he really believed he'd left that world behind. As if one kick of the spurs wouldn't send him back into a fight to the death.

"Come home," said Lionel. It was an order.

Julian had grown straight and tall, with eyes like the sea, able to lull you to sleep or suck all the breath from your body. "Welcome back," he said, as Lex entered the vestibule with his bags.

Twenty-six. Lex had been in Smallville for two years. Dad treated it like the parable of the steward and the talents; send one son to a crap factory, and compare what he brings back with the best gifts of the other son.

Julian was still too young to have a crap factory of his own, though, and Lionel showed no inclination to be parted from him, so what precisely Lex's stewardship would be compared with had not been shared with him. Really, though, you had to give Lionel credit for that—much more Orwellian this way; you never knew whether to expect grudging approval or mockery.

Smallville seemed to have an extraordinary number of accidents for so small a town, but Lex gave no more than minimal thought to the mystery; his mind was elsewhere. He flew along the back country roads in his cars, ignoring the stares, but he never became part of the town.

Dad came on his birthday. Lex had not been told to expect him, and only discovered this uncalled-for honor when he was eight miles north of town, and it suddenly occurred to him that the car ahead looked oddly familiar. Generally Lionel took the helicopter or the limo, going for speed or the ability to work during the drive; but when he was in the mood, he could wield a sports car like a weapon, grinding out his aggression on the helpless gears.

From Lex's point of view, it was meant to be a sedate drive back to the mansion. He wasn't even sure his father had spotted him—not till he tried to pass.

The two Porsches took the curve outside the Benson place at 85, then pulled up to 120 on the straight line of Hickory Lane. They blasted past the Kent farm, Lionel in front, Lex gaining ground. A frightened cardinal took off from a fencepost in a blur of red, and Lex had the impression of some flannel-clad farmer standing, mouth open in shock, as they thundered past.

Lex moved into the oncoming lane to overtake Lionel. One-twenty. One-thirty. As they reached Turner's Bridge, Lex saw an oil truck coming from the other direction. He hit the gas, hard—knowing Lionel would be doing the same thing—and then reality set in. Lex knew he could do a lot of things, but he couldn't change the laws of physics through will alone. He braked and fell in behind his father's car.

They reached the mansion at the now vaguely unreal speed of 35 miles an hour. The car doors slammed, one after the other. "You would have made it," Lionel said, "if you hadn't lost your nerve."

A little revisionist mindfucking. No, he wouldn't have made it; he'd have been chopped hamburger on a rural road, and that's no way for a Luthor to make an exit.

Wouldn't he? Lex pictured the oncoming truck again, mentally reviewing the space between them . . . *Stop it.*)

"The same make and model of car, both in peak condition; what could be the difference? Ah, yes—the quality of the driver. I begin to see why you begged off from extreme skiing; without the inner will, the body is a brittle shell."

Really, the man was outrageous. For a second, Lex almost liked him.

Dinner was like old times. After Lionel had grilled Lex on the status of the plant, the amount of attention he'd paid to the acquisition of Bendell by LuthorCorp, and the sayings of Clausewitz on total war, his father seemed almost mellow.

"I'm surprised you didn't bring Julian along for 'Final Jeopardy,'" said Lex.

Lionel smiled over the tiny, perfect square of chocolate mousse. "I considered it. Your brother's at the lake house studying for finals."

"Like Julian needs to study."

"He'll be graduating in a month," Lionel remarked. He added, as though it were an afterthought, "I have an idea about that."

Fuck.

"Oh?"

"Your tenure in Smallville has been . . . adequate."

"Gee, thanks, Dad."

"I'm thinking of posting Julian to Plant 26."

"North Carolina? A bit far, isn't it? You usually don't let him out of your sight." A crooked smile. "Almost as if you were afraid to."

His father laughed delightedly. "Your brother's old enough now to come into his own."

"Really. And what 'own' would that be?"

"Why, that's up to you, Lex. You'll each get a plant of your own to run, like good boys." Lionel put the crystal salt shaker next to the pepper, as though graphic accompaniments were necessary. "At the end of a year, we'll see who's increased profits the most. The winner gets groomed for his inheritance."

"And the loser?"

"Oh, I don't know. Perhaps a commemorative pen set?"

"Dad—"

"Nothing. Ever. Both your trust funds were left to my discretion, and I'll cut one of you off without a penny."

"I see," said Lex thoughtfully. "You want a fight to the death."

"What else makes it worthwhile? You won't show what you're made of unless I force you, Lex. Consider yourself forced." He pulled a cigar from his breast pocket. "Oh, and did I mention? The plant of the loser will be closed, with minimal severance for its employees."

Lex sat there silently, considering his options.

Lionel said, "I know you've got the killer instinct, Lex. You keep burying it. I won't tolerate that anymore."

He stood, and Lex stood as well. "Morituri te salutamus," said Lex ironically, giving a sketchy bow. *We who are about to die salute you.*

Lionel recognized the ritual response of the gladiator about to enter the arena, and he laughed, pleased. Lex watched him as he walked out of the room.

Killer instinct. Lex didn't mind bringing it forth, but doing it for no other reason but the entertainment of the emperor diminished the act.

He went to the library, opened his laptop, and brought up the numbers for Plant 26. Then he made a phone call.

"Hello," said the voice at the other end.

He waited, unmoving, in his chair. The tick of the Swiss clock across the library was clearly audible, only deepening the silence.

"Lex?"

Who was he hiding from, really? "I just had an interesting discussion about commemorative pens."

"Ah." He could hear the slight smile in the voice.

"All right," he said, "you've convinced me."

"Mmm," said the voice, a smug purr. "That's what I love about you."

Lex made sure that every minute of his remaining time with Lionel was accounted for. He took Gwen Tarquinio, an AVP at the plant, to bed, despite the complications it would certainly cause later. She had a reputation for plain speaking that could be useful, should a witness be necessary.

The next morning, over juice, yogurt, and fresh blueberries, Lionel paid court to Ms. Tarquinio. She blushed—a fine look with her dark hair—and cast confused glances toward Lex, who smiled blandly, excused himself, and went to the library.

He made another call.

"Hello," said the voice at the other end.

"It's me."

"Where are we?"

"Still at breakfast. Are you sure you can—"

"Leave it to me, Lex. Just keep your hands clean and smile like the good son you are."

Lex started to pace back and forth in front of the fireplace. "What if he leaves the Porsche and takes the limo?"

"You said he was feeling young and aggressive."

"Yeah, but that might mean he'll want to sit in the back, make a few phone calls, and destroy a small country."

"So see that he doesn't."

Lex found he was reviewing his decision. He generally didn't give in to second thoughts—didn't acknowledge them, if he could help it; they were nearly always spontaneous emotional mistakes that ruined the beauty of a good plan. Still . . .

"Lex, tell me something." The voice was low, breathy. For one shocked second, Lex could picture Julian sprawled back on the divan in the house on the lake, touching himself.

"What?" It came out sounding stranger than he'd intended.

"Does this turn you on as much as it does me?"

Lex hung up to the sound of his brother's laugh.

Dusk. Lex stood at the top of the curve that led down to Ophiuchi Gorge. He could see, below, the crumpled piece of origami that used to be the hood of the car. Porsches have exceptionally soft front noses; when you buy a Porsche, they teach you a special technique for closing the hood, so your handprints don't change the shape of the metal.

He found himself staring as though the shape of the crumple were some kind of beautiful fractal, packed with information just for him.

Julian, confident and graceful in his twenty years, walked over and joined him. "It's a nice day for a white wedding," he sang softly. The wind ruffled his dark hair as he looked over the edge.

Lex was silent.

Julian looked over at him and smiled. "Would you prefer a more liter-ary quote? 'When you look into the abyss . . .'"

"I get it, Julian. Till death do us part." He glanced back at his brother and raised an eyebrow. "If you're waiting for me to strike a match . . ."

"Sorry." Julian leaned over the edge and focused on the car. A few sec-onds later the engine caught fire. "There. Nobody could survive that."

"Huh. He'll be clawing up from the grave, like the end of *Carrie*."

"He's gone, Lex. We're free. *Free!*" The smile Julian turned on Lex was one he'd never seen before: full-throttle, radiant, incandescent. Where the fuck had he been hiding those? The sociopath reborn, into—what?

Lex turned back toward his car, and Julian followed. "You sure about this?"

"I'm not an administrator, Lex." He whirled, laughing, arms out to catch the last of the sunlight, pleasure on his face without a trace of guilt. "I wouldn't want to be. I'll do my part and take my share; you were always going to inherit, anyway."

"Maybe not."

"That's the paranoia *he* fed you talking. You believed that crap about Darwinian selection?" Julian shook his head. "If it were anything else but our family, you'd have seen the truth years ago. That man—" (What hap-pened to "father"? Lex thought) "—would never have handed his empire to anyone but his own blood. Adopted sons are for pacing the real ones." There was a bitterness in the tone that had never been allowed out while Lionel lived. Lex said, "And yet, he treated you—" *With affection.* "—with more consideration than he did me."

"Really. You know why Lionel was always smiling, when we came out of the study?" Lex looked at him. Julian's voice was flat. "Because he had a piece of meteor embedded inside his watch. He'd insist we shake hands before we leave. He knew it would bring me to my knees."

Christ. Lex wondered if it would have made any difference to the dy-namic had the third Luthor son, Napoleon, lived. But then, maybe not; and two brothers were complication enough.

They reached the car. Lex started to open the door, and Julian slammed it shut again. Lex turned to find his brother standing almost pressed against him, arms braced against the car, imprisoning Lex in his personal space. Dark hair, golden skin, drowning eyes. Lex breathed in, hard, seeking air.

"You knew."

"Of course I knew. You don't look at someone like that because you're checking on how well they did their term paper."

The moment hung on the wind from the gorge. Lex didn't move.

Maybe they wouldn't—

Julian leaned in and Lex's mouth opened as naturally as if they'd been doing this for years. As though there were a law somewhere that said, however the bag were spilled, these two pieces were meant to fit together. It would have been so easy to be enemies, if the gravitational force toward alliance hadn't been even stronger, hadn't frightened Lex into leaving Metropolis and staying away until his brother grew up and Lionel forced them back together.

Julian pulled away, and it was still so natural, not like a first kiss at all; Lex found himself getting into the driver's seat of the car without even questioning it. Julian sat beside him.

"What now?" It was the question that had rolled beneath the black sea of Lex's nights in Princeton and New Haven. How could he have this certainty that if the two of them worked together, the world would *change* in some way—some exhilarating, frightening, perhaps horrifying way?

A turn of the head as Julian buckled the pointless seatbelt, and then Lex got one of the old, sly grins. Julian's voice was dark and full of promise. "Anything we want." Lex felt the shiver of it as he pulled out and headed for the highway. Julian settled his long legs in as comfortably as he could and leaned back. "Why ask me? I'm just the broad-strokes guy. You're the mastermind."

Lex laughed, and though the sun was going down it felt like the morning of the world. "There'll be an emergency meeting of the Board of Directors tomorrow morning, and they'll be voting on a new president by the end of the month. You need to use your powers to get dirt on every single one of them . . ."

They left Smallville at 110 miles an hour. Hurtling toward Metropolis and the world.

Petrie Dish

No one could have faulted her professionalism as she entered the conference room. At thirty, she was the youngest person there, and if she felt under a spotlight, it was only because she was.

There was only one other woman present: McAvoy, from Navy Intelligence, in her sixties now. McAvoy spoke Mandarin as though to the Forbidden City born, and had spent two years in a Korean prison. Would she be a help or a hindrance? Naive, of course, to make assumptions based on gender.

Brass lamps gave enough illumination to compensate for the lack of windows. The red plastic folder that housed her report was there, set neatly in front of each member of the committee—every copy scrawled on now with the notes of the recipient, made individual with a haze of yellow Post-its. And there was her audience: Lezak, from the CIA; Marty Grimes from the Pentagon; Printz and Hellerstein from the White House; and Rick Bayard from the Senate committee that had been hastily formed, and that would never bear an official name.

Martha pushed a wing of red hair behind one ear, straightened her gray blazer, and met their eyes coolly. Her father's twenty years in the CIA, with cover at a Metropolis law firm, made her an auxiliary member of this world, privileged in a way she might not have been by herself. Her two years in the army made her reliable in their eyes. And her specialties of social psychology and anthropology made her the closest thing to an expert on aliens. She'd hammered that point home in her report—all very well for generals and administrators to give opinions, she'd implied; but how many had spent years wrapping their brains around ways of thought that weren't normal to them?

Grimes said, "Miss Clark, we've read your report. It contradicts the majority recommendation of our advisors."

"Yes, sir."

"And yet you feel confident in your dissent."

"I do, sir."

McAvoy leaned back, misleadingly casual. "All right, Miss Clark. Tell us why the military experts are wrong, and you're right."

Martha hit a button, and a slide of the Subject appeared on the wall. He was playing with a set of colored building blocks she'd given him to test his spatial coordination. She'd been careful to make sure every test she gave was fun—even then, she'd been planning strategy. "The Subject gives every behavioral indication of being a human male, aged three to four—"

"And yet," Bayard said, "The Subject is *not* a human male. And according to the report of our medical team, its cells are becoming imperceptibly denser each day. Soon we won't be able to take blood from it. The day will come when we will be unable to kill it. It could grow into anything, and you would have us leave this creature alone until we're at its mercy. Cut to the chase, Miss Clark. Why?"

"Why kill it," said Martha, "when we can absorb it?" She brought up another slide; a monkey clinging to a washcloth dummy. "Primates seek contact with other primates. Given a situation where it's shocked at irregular intervals, this monkey will hug a soft dummy and seek comfort from it, rather than from the wire dummy that dispenses milk. That need for physical contact is built into us, hard-wired; we can't help ourselves."

"The Subject," said McAvoy patiently, "hardly qualifies as a primate. We're closer to that monkey than we are to it."

Another slide: the Subject, eyes trusting and needy, opening arms to be hugged. Martha gave McAvoy a cool look. "Tell me that again, ma'am. With all due respect."

She hit them with statistics, case studies; feral children brought up in attics, unsocialized. The alien's scores on IQ tests that were as culture-free as she could devise. "It has the same reflexes we do. The same emotional weaknesses. If we bring it up as one of us, it will *be* one of us, loyal to our standards and morality. We can use the same technique that worked on chimps who were taught sign language—one trusted caretaker, physical affection, a comforting and secure environment." She paused, and looked around, meeting their eyes. "Why destroy a prize when that prize can belong to us?"

McAvoy smiled suddenly. She glanced at her colleagues. "Well done, Miss Clark."

"Well done?"

"The minority report has been accepted. This was your graduation exercise."

She took a deep breath and felt a sudden impulse to sit down. She trampled it. "Then, may I ask—that is, I wish to request—"

"Yes," said McAvoy. "You may be the caretaker. I assume that was the request?"

She hadn't expected it to go this well. "I want to thank the committee for this magnificent research opportunity—"

Lezak smiled. "But not alone."

She froze. "Pardon?"

"Well, we can hardly tell you to take the alien and run along, can we?" He opened a large yellow envelope and slid some photos toward her. "Fortunately, we have a friendly area."

"A . . . friendly area."

"A controlled environment. We call it Smallville. For the last few decades we've used it for testing agents, and for retiring certain government witnesses, as well as . . . other people we want to keep an eye on. About half the citizens there are covert; the other half are normal population. You won't be able to tell which is which, and neither will they. That's how it works."

Damn. She'd planned on going back to Metropolis. Still, it was a small price to pay. "I take it there's surveillance?"

"The streets and shops are covered. The school will be, too. As will every room of the house where you and your husband will be living."

Husband?

McAvoy passed her another folder, as though the idea were a minor postscript. "Jonathan Kent, currently a sergeant in the marines. His family has a farm in the area. It's really the best way to establish your cover."

Martha stared at the photograph in shock. He wasn't a bad-looking man, but . . .

"Miss Clark?"

She looked up. "I beg your pardon?"

"I was asking," McAvoy said, "if you've given thought to what you'll tell the Subject if he recalls his time here at the facility."

"Yes. I'm going to say that he was in a hospital for a few days. It's unlikely he'll remember—the language difference, the trauma—"

"But you have a backup plan in place. Good. Excellent work, Miss Clark." Martha looked up from the photo again to find that McAvoy had a hand outstretched. Martha shook it. Then she shook hands with the White House, the Pentagon, the Senate, and Navy Intelligence.

She walked away from the meeting, dazed. *Smallville.* Dear god, was that the best name they could come up with?

Five days later:

Martha led Clark by the hand till they reached the elevator. His eyes, curious, roved all over the hallways, and she wondered what they would do if his powers reached the point where he could sense hidden cameras. Another bridge to be crossed when they came to it, she thought, as he gestured and she lifted him up.

Jonathan stood at the elevator bank. "Thanks for waiting, honey," she said, trying on the endearment for size. It fit with the awkwardness of a new bathing suit.

He smiled back, just as awkwardly. He seemed like a nice man—for someone she was sure had orders to report on her as well as the baby. She hadn't had the balls yet to ask if sleeping together was considered part of routine cover.

Inside, she set Clark on his feet again and they stood together in the empty elevator, a perfect family. "Uh, honey?" he said. "Can I ask you something?"

"Go ahead . . . Jonathan."

"I heard you swung the entire committee over to the minority view. I know you couldn't make any kind of maternal plea—if you didn't keep it professional, they'd never have taken you seriously. But . . . did you do it strictly for science and country? Or for *it*?"

"Him."

"God. Yes. Him, I'm sorry." Clearly he was sorry for not settling into cover quickly enough, not for any other reason.

Clark watched the numbers on the elevator with big, dark eyes, oblivious to the language of aliens spoken over his head.

"You think I want a child that badly, Jonathan? Surely there are easier ways."

"Oh, yeah, I didn't mean anything."

She tuned him out as she straightened Clark's jacket on his little shoulders and gave him a peck on the cheek. He put his hand in hers unhesitatingly, and she thought, "*This* is the child I want. I'll get you through this, Clark. Whatever it takes."

And she gave Jonathan a bright, professional smile. He returned it, uncertainly.

Perhaps she could learn to knit.

Bleeding Kansas

Pete knew what you were *supposed* to do with green rock; everybody did. You left it where it was and notified someone in charge.

But the stories were that the green rock could grant you your deepest wish. Urban legend, some said. And if it granted your deepest wish, how come a handful of the men and women who worked near the thickest part of the meteor landing had bumps beneath their clothing, marks of amputation, in the very same places?

Though Pete knew the answer to that too: because everybody's deepest wish was the same.

And Pete was no different; just more determined. That's why he collected the rocks whenever he found them and stored them under his bed, and lay awake at night tracing the lines of his Wish.

Maybe he should never have hidden in the Kent barn. But he needed at least one more day, one more full night of practice, to make his wish come true, and he had to hide *somewhere*. So he lay among the hay bales, waiting for darkness, listening to the blessed quiet. No sirens. No helicopter blades cutting through the blue Kansas sky. Just silence and birdsong and the distant lowing of the cattle, until . . .

"Come out."

Clark's voice. Pete froze behind the hay bale. Clark couldn't possibly see him from there, and Pete knew how to be quiet. You learned things like that early.

"Come on, I can see you." Clark didn't sound angry. But how the hell could he see him? Pete sighed and rose to his feet.

"Clark."

"Pete, what are you doing here?" Pete didn't answer; it was fairly obvious, he thought, what he was doing there. Clark shook his head. "They're talking about you on the local news station."

There was no accusation in Clark's voice, and Pete was glad of it. The Kents had always seemed like good people; he'd even played with Clark a couple of times, when they were both very young. "Guess I'm famous," Pete said. "They got the schoolkids out looking yet?"

"Probably by tomorrow," Clark said. "They're pretty sure you're still in the county." He handed Pete a candy bar. "You look hungry."

Unexpected kindness. Pete glanced down at the bar, the letters blurred and meaningless. He ripped it open and took a few bites, and felt his stomach almost leap to greet the sugar. His body had changed, since he made the Wish—the engine inside ran hotter and faster.

"Thanks, man. I never had one of these. What do they call 'em?"

"Snickers." Clark sat down on another hay bale, just as if he expected Pete not to run away from him, and it was hard to ignore that kind of trust. Suddenly he felt as though he'd been rude.

"Sorry about being in your barn. I wouldn't want to get you in trouble."

"You won't get me in trouble." The smile was kind, too, and Pete felt himself relax for the first time since he'd changed. Maybe he'd come to the right place. Why should the Kents turn him in? It wasn't as though they were that big a deal themselves; small-time farmers barely eking out a living.

Don't fool yourself. There's a continental divide between them and you, and the reason why is branded on your ankle.

"My parents aren't home, but I could make you eggs and toast at the house." Pete felt himself stiffen, and Clark must have seen it too, because he went on, "Or you could stay here, if you're more comfortable." Jesus, but the Kent kid was polite. It suddenly brought to mind that summer, years back, when Clark could barely talk—funny, because he'd seemed bright in all other ways—and he'd hauled out his toys for them to play with on the banks of the creek, on those long afternoons. They couldn't have been more than four or five, and Mrs. Kent would be hanging sheets on the line, glancing over at them from time to time, smiling, clothespins in a bag on her hip. She'd said that she liked the way the sheets smelled when they were hung, fresh and full of the scent of wild prairie roses that grew on the banks.

But probably they just hadn't wanted to spend the money on a new dryer. It was hard to tell, with the Kents. Pete had heard Mr. Kent once, when Gabe Sullivan brought Pete to the store on a supply run, talking knowledgeably with the other men; saying what a shame it was a few bad slaves got ideas and spoiled it for the others. Kent didn't use slaves himself, though he used to borrow a couple during harvest. Now that Clark was older, he'd stopped. One kid couldn't take the place of two or three grown men, so Pete had figured it was about money.

But now he thought maybe it wasn't. Maybe Kent was a secret freedom-runner. Maybe he talked that way at the store to throw his neighbors off. Maybe Pete could ask Clark to take him in the house and wait for his parents, and they'd feed him and get him north—or even south; there were no slaves in Mexico.

Yeah, Pete. And maybe they'll fly you there in a LuthorCorp helicopter.

Clark was watching him, now, in a sidelong, thoughtful way. Finally he spoke. "Pete, what's behind you? On your back?"

"Just my extra clothes." He made sure his voice was careful and even.

"No it's not."

He wondered, again, how Clark knew these things. Clark waited—not resentfully, not suspiciously; calmly, as though he trusted Pete to tell him.

Finally Pete unbuttoned his shirt. He moved to the center of the barn, to give himself room. He threw the shirt to the floor and stretched, and felt the weight shift as he . . . unfurled.

The light bones folded out, and out, and out again. You would never believe the things could fit in so small a space if you hadn't seen it, felt it. Light, light as silk they were, soft, and strong as sailing canvas; in the glow of sunlight through the door they shone with a reddish brown tinge like the fire of a deeply buried sunset. The fire of a wish.

A thing of Earth, not heaven. Not angelic, but with the pure magnificence of nature.

Clark stared, awestruck. Pete's wingspan was a good twelve feet, at least, maybe fifteen.

Clark reached out a hand, and Pete nodded. Clark touched the silky feathers, and saw the ripple that moved out from that touch. "Can you *feel* them?"

He nodded again.

"What does it feel like?"

"Good. It feels good."

"Aren't they—isn't it too much weight, when you're trying to walk?"

"Not really." And it was a burden he was happy to bear.

Clark looked at Pete for permission and then touched them again. "So *soft*," he whispered, as though he were in church. Pete *flicked* at him with an edge of the wing. A wide, disbelieving grin took over Clark's face, and suddenly Pete found he had one to match, and then they started to laugh.

Clark sat down again. He waited a minute, as though wondering how to put this, then asked simply, "And you don't mind being different?"

"Are you kidding? I'm glad to be different. C'mon—don't tell me you never wondered what it would be like to fly."

"You flew with these?" He didn't sound convinced.

Pete grinned smugly. "Last night, first time I'd call it real flying. Ferguson's Hill. I was up for two minutes and forty-five seconds."

"You *counted*?"

"Damn straight I counted. Twelve seconds, first time I tried. I'm working my way up."

"Wow. I didn't think they'd actually . . . well . . . function."

"They're from my *Wish*, Clark. They're made to fly."

"Oh, god, Pete, you're not talking about the rocks, are you? Because you should stay away from those."

"I'm fine."

"Really. You should never touch those things. Tell somebody, and they'll take them to the hazardous disposal—"

"Oh, crap. They take them to the LuthorCorp trucks that are going to Metropolis. I should know, I worked on three LuthorCorp experimental farms, and it was always the same story. Like they thought we were dumb." He smiled, not nicely, at Clark's disconcerted look. "Somebody in Metropolis has got a mighty big wish."

There was a sound in the distance. A truck engine. Pete froze again. "I think your parents are coming back."

Clark said nothing. Pete went to the entrance to check, and far down the road he saw it: the familiar blue supply truck. Maybe he couldn't read, but he knew the words for LuthorCorp by now, and the logo. It was the same logo that was burned into his ankle.

"You called them!"

"Before I came in."

And despite his panic Pete had to wonder how Clark had known, before he even entered the barn, that he was hiding there.

"Clark, you gotta hide me. I just need time. Please. If I could get to Canada—or just Illinois—"

Clark didn't look happy or triumphant or even mean. He looked miserable. "Illinois wouldn't make any difference. They'd just send you back. The Supreme Court upheld the Dred Scott decision—we read about it in school."

Clark said that as though Pete would know what the Scott decision was, or why one court was more supreme than another. And then Clark took his hand earnestly, as though he could transmit his own certainty. "It's the right thing to do."

Pete shook him off. He looked wildly around the barn. He could run through the fields, jump the creek, try to get past the Bensons', down the road, and—

—and they would have cell phones and radios and by now the sheriff was driving from town, and his deputies would have the north end of Hickory Lane covered. The Bensons would have let their dogs out. And his picture was all over the fucking news, from what Clark said—

And you know what happens, Pete, when you make them run after you. When the blood starts pounding and they get pissed as hell. You've seen it when they brought other people back.

But I have wings now!

Too soon. Not enough time to learn how to use them.

The truck parked outside the barn. Gabe Sullivan got out, along with three supervisors from the farming division. They wore holsters. "Clark?" Mr. Sullivan called.

Clark walked outside into the sunshine. "He's kind of scared, Mr. Sullivan. I don't think he wants to make any trouble. Can't you take it easy on him?"

"Nobody wants to hurt him," Mr. Sullivan said soothingly. He raised his voice. "You hear that, Pete? We've just come to take you home." His gaze raked through the shadows just inside the barn and came to rest on Pete. He nodded to the supervisors, and two of them came and grasped Pete's arms. They pulled him outside.

"Just take it easy," Mr. Sullivan said. "You're in enough trouble already, right?" He turned to Clark. "Thanks for the help, son. Your family's always been good neighbors."

They pulled Pete toward the truck and suddenly he came to life again. He kicked out, yanked an arm away and whirled, surprising himself, toward *Clark*. If Clark *knew* things, maybe there were other—powers—Clark had. Anyway, he was Pete's only hope right now.

"Clark, man, you don't get it! *They'll cut them off!*" His arm was grabbed again, more roughly this time, and they hustled him to the back of the truck. Cuffs clicked onto his wrists.

The man he'd kicked hissed, "You'll be lucky if we use anesthesia, you fuckin' psycho. Want we should get the ax out of the cab?"

"Not in front of the kid," said Mr. Sullivan, and by "the kid," he obviously meant Clark.

He was dumped unceremoniously into the back. "Clark, fuck this, help me, I can fly! I have to fly! Don't let them—"

Clark walked a few steps closer, clearly upset, eyes shining with unshed tears. "It's the right thing to do, Pete. They'd only shoot you down."

Gabe Sullivan started the motor. The three supervisors climbed in the back beside him. And the truck rumbled down the road, with Pete gazing out at the square picture postcard of dust and sunlight and the Kent farm, and a boy in the distance growing smaller and smaller.

Clark watched for a while as the truck disappeared down the road. He was unhappy for Pete, but the worst of the pain would soon be over, and he'd get the best medical care. LuthorCorp knew how to keep its property well.

At least this way, Pete was alive. And stealing was wrong; Clark knew that, it had been explained to him. Even when what you were stealing was yourself, it was still wrong. You could try to make the excuse that it wasn't a large theft, but slaves weren't cheap; and ultimately crime is never an abstraction. In the case of LuthorCorp, you were taking from the stockholders of the company, real men and women, some of whom were retirees on fixed incomes.

Clark believed in ideals. He believed in truth, justice, and the American way. So he turned from the road and walked back toward the house, hoping his parents would be proud—a good boy, a good student, a loving son; and stalwart defender of civilization as he knew it.

Footnote: In the years before the American Civil War, slavery was a particularly bitter issue. When Kansas was still a territory, it was decided that the people in that area would settle the question for themselves—they could vote on whether to enter the union as a slave or a free state. Immediately pro- and antislave forces rushed in settlers and agitators to influence the vote. Argument soon turned to murder—over two hundred men were killed, the free-soil city of Lawrence sacked, and several (apparently) proslavery settlers were hacked to death by John Brown. It became a tiny microcosm of the war to come, and so great was the violence and enmity, that the years 1854 to 1856 in that place became known as "Bleeding Kansas."

The Dwarf's Tale

Title: They Say of the Elves (2002)
Author: Brancher
Fandom: *Lord of the Rings*
Rating: Mature (slash, Legolas/Gimli)

Introduction

J. R. R. Tolkien's *The Lord of the Rings* inspired a fandom almost immediately after its publication in the mid-1950s, not only among the science fiction and fantasy readers who you would imagine to be its target audience, but also more broadly among the young people who came of age in the 1960s.[1] Tolkien's stories motivated people not only to create fiction, music, and art, but also cultural histories of Middle Earth and glossaries of the various Elvish dialects, and of course Dungeons and Dragons–style gaming and cosplay. The fandom only grew with the release of Peter Jackson's Oscar-winning trilogy of films, although—as is sometimes the case[2]—there was some friction between book fans and movie fans. Fans not only wrote fanfiction about every possible character in *Lord of the Rings* (as well as about a variety of relationships, literally fleshing out Tolkien's profoundly romantic but sexless universe) but also about the tightly knit cast of actors[3] in Jackson's films (a genre called LotRiPS, for *Lord of the Rings* Real Person Slash). Many, if not most, fans of *Lord of the Rings* were both book and film fans, writing about the book characters but basing their descriptions on the visuals from Jackson's films.

The following story is beloved by many in *LOTR* fandom because of the way in which it bridges the Jackson movies and J. R. R. Tolkien's prose.

According to its author, Brancher, "They Say of the Elves" is a completely book-based story, "something that plopped out of my brain after I finished rereading them." Written two weeks after the first film came out, "They Say of the Elves" was posted to a small mailing list devoted to Tolkien fanfiction. "It had been a tiny sedate little fandom," Brancher remembers, "and the movies exploded it." The story was embraced by *LOTR*'s rapidly growing fan base, which, excited by the films, returned eagerly to the books: 30 percent of the copies of *The Lord of the Rings*—the second best selling book of all time—were sold after the movies came out.

"They Say of the Elves" is written in the lush language of Tolkien's world even as it is about a subject that Tolkien never discusses: sexual attraction. It opens with a lovely image of Elves who'll "tumble you as soon as look at you; seducers, coquettes, you'll wake with only a handful of leaves and a sweet taste in your mouth," immediately evoking the racial distrust between Elves and Dwarves in the novels. The story is set firmly within canonical events and characterizations: in Tolkien's books, Gimli is not "a squat object of ridicule, as he is in the movies," as one fan described him,[4] but a romantic, as well as a poet. In the books, Gimli's description of the Glittering Caves is so beautiful ("There are columns of white and saffron and dawn-rose, Legolas, fluted and twisted into dreamlike forms") that Legolas, moved by his words, agrees to visit them: "Come! Let us make this bargain—if we both return safe out of the perils that await us, we will journey for a while together." "They Say of the Elves" is set during this canonical journey that Legolas and Gimli take together.

Over the course of *The Lord of the Rings*, Gimli and Legolas overcome strong mutual prejudice to become the most intimate of friends: as Brancher notes, their canonical progression in Tolkien's text "from mutual, even racist distrust, to grudging respect, to friendly rivalry, to blood brotherhood is one of the great modern romances." The bond that Legolas and Gimli develop as Elf and Dwarf is already much more taboo-shattering—and consequently much more romantic—than any sexual (or even homosexual) relationship; gender is not the boundary being transgressed here. It's clear in Tolkien that the culture clash is what's significant, and consequently, it's the culture clash that's emphasized in Brancher's story. "They Say of the Elves" shows us the characters overcoming rumor ("they say") as well as their inherited fears of each other. Brancher's story turns on Gimli's (and the reader's) discovery that Legolas is as scared of being hurt by Gimli as Gimli is of Legolas, for as

Legolas blurts, "The hearts of Dwarves, they say, are like the hearts of mountains, difficult to reach, and seldom moved."

The moment of emotional connection that follows bridges Tolkien's canon between Legolas and Gimli's journey and the fact—it is one of the last given to us in Tolkien's appendix—that Legolas and Gimli stayed together for the rest of their lives.[5] While many people think fanfiction is about inserting sex into texts (like Tolkien's) where it doesn't belong, Brancher sees it differently: "I was desperate to read about sex that included great friendship; I was repurposing Tolkien's text in order to do that. It wasn't that friendship needed to be sexualized, it was that erotica needed to be . . . friendship-ized." Many fanfiction writers write about sex in conjunction with beloved texts and characters not because they think those texts are incomplete, but because they're looking for stories where sex is profound and meaningful. This is part of what makes fanfiction different from pornography: unlike pornography, fanfic features characters we already care deeply about, and who tend to already have long-standing and complex relationships with each other. It's a genre of sexual *subjectification*: the very opposite of *objectification*. It's benefits with *friendship*.

Suggested Further Reading

Tolkien fandom is enormous, and the world of Tolkien scholarship is enormous; Tolkien is of course the father of all modern fantasy and beloved by science fiction and fantasy fans, gamers, world-builders and medievalists, folklorists, and philologists alike. Works dealing particularly with media fandom's engagement with Tolkien include Daniel Allingon's 2007 article, "'How Come Most People Don't See It?' Slashing *The Lord of the Rings*," in *Social Semiotics*, and Robin Anne Reid's 2009 essay "Thrusts in the Dark: Slashers' Queer Practices," in *Extrapolation*. Janet Brennan Croft's essay collections *Tolkien on Film* (2005) and *Perilous and Fair: Women in the Works and Life of J. R. R. Tolkien* (2015) are particularly of use to fanfiction scholars, and feature essays like Amy H. Sturgis's "Make Mine 'Movieverse': How the Tolkien Fan Fiction Community Learned to Stop Worrying and Love Peter Jackson," Susan Booker's "Tales around the Internet Campfire: Fan Fiction in Tolkien's Universe," and Una McCormack's "Finding Ourselves in the (Un)Mapped Lands: Women's Reparative Readings of *The Lord of the Rings*."

They Say of the Elves

Brancher

Then Gimli bowed low. "Nay, you are excused for my part, lord,"
he said. "You have chosen the Evening; but my love is given to
the Morning. And my heart forebodes that soon it will pass away
forever."[1]

—"Many Partings," Book III, *LOTR*

You know what they say of the Elves, that they'll tumble you soon as look
at you; seducers, coquettes, you'll wake with only a handful of leaves and a
sweet taste in your mouth.

Well, I have traveled far and seen enough to give lie to many of the tales
old Dwarf-dams tell in the mines of my youth. But still and all, I kept my
eye on him. Legolas, a tall luminous shape in the edge of my vision; never
far from me, a gleam of sunlight at my shoulder. And when the war was
over, and he made good on his promise to travel with me, I knew what he
was after. I thought I knew.

Durin's Beard, he wasn't subtle, was he? "Visit the tunnels and caverns
of your people, Gimli, my friend," indeed. I just bet he was eager to visit
my caverns. Elves are all the same.

---

1. The epitaph comes from *The Return of the King*, where Gimli and Eomer have been arguing
about who is fairest. As Brancher points out, Gimli's speech can (and has) been taken two ways:
"The superficial reading is that he is contrasting Arwen, who will stay with Aragorn in Middle-
Earth, with Galadriel, who is slated to 'diminish and go into the West.' But . . . the 'Morning' he
refers to here could just as easily be Legolas, from whom he's been inseparable for three books,
with whom he's about to go on an epic camping trip, and who is also fated to one day pass over
the Sea. The ambiguity here is so strong that one wonders what Tolkien thought he meant by
it."—Ed.

So off we went, and I was dreading it and dreaming it at the same time. I wanted to taste him, I wanted to touch: would it be as good as legends say? And yet my heart within me felt forged of iron, for once he'd had me he would surely leave. I feared the fistful of leaves and grass, the fading song on the wind.

For I had grown overfond of him.

We passed first through the Glittering Caves, and there I was sure it would happen. I led him down the path into the earth, and in the first great chamber our torches flared and he cried out, and was then silent for a time as we passed under curtains of marbled rock, glinting white and rose, like the hem of the cloak of Galadriel; and thence to glittering passages lined in gems, sharp enough to the touch to draw blood.

In the central passage, where water falls drop by drop into pools of different depths, we stood quietly for a time. The music of the pools lulled me. I stood entranced, I know not how long, and did not look to Legolas, not until I felt the heat of him behind me, and the touch of his long-fingered hands on my shoulders.

I thought my breath would stop in my body. I could not speak. But he did not move his hands from my shoulders, and merely stood close to me, close enough that I could hear his breath.

"*Vanya*," he said at last. "*Lama alcarinqua.*"[2]

And that was all he said, and the only touch of his hands that I received in that place.

We came up out of the caverns in silence, each of us in our own thoughts. To the others, the wizard and the hobbits, Legolas said only that he had no words, that it was for me to speak of the beauty of the Caves of Helm's Deep. And I, for my part, said nothing to anyone.

I did not know what I felt. The first time I walked in the Glittering Caves, the sight had driven me to poetry, even as we rode from battle. Legolas said then that he had not heard me speak so before.

And it had seemed to me, then, that he was the one I should tell of the Caves, that he would take their beauty and my heart's burden and hold each in his safekeeping.

Yet now . . .

At the evening meal the young hobbit, Meriadoc, started up with a song, and I took my meat and bread and moved away from the fire. They

---

2. Translated from Quenya, one of Tolkien's Elvish languages (Tolkien was of course first and foremost a scholar of languages). *Vanya* = Beautiful. *Lama alcarinqua* = glorious sound.—Ed.

were used to my ways by then, and said nothing, but Samwise muttered that I must be loathe to depart from Helm's Deep, since I loved it so; and from the corner of my eye I saw Legolas look after me, bright against the evening sky, though I could not read the look on his fair face.

Then the Fellowship was broken, and we two journeyed alone to the forest of Fangorn. I had hoped that the elf would at least roll me on my own ground, at Helm's Deep, and not wait until we were shadowed by leaves and moss. But it seemed that was his plan.

At the forest's edge I balked; strange scents came to my nose, green and wild. But Legolas took my hand, then, and led me into the wood.

Rightly do they call him Greenleaf, for soon I could scarcely tell him from the ivy and the oak; I kept my eyes on the path before us, and on the pale hand in my own. Presently he spoke to me: "Gimli, look up," and I did.

We were in a hall of living trees. Stout and aged they were, with bark as hard and cold as forged steel, and yet if one watched long enough it seemed they swayed, this way and that, though I could feel no breeze. These were trees such as there were when the world was young, Legolas whispered to me, and his fingers interlaced with mine, even as the branches interlaced overhead.

This and other alien wonders he showed to me, and I was amazed. He led me ever deeper into the Entwood, among trees whose roots alone were like fortresses raised above my head. And my heart beat ever in my ears, like a drum.

At nightfall we camped at the root of a great tree, and when I lay down in my bedroll in the dark I could still see him perched on a great root above me, for elves need little sleep.

I did not sleep, either. All night it seemed I waited for the touch of a delicate hand, the featherweight of his body settling against mine. I waited with impatience and with dread. The bedmanners of elves are well-known, as I have said; but my own people take but one mate, and many who cannot claim their desire, be it man or woman, will have none.

I had already come to know that it would be thus with me. And so trembling I lay awake all night, as the stars moved above the canopy of leaves, and my doom glimmered on his perch above my head, like something wrought of mithril, still and bright.

For my trouble I rose in the morning with a stiff neck. Legolas was boiling water over a little grass-fire for tea.

We came out of the forest that afternoon and set out north for Mirkwood and the Iron Mountains beyond. My heart was heavy.

He did not take me in the caves, for all his innuendo, I thought to myself. I had thought he might draw me down to the sandy cave floor and . . . but naught came of it.

He did not ravish me in the forest, I thought. It was his realm, not mine, and he could have cast a charm on me and laid me low in a bed of moss and fallen leaves. He could have peeled my armor from me piece by piece, until I was exposed to him, my pale belly, the places no one has caressed . . . I would have given that pleasure to a smooth-handed Elf.

But no.

It could only be that I was too unlovely for him.

No one has ever called me *Vanya*, no one has ever said *lama alcarinqua* to my harsh dwarf's voice. Elves love beauty; I am none. And I grieved, for I loved him, and I would lose him now with not even so much as a handful of leaves to keep by me.

So we walked in silence, and the sun sunk low in the West.

Then Legolas said, "We could come south."

He had not turned to look at me. "What?" I asked.

"We could bring our people south, you and I. My folk could dwell in Ithilian; it must be won back from years of fell things and wildness, but there is forest there such as my kin would delight in. And you . . . you spoke of bringing craftsmen to Helm's Deep." Here, he glanced at me, his light eyes slanted as of old. "You spoke of opening the caves and chambers, a single hammer-stroke in a day of anxious work."

He threw my words back at me exactly as I had spoken them, months before. I was startled, and it roused me somewhat from my despair.

"Ithilian is not so very far from the Glittering Caves," I said.

"No," said he, "not far by elf-roads. It might be a good life, for two such as we."

"Such as we?" I echoed.

"Gimli," he cried suddenly, "my friend, speak now and tell me how it is with you! For my people must follow their hearts; but the hearts of Dwarves, they say, are like the hearts of mountains, difficult to reach, and seldom moved."

I stood speechless. He pressed on: "And they say of the Dwarves also, that they take no joy in the pleasures of the flesh, but carve their children out of stone and so continue their race. I no longer doubt it: A fortnight we have traveled together, and you have made no move toward me; not when I touched you, nor when I took your hand. And yet . . . and yet, my heart cries that I have found one closer than a brother, a companion for my life. A companion for my bed," he added quietly, "if only you would have me."

And he covered his fair face with his long-fingered hands.

I looked at him a long time, for he was very beautiful; and then I looked away for even longer, as the sun set over the Misty Mountains.

Then I turned to Legolas, and took his hands away from his face and held them in my own. He gazed at me, his light eyes wide. I kissed his hands and spoke.

"You should hear what they say of the Elves," I said.

The Pop Star's Tale

Title: The Vacation (2002)
Author: Kaneko
Fandom: Popslash (*NSYNC)
Rating: Mature (slash, Joey Fatone / Lance Bass)
Additional tags: robots, robots and artificial lifeforms

Introduction

Popslash, a media and music fandom organized around the members of boy bands *NSYNC and the Backstreet Boys, has been wildly influential on fandom as a whole. It's not simply that popslash paved the way for juggernaut music fandoms like One Direction, K-Pop, and Fall Out Boy, but that its tropes and thematic concerns affected the entirety of fandom, so that it is possible to speak of pre-popslash and post-popslash aesthetics.

First of all, the large cast of boybanders—memorably described as "Puppies in a Box"[1]—brought into vogue "smooshed" or portmanteau pairing names, which have in most cases replaced the traditional punctuation marks ("/" or "x") fans used to describe a relationship featured in a story. If you currently ship "Johnlock" (John Watson / Sherlock Holmes) or "Pepperoni" (Pepper Potts / Tony Stark), you owe something to popslash's "Timbertrick" (Justin Timberlake / Chris Kirkpatrick) and "Trickyfish" (Christopher Kirkpatrick / Lance Bass).

Popslash also shattered fandom's taboos against "RPF," or real-person fiction; previously, fans felt that writing fanfiction, particularly romantic or sexual fiction, about "real people" (actors, musicians, celebrities) was disrespectful or in bad taste. This was particularly true of "RPS," or real-person slash, both because homosexuality was then more negatively viewed by the larger culture and because of the corresponding fear of inadvertently "outing" someone. But, as Kristina Busse notes in her essay "'I'm Jealous of the Fake Me': Postmodern Subjectivity and Identity Construction in Boy Band Fan Fiction," the "real" public lives of boy band members can become "a narrative often unrecognizable to the stars themselves: Justin Timberlake (2003), for example, points out that his life in the media is more interesting and appealing than his actual life."[2] This leads to the quote in Busse's title: Timberlake is "jealous of the fake me." But once a celebrity's public self is understood to be constructed—a *story*, in other words, albeit one told across tabloids and entertainment shows and DVD extras—then why *not* write fanfiction about it?

Are celebrities "real people" or are they characters? The Beatles, that original boy band, played themselves as characters in films like *A Hard Day's Night* and *Help!* Those movies were scripted as well as directed, and they put the Beatles into neat little characterizational boxes: John was the smart one, Ringo the funny one, and so on. But were they? It may be that a postmodern identity crisis is part of the boy band DNA: in one notable scene in *A Hard Day's Night*, John Lennon manages to convince a fan that he isn't himself, asking her to notice that his eyes are lighter, and his nose is wrong. At the end of the scene, the fan peers over her glasses and agrees, "You don't look like him at all."

While the Beatles were often depicted doing surreal and impossible things, popslash fans went even further, exploring postmodern questions of identity using the techniques and tropes of speculative fiction. If, as Mary Ellen Curtin has theorized, fanfiction is speculative fiction about character, then nowhere was that speculation wilder or more "out there" than in popslash. What if Justin Timberlake and Lance Bass accidentally switched bodies? What if the members of *NSYNC were fish? (Literally, fish.) What if all the different fanfic versions of the popslash characters were alive and living together in a dorm somewhere while they waited for their authors to finish writing their stories?[3] One of popslash's most influential stories is Helenish's "The Same Inside,"[4] whose legendary, endlessly replicated opening line ("Somehow, in the night, Chris had turned into a girl") is feminist speculative fiction that draws from the same well as Kafka's "Metamorphosis" ("As Gregor Samsa awoke one morning from uneasy dreams he found himself transformed in his bed into a gigantic insect") and for similar reasons. Helenish, like Kafka, dispenses with science fiction's obsession with the whys and hows of plot (What turned Gregor Samsa into an insect?

How did Chris Kirkpatrick turn into a girl? *Who cares?*) to focus on the real story: what it's like to occupy a marginalized position. In Helenish's story, Chris explains that he doesn't *feel* like a girl. "I feel the same inside," he insists, prompting his bandmate Lance to reply: "Yeah. well. girls probably feel the same inside, too" (*sic*).

Author Kaneko describes the story that follows, "The Vacation," as "a 'Same Inside' rip off," by which she means it is a science fiction story similarly disinterested in the whys and hows of its premise. In "The Vacation," *NSYNC's Lance Bass takes a vacation and sends a "T21 Mark 5 Robot" to take his place on tour.[5] The robot looks, acts, sings, and dances exactly like Lance; in fact, practically speaking, the robot is better than Lance in almost every way, because the job of a boy band member is to pretend to be and want and like whatever his public narrative requires, and a robot does that more easily than a human being. Lance's bandmate Joey Fatone has a hard time adjusting to the robot, because they don't have anything in common: "Lancebot, it turned out, actually did like football and hockey and all of the other things Lance only pretended to like," including women. (The real Lance Bass came out of the closet in 2006, four years after this story was written, but popslash fans had long speculated that that one or more members of the group was gay, and made a game of scrutinizing *NSYNC's public performances for clues. A similar game is being played at the current moment with One Direction.) In this story, Joey, too, is in the closet, and so to lose Lance—one of the few people who knows the real him—is to lose his own grip on reality. In "The Vacation," Joey is provoked into an existential crisis—seemingly brought on by the Lancebot but really brought on by a boybander's life of constant consumer-oriented, PR-scripted performativity. In a world where he can't be who he is or like what he likes, Joey begins to doubt that *anyone* is real, that even he *himself* is real: "Would one robot recognize another, Joey wondered. Would the robots even know if all the real people had been pied-pipered away?" Here we see Kaneko using the science fiction trope of robots to tell a character-driven story about the commodification of the self and of desire in consumer culture, as well as the surreal disassociations of the closet.

*NSYNC were particularly suited for this kind of postmodern narrative: on the cover of their wildly successful 2000 record "No Strings Attached," the band are portrayed as marionettes. This image of the band as puppets—replicated in their videos and tour choreography—was meant to highlight the ways *NSYNC were both controlled by the music industry and actively resisting that control. (The group took legal action against their managers and record company when they felt they were being defrauded.) Through this iconography, the band made their struggle for control visible to fans, though they always framed themselves as seeking legal and economic control, not more authentic self-expression. Today, the real Lance Bass talks about being closeted under massive public scrutiny. "I didn't tell a single person [I was gay] when I was with NSYNC, I didn't tell a friend, a family member, nothing like that. As long as I was with NSYNC, I didn't date a guy, I was completely asexual."[6] Popslash invented new ways to articulate this repression and alienation from the self—and while the particular band or celebrity may change, the song remains the same.

Suggested Further Reading

The foundational article about female fans and boy bands is Barbara Ehrenreich, Elizabeth Hess, and Gloria Jacob's "Beatlemania: Girls Just Want to Have Fun," in Lisa A. Lewis's *The Adoring Audience* (Routledge, 1992). But because of its experimental narratives and postmodern orientation, popslash has attracted more than its fair share of scholarly criticism. Kristina Busse has written several important pieces about popslash and postmodernism, including 2005's "'Digital Get Down': Postmodern Boy Band Slash and the Queer Female Space," and the article referenced above, "'I'm Jealous of the Fake Me': Postmodern Subjectivity and Identity Construction in Boy Band Fan Fiction." More recent work on boy bands and RPF includes Bronwen Thomas's 2014 "Fans Behaving Badly? Real Person Fic and the Blurring of the Boundaries between the Public and the Private," in her collection *Real Lives, Celebrity Stories: Narratives of Ordinary and Extraordinary Experience across Media*," and the *Transformative Works and Cultures* essays "Queer Bandom: A Research Journey in Eight Parts," by D. Wilson (2012) and "Real Body, Fake Person: Recontextualizing Celebrity Bodies in Fandom and Film" (2015) by Melanie Piper.

The Vacation

Kaneko

The first they knew of it was when Lance called a group meeting.

It wasn't much of a group meeting. When Joey told Chris about it, Chris just growled sleepily and hung up, and JC was spending the weekend with his parents. Joey and Justin were there, though. And Lance of course.

"I'm taking a break, and going to Bermuda," Lance said. He was wearing a pink Hawaiian shirt, and he smelled coconutty and warm, like he was on vacation already.

"*What?*" Joey said. "What the *fuck?*" He had to stop then, because he'd breathed in Diet Coke. When he'd finished coughing, Justin was talking.

"You can't do that, dude," he was saying, patiently. "I know you're tired—we're all tired. But we've sold tickets for the next twenty-eight shows, and we have to—"

"All taken care of," Lance said. He patted Justin's shoulder and made for the door. "Gotta go, my flight's in an hour."

"But—" Joey started.

"All taken care of," Lance said again, over his shoulder.

"Well," Justin said. "That was weird."

Joey shifted uncomfortably. "Someone's gonna have to tell JC."

Lance walked back into the room a few minutes later.

"Jesus," Joey said. He collapsed onto the sofa, his legs wobbling. "You totally fucking had me going for a—"

Lance held up his hand to stop him. "I'm not Lance," he said. "Lance

105

is on vacation. I'm a T21 Mark 5 Robot, and I'll be doing the shows while he's away."

Joey laughed nervously. Lance wasn't in his Hawaiian shirt anymore. He was wearing something green and soft that matched his eyes.

"I've watched the videos and memorized the choreography," Lance continued. "And the singing parts, of course. I'm confident I'll be able to perform up to Lance's usual standard, but I'm open to constructive criticism."

"You are fucking weird, you know that," Justin said.

Lance nodded calmly. "You need proof. I understand."

"So fucking weird," Justin said. "And not in a—" He stopped.

Lance had pulled off his arm. "I hope this is adequate," he said, holding it up so they could see the metal cords hanging out of it.

"—not in a good way," Justin finished in a whisper.

Joey ended up being the one to call JC. "Lance went to Bermuda, but he left a robot to fill in for him," he said, and hung up.

"Wimp," Justin said.

JC was much cooler about it than Joey expected. He turned up three hours after Joey's phone call, looking grim, and demanding that Lancebot do a full dress rehearsal on his own. Then he watched with his arms folded over his chest, muttering "*two* three four, *two* three four" under his breath.

By "Tearin' Up My Heart," he'd relaxed a bit, and he was even nodding occasionally. And when Lancebot did the jumping and singing part of "It's Gonna Be Me" without Lance's usual voice-wobble, he actually smiled.

"Yeah, this'll work," he told Joey. He jogged over to Lancebot, and touched his shoulder to stop him dancing. "That's good," he said.

Joey tried not to stare too hard at Lancebot's skin—golden and perfect under JC's hand, and gleaming with sweat just as if he were real. "Where did Lance get you?" he asked. It came out a little accusing.

Lancebot shrugged. "He knew somebody who knew somebody," he said.

Chris was the one who freaked. When Lancebot did the arm thing for him, he screamed and stumbled back. "What—" he said, and his voice was shaking. "What have you done to Lance?"

"Lance is on vacation," Lancebot explained, talking slowly, like Chris was retarded. "I'm just filling in for him."

"Yes, but." Chris looked at Joey appealingly. "Joey, he pulled off his *arm*."

Justin put him to bed with a bottle of tequila.

"He's fine," he said, when he came out of Chris's room. He shut the door quietly behind him. "He has some kind of robot phobia or something, but he'll be fine for the show on Monday."

Joey took a deep breath. He felt sick. "So now what?" he asked.

"Well." Justin shrugged helplessly. "I dunno. I guess we just do our normal thing."

Joey turned to ask JC for his opinion, but JC wasn't paying attention to them at all. He was looking at Lancebot almost hungrily.

"I bet," JC said. "You can do some cool things with your voice."

At first, Joey tried to get to know Lancebot a bit, dragging him out to a newly opened club that the real Lance would have adored.

"Do you um. Do you drink?" asked Joey hesitantly.

Lancebot smiled proudly. "I can do anything that a person can do."

"Cool," Joey said.

It didn't work out so well, though. For one thing, they didn't seem to have anything in common.

Lancebot, it turned out, actually did like football and hockey and all of the other things Lance only pretended to like.

For another thing, Lancebot was apparently irresistible to women. "My friend kind of likes your friend," at least five of them told Joey. "Does he want to um—?"

Joey spent the night nodding and smiling while Lancebot said things like: "Gerard Moroni's been in fantastic form this season. I'm thinking he's going to bring the whole team with him to the playoffs. But *Smith*, now—" until Joey wanted to stab his own eyes out.

To top it all off, while Lancebot could drink, it seemed he couldn't get drunk. After seven shots, he was still dancing about a thousand times better than the real Lance, who, offstage, had like two moves—The Dork and The Doofus.

Joey told himself it wouldn't work: the fans knew too much shit about them—pets' names, favorite foods. They fucking knew which soap Joey liked, which was crazy, because Joey never remembered himself until he saw the packaging at the supermarket. It *couldn't* work. The fans would see through it, and Lance would have to come back. It would be like the space thing and the acting thing, and all the other times Lance had overreached himself.

Lance had kissed him about a week before he'd left. He hadn't even been drunk.

"We can't," Joey had said, angry that Lance had made Joey be the one to have to say it, and feeling absurdly cheated: he was probably only going to get one kiss with Lance ever, and he hadn't been ready for it. Already, his memory of it was kind of blurred—like it was something that had happened years ago. Joey licked his lips, trying to get the taste back.

"Why not?" Lance looked tired and resigned and like he wanted to cry.

Joey shook his head. "You know why."

Lance always tried to overreach himself.

In some ways, it was like Lance had never left. On the bus, he still shouted at Joey for leaving dirty shirts on the floor, and when he reached across Joey for the coffee, the skin above his jeans was still milk-smooth and touchable.

He didn't confide in Joey anymore, though. He didn't watch videos with him, or listen to him rambling about things he'd seen on infomercials. Instead, he watched CNN, and talked about politics and world events and sports. Once, he said something in a British accent that made JC fall onto the floor, giggling.

"Tony Blair," JC said, when Joey looked at him, mystified.

"Oh," Joey said. He wrapped his arms around himself, and watched Lancebot illustrating his words with Lance's pale hands, laughing in Lance's voice. When he laughed, the curve of his throat was achingly familiar, and Joey found himself wondering what his skin would taste like— what Lance's skin would taste like.

Joey told himself he wasn't jealous, not even when Lancebot started giving JC the sly half-smile Lance usually reserved for Joey. He couldn't deny they were spending a lot of time together, though.

"Dude, you would not *believe* some of the stuff he can do!" JC said, when Joey brought up the subject as casually as he could. "He has like a thousand more muscles than a human. And his *voice*."

"Go figure," Joey said, flatly.

He missed Lance a lot. He could admit that. He missed Lance's dry sense of humor, and the way he'd slide into the seat next to Joey's—his arm warm against Joey's side, because Lance loved to sit in the sun. Most of all, Joey missed the way Lance would send him panicked looks sometimes in interviews, the way Lance would grin at him red-faced when he fucked up the choreography. Lancebot never fucked up the choreography.

"He used to make me sandwiches when I couldn't sleep," Joey told Chris, gloomily. "Really disgusting sandwiches—fried peanut butter and banana."

"Well that explains a lot," Chris said, patting the curve of Joey's stomach.

Chris had pretty much gotten over his freak-out, though he still looked at Lancebot sometimes like he thought Lancebot might start screaming, "Exterminate, exterminate!"

"I saw *Westworld*," he said to Joey meaningfully.

Joey thought it might have more to do with Chris trying to fuck with Lancebot early on. "This is Lance's lucky shirt," Chris had said, holding up a sparkly, lime-green Fuman top. "He'd want you to wear it to the Grammies, man."

Lancebot had punched him.

"Ow!" Chris had grabbed his jaw, looking more angry than scared. "What the *fuck*?"

Lancebot shrugged apologetically. "Lance left some pretty specific instructions."

At least part of the problem was that Joey couldn't seem to get hold of Lance.

"We have no one by that name, sir," the concierge of the Ritz told him. So did the concierges of the Hilton and the Hyatt, and the secretary of the Holiday Inn.

"What about a Clint Black?" Joey said desperately. "Garth Brooks? Or, um. That guy from Duran Duran?"

"Tell him it's Joey," he said over and over again. "Tell him I miss him. Tell him . . . tell him I miss him."

"Face it," Justin said to him when Joey had exhausted Bermuda's hotel list. "Lance doesn't want to be found."

"Yeah," Joey said. He crumpled the list up and threw it on the floor.

The next day he uncrumpled it and started calling again.

He sent a bunch of letters to Lance's mom, all addressed to "The Real Lance." They all said the same thing: I miss you, please come back. Lance's mom phoned him a few days later. "Did you and Lance have a fight, Joey?"

"No, no, Mrs. Bass. I just thought you might—"

She interrupted him. "I'm not going to be a go-between, honey. You two are grown men now. I will tell you this, though: friendships like yours are damn rare."

"Yeah," Joey said, tiredly.

"Go talk to him, Joey. Right after you get off the phone. I mean it."

"Lance's mom forwarded me some mail," Lancebot told Joey a week later. "Do you want me to keep it for Lance, or—"

Joey shook his head. "It doesn't matter."

He thought about the kiss a lot—replayed it in his head. One of the things he missed most was being able to touch Lance whenever he wanted.

On his second day, Lancebot had pushed Justin's legs off his lap and elbowed Chris back to his own side of the couch.

"Okay, that's *enough*," he'd said.

He stood up and drew an imaginary circle around himself with his fingers. "This is my personal space. All of you have to respect it."

"Okay." Melissa crunched on an apple and tossed them each a CD. "Spark Girls," she said with her mouth full. "They're the latest Jive recruits, and from now on, you're their best friends—Lance, you have a crush on Suzie. And all of you *love* the new album."

"Sweet mother of God," Joey said when Melissa had left. He had to say it loudly, because Justin was beatboxing to the girls' first single. "Just once, just *once*, I wish she'd come in here and tell us to like good music."

"So Joey," Chris said. He held out his CD like a microphone. "What do you think of the new Sparkly Girls album?"

"Spark Girls," JC said.

"Right."

Joey leaned in. "Yeah, I'm all about flat singing at the moment. Repetition's where the scene is *at*."

"And you, Lance?" Chris leered. "A little bird tells me you have a hard-on for Suzie."

And for a fraction of a second, Joey forgot, turned smiling to hear what Lance would say.

Lancebot smiled easily. "She's great," he said. "And I love the album."

Some of Joey's favorite times ever were leaning against Lance on their bus, while they watched MTV and drank beer.

"There's a thousand words that I could say," Lance would croon. "But I won't stoop that low." And "*There* we are. Oh wait, no, that's still Justin. Wait, wait . . . *There* we are . . ."

And Joey would giggle and feel the rumble of Lance's laughter against his skin, and think: this is enough. I can live with this.

Rosie leaned across the desk. "So hey, what have you guys got in your stereos?"

"Well, uh. I have the Spark Girls in my car," Joey said. "*Great* album."

"Yeah?"

"Yeah, I crank it up when I'm in traffic, and—"

"And we met them!" Chris interrupted. "We've uh. We've been hanging around with them—sweet girls."

"And Lance has a crush on Suzie!" Justin crowed.

Rosie laughed. "No way!"

Lancebot ducked his head, smiling. "She's great," he said.

Joey had been sure someone would notice. But sound checks went by and concerts, radio interviews, and charity appearances, and nobody said a word.

After a while, Joey started to wonder if maybe the fans actually liked Lancebot more than they'd liked Lance.

On *TRL*, Lancebot grinned and said, "I love women," and the audience erupted into cheers.

On another show, the presenter told Lancebot he looked fantastic before they'd even settled into their chairs. "Been working out?" she said.

"Uh. A little, yes." Lancebot nodded through the audience's screams.

He'd started to look less like Lance—rougher or something. He didn't shave as often, and his arms seemed more defined.

"Marry me, Lance," said one of the signs. "Suddenly hot," said another. It had a blown-up photograph of Lance's ass. Joey wondered how far he was gone if he recognized Lance just from his ass.

"And Joey. Are you enjoying the tour?"

Joey smiled automatically. No, he thought. "Yes," he said.

That night, he watched the show, feeling weirdly dislocated. The Joey on the screen smiled and laughed and flirted with the presenter. He high-fived Justin, and said things like "I never get tired of touring," and "If you've got it, flaunt it, baby," to a girl with big breasts. He seemed no more Joey than Lancebot was Lance.

"I hear you're a ladies' man, Joey," said another presenter in Washington.

Joey looked at her with dislike; her tone had been a little flirty, a little contemptuous, and a little nudge, wink. *I know you like boys,* it said.

I like boys, Joey thought to himself. He tried it out inside his mouth. I like boys. The pure possibility of saying it loomed large. He could say it. He could say it, he could knock that expression right off her face.

Justin shifted beside him. He was smiling his not-another-interview smile, which meant he was bored and tired and he hadn't eaten since breakfast. Further along, Chris looked like he wanted to scream, but he was confining it to tapping his foot against the leg of Justin's chair.

"I—" Joey felt a trickle of sweat slip down his side, and more sweat prickle on his forehead. He squeezed his hands to remind himself not to wipe his face—the makeup people would kill him. Justin looked at him, and his smile went real for a second. Joey forced himself to smile back. He could say it. He could.

He took a breath. "I—I love women," he said. "What can I say?"

The audience's cheers sounded tinny—like a recording of a recording.

As soon as the cameras stopped rolling, Joey ripped off his microphone and ran to the bathroom. He threw up for what felt like an hour. He was real, he told himself. He was real, he was real, he was real, he was *real*.

Someone rattled the door. "Joey?" It was Chris. He sounded anxious.

"Fine," Joey wanted to say. "I'm fine." But all that came out was "Lance. I want Lance."

"I know," Chris said, gently. "Joey, open the door."

Joey wiped his mouth. He took a shuddering breath. He wiped his forehead with his other hand. He opened the door.

"Hey," Chris said. He was back to his noninterview self—shifting from one foot to the other, restlessly, almost jogging in place. He smiled and rubbed Joey's arms. "You okay?"

Joey shook his head. "I want Lance," he said.

"Yeah." Chris pulled him into a hug. "I miss him too."

Chris took him out and got him very, very drunk. When Joey finally stumbled back onto the bus, it was 4:00 a.m. Lancebot was still up. He was plugged into his recharger, reading something fat with small print.

Joey pulled it out of his hands.

"Hey!" Lancebot said.

Joey touched Lancebot's face. It felt just like real skin. "For someone who isn't Lance," he said. "You're a pretty hot guy."

"Robot," Lancebot said.

"Whatever."

Lancebot sighed. "Joey," he said. "Can I have my book back?"

Joey shook his head. "You feel real," he said. He pressed his hand to Lancebot's chest where his heart would have been if he'd had a heart. "Do you feel real?"

"Well." Lancebot shifted uncomfortably. "It's not really something I think about."

"Oh," Joey said.

"I think it's more of a human thing."

"Yeah?" said Joey, hopefully.

"Sure. That's why human teenagers get stoned and wonder if the green they see is the same green everybody else sees. But they get over it. They read Sartre, Camus, get bored, and get over it."

Joey stared at him. He could have been speaking Russian for all the sense he was making. Lance would never have said that. And Lancebot wasn't Lance, but he looked like Lance, and he smelled like Lance.

Joey surged forward and kissed him awkwardly.

"Joey." Lancebot grabbed his shoulders and pushed him away a little. "Joey, you're drunk."

"I don't care, I don't care," Joey said, insistently.

"Joey, I like girls."

"You like girls?" Joey said, shocked. "But. But Lance doesn't like girls."

Lancebot sighed. "I'm not Lance. Lance is on vacation," he said, sounding tired. He frowned suddenly.

"Hey, all that stuff about being real. Are you having an existential crisis?"

"What?" Joey blinked at him. He wasn't sure that would have made sense, even if he were sober.

"Because you have to tell me if you are. There are warnings on the box about it."

"You came in a box?" Joey asked, distracted.

Lancebot waved his hand. "That's irrelevant."

Joey shook his head. The room was wobbling a bit. "Um. I don't know."

"Hmm," Lancebot said. He sounded suspicious.

Joey crawled out of his bunk the next day, and found Lancebot on the couch, staring out of the window.

He slumped down next to him. "Um, about the—"

"The crisis?" Lancebot sounded nervous, and Joey wondered if it were because he really felt nervous, or if he'd been programmed to sound nervous in gay situations. Was this a gay situation?

"The kiss," he mumbled.

"*Oh*, oh." Lancebot looked weirdly relieved. "Hey. You were drunk—people do crazy things when they're drunk."

"Okay."

"Forgotten already. Never happened."

Joey covered his face. His head hurt. "Okay."

Joey avoided Lancebot a little after that, and—watching Lancebot step around him carefully at the breakfast table and disappearing when Joey came to rehearsal—he had a feeling Lancebot might be avoiding him too.

They were in a band though, so spending time together was sometimes unavoidable.

In Chicago, they had to open a club owned by Leo or Sly or someone important.

"Okay," said Monica. "You have a choice." She held up two suits. "Black with silver trim or white with mauve."

Joey looked from one to the other. "Can't I just wear a sweater and jeans or something?"

Monica smiled tightly. "Don't do this to me, baby." She switched the suits around. "White with mauve, black with silver," she said enticingly.

"I have some nice sweaters."

"Honey. Honey, honey." Joey could almost hear her grinding her teeth. "Everyone's waiting."

"Black," Joey said, feeling like he was five years old.

"Ha! You went with the black too," Chris said, when Joey came downstairs. He did a quick spin. "Spill-proof, baby."

Lancebot smiled mildly. Joey saw he'd gone with the white.

"So I was thinking of buying a new car," Joey told Justin on the way to an early morning radio appearance.

"Yeah? Cool." Justin sipped his coffee. "We could like go driving together after the tour—do a road trip or something."

"One of those new Porsches with the—"

"Oh hey, hey," Justin looked puzzled. "No, man. BMWs for five years. Remember? We signed with them in January?"

"Um," JC said in a rehearsal break. "I haven't been spending much time with you lately, huh?"

"Oh hey, it's—" Joey shrugged. "It's okay, it's been a weird couple of months."

"Yeah." JC stared at his shoes. "So um. So okay I don't know how to say this. But Lancebot told me you kissed him."

"Jesus!" Joey looked around quickly to check that no one had heard. "He *told* you that?"

JC's face was pink. "Uh, yeah. Lance had him programmed to confide in me if he couldn't process anything."

"Oh," Joey said. He remembered the first time he'd met JC. Joey had been shooting hoops with Steve in their driveway, and JC had wandered over from across the street. JC had been older than both of them, but he'd seemed younger—a dorky kid with a sweet smile and the ugliest haircut Joey had ever seen.

"I'm worried about you," JC said quietly. "We're all worried about you."

Joey gulped his drink, embarrassed. "You don't need to be," he mumbled.

"But we are. You miss him. It's okay to miss him."

"That's not why!" Joey said. He saw the bodyguards turning to look at them, and lowered his voice.

"That's not why . . . the kiss . . . It's not like that."

JC fiddled with his water bottle. "Okay."

"It isn't," Joey insisted.

"Okay, Joey," JC said again. He looked tired.

JC went back to the dance floor after that. Joey watched him in the mirror. He seemed smoother, more elegant than the kid Joey had met playing hoops; it was hard to believe they were the same person. Joey wrapped his hands around his glass. He'd know if JC wasn't JC, he told himself. He would.

He found himself watching them all more closely, though.

Justin was so beautiful that he sometimes made Joey's heart ache—not in a sexy way, Joey told himself hastily—more like when he looked at a beautiful painting or sculpture. He was good at everything, too—sports, singing, song writing, math.

Chris bought Joey a fruit basket out of the blue. "Pink Lady apples are in season," he said before Joey could say anything. He grabbed one for himself and bit into it.

"You're not a bot, are you?" Joey asked abruptly. Lancebot was always bringing him vegetables and telling him to eat better. Joey thought it was easy enough for him to say—Lancebot didn't have to eat at all if he didn't want to.

Chris frowned at him. "No, you paranoid fucker. I'm worried about you. You've been moping about Lance so, hey—one fruit for another." He winced as Joey smacked him. "Ow. Jeez, Joey."

"It wasn't funny," Joey said, rubbing his hand. Chris's arm was like steel.

Chris and JC maybe talked to Justin, because Justin dragged him to a club to "cheer you up, or at least get you wasted."

When they got there, the room was full of people so beautiful it was hard to believe they were real. Joey stared at them: poised and attractive and laughing at jokes Joey didn't find funny at all.

"Love your shirt, sweetie," said a woman he'd never met. She kissed his cheek. "D&G? Lacroix?" She had perfect cheekbones, perfect makeup.

"Um—I don't—" He started, but she'd already turned away.

Someone else clasped his shoulder. Joey didn't recognize him, but his teeth and smile were like every other person's in the room, so he still seemed strangely familiar. "Great record, Joey. Wonderful record."

Joey watched him weave his way through the crowd, patting people on the back. "Love your record, wonderful record," Joey heard faintly.

Either of them could have been a bot, Joey thought. Maybe they were both bots. Maybe everyone in this room was a robot, and their real selves were on vacation.

He watched Justin slap people on the back and laugh—Justin blended into this crowd like he belonged, like he was made for it. Joey was the only one who didn't. He shuddered. He felt like he was in the eye of a storm: stationary while the whole world blurred around him.

"Is this our life?" he said. "Is this really our life?"

Justin put his arm around him for a photograph. "Surreal sometimes, huh," he answered, grinning widely for the camera.

Joey had promised himself he wouldn't try to kiss Lancebot again—he still felt sick with humiliation whenever he thought about it. But the next time he got drunk, he found himself with his face buried in Lancebot's neck.

"Lance," he mumbled. "Lance."

"Joey." Lancebot wriggled out of his grip. "I'm not—"

"I know, I know," Joey interrupted. "You're not Lance. But—" He swallowed nervously. "But maybe you could—I thought maybe you could pretend. We could both pretend. Just for a while. Just—" He reached out to touch Lancebot's mouth. "Just for a little while."

"*Joey.*" Lancebot grabbed his hand and pulled it away. "I'm not like that."

"But I thought—"

"I've been *programmed*. I'm not like that, and I can't be anything I'm not."

"Why not?" Joey said. He felt like he was going to cry. "Why not? Lance pretends. Lance pretends all the time."

"Of course he does." Lancebot sounded confused. "He's human."

Would one robot recognize another, Joey wondered. Would the robots even know if all the real people had been pied-pipered away? He looked down at his hands. It was surprisingly easy to picture his real self somewhere on a beach with Lance.

He frowned and looked at his hands closer, felt the hairs at the back of his neck rise. The nail on his index finger had been black the day he met JC, he remembered suddenly. He'd caught the ball wrong the week before. He stared at his hands now. His father would have said they were the hands of someone who'd never worked a day in his life; they were clean, and the nails were smooth and perfectly round. They didn't seem like his own hands at all.

"Am I a robot?" he asked when the others arrived for breakfast.

"No baby, you don't dance well enough," Chris said. He was sort of smiling, but his eyes had narrowed.

Joey's heart thudded. "Is it something we're not supposed to talk about?" he asked. "Am I defective if I know I'm fake?"

"Joey," Chris said. He took a few steps towards Joey slowly, like he knew Joey was defective. "Joey, calm down."

"Am I a defective robot?"

"No, of course not." Justin's frown was identical to Lancebot's. Joey jerked back from him.

"Because I think I am," he admitted. He might as well get it over with. "I think I'm defective. I like boys. I like Lance."

"Okay," JC said, soothingly. "Okay, good for you, Joey."

"It's true, isn't it?" Joey said. He sucked in a panicked breath. "It's true!"

"Joey, you have to calm down." Now Justin was coming towards him too.

Joey backed away from him. "You're all replacements, and I am too!"

"Aren't there warnings on the box about this kind of thing?" Chris said to Lancebot.

"I came in a box! And you did too! You—all of you—"

"Fuck!" Chris said.

And Joey looked back just in time to meet Chris's fist.

There were crappy souvenirs on the bedside table when Joey woke up—figurines made of shells and a T-shirt saying "I escaped the Bermuda Triangle."

Lance was sitting on the edge of the bed. Joey was fairly sure it was Lance—his face was blotchy like he hadn't slept in a while, and his hair needed a wash. Joey had imagined that when Lance came back, he would look sleek and rested, but he mostly just looked tired.

"Hey," Lance said awkwardly when he saw Joey was awake. "So um. So I'm back."

Joey shifted and winced. "How long ago?"

"A couple of hours." Lance touched Joey's cheek lightly where Chris had hit him. "I heard you went a bit nuts."

"They told you." Joey closed his eyes. His head ached—unrelenting and impossible to ignore, like a voice jeering that he was real, that there was no more plastic to hide behind. It was, he thought, like waking up with a hangover and knowing you'd behaved like a fucking idiot the night before.

"They kind of had to," Lance said. "It was part of the conditions on the box."

"Oh."

"Chris was pretty freaked."

"Yeah." Joey swallowed. "Yeah, me too."

"So," Lance said, and something in his voice made Joey open his eyes. "So," Lance said again. He wasn't looking at Joey at all; he was staring at the bedspread, tracing the line of the seam, and his hand was shaking. "You like boys. You like me."

"You knew that," Joey pointed out.

Lance looked up at him. "I never heard you say it."

Joey nodded, because that was fair enough. That was fair. And Lance's hand was shaking and it somehow made it easier—knowing that Lance was scared too. He swallowed. "I um. I like you."

Lance looked concerned. "That's pretty defective, Joey."

Joey grinned at him wanly. "Fuck you."

Lance smiled then—the sly smile that was just Joey's. "You know I like you too, right?"

Joey grinned wider and leaned in to kiss him. As kisses went, it wasn't perfect: Joey's head still hurt, and Lance's lips were a little chapped. And they were interrupted in the middle of it by the phone.

It was a Boston radio interview—Joey had completely forgotten about it.

"I love touring," he told the DJ as Lance sighed and flopped onto his stomach next to him. Joey raised an eyebrow at him. "It's a much more intimate tour this time."

Lance snorted and poked him with his foot.

Joey nodded and murmured answers, watching Lance help himself to an apple from Joey's fruit basket. He bit into it and a trickle of juice ran down his wrist. Joey wanted to lick it off.

"Yeah, the Spark Girls CD," Joey said. "It's really—"

Lance made a face and pretended to stick his finger down his throat. Joey started laughing. "It's great," he said. "I really love it."

> The Electric Monk was a labor-saving device, like a dishwasher or a video recorder. Dishwashers washed tedious dishes for you, thus saving you the bother of washing them yourself, video recorders watched tedious television for you, thus saving you the bother of looking at it yourself; Electric Monks believed things for you, thus saving you what was becoming an increasingly onerous task, that of believing all the things the world expected you to believe.
> —Douglas Adams, *Dirk Gently's Holistic Detective Agency*

The Spymaster's Tale

Title: Queen of Spades (2006)
Author: astolat
Fandom: James Bond (Craig movies)
Rating: Het, explicit (James Bond / M)

Introduction

While Ian Fleming's James Bond is one of the world's most popular transmedia characters, a hero whose adventures have taken him from books to comics, movies, video games, and beyond, he has not historically been popular with female media fans. Overshadowing the Bond franchise in the hearts of fans is the Bond-inspired television show *The Man from U.N.C.L.E.* (1964–1968), which may have been the first true media fandom, and which certainly helped lay down the template for other fandoms that followed. *The Man from U.N.C.L.E*, known as *MUNCLE* to fans, teamed American spy Napoleon Solo (a character created for the show by Fleming) with Russian partner Ilya Kuryakin to fight THRUSH, a global organization akin to Bond adversaries SMERSH and SPECTRE. *The Man from U.N.C.L.E.* may have been more congenial to the subcultural desires of female fans: unlike Bond, who was truly a solo act, Napoleon Solo was given a partner at the insistence of the show's early fans, and one who was almost as alien as Mr. Spock to Americans in the Cold War era. *MUNCLE* and *Star Trek* were 1960s utopian fantasies of collaboration, of nations and races coming together despite their differences, which may have inspired more subterranean fantasies of gender and sexual equality; in any case, they were the fan favorites. In contrast, James Bond the solitary cold warrior was largely left out in the cold by fandom, more often the subject of critique than the object of fantasy.

This historical dissatisfaction with Bond was sexual as well as political. The Bond series arguably helped to mainstream a pornographic gaze during the postwar era, both in the books—which drew particular attention to the physical features of its female characters and depicted Bond himself as a reader of erotic, and even sadomasochistic, literature—as well as in the early films, where Sean Connery served as a sexual tour guide to the Bond Girls of various exotic locales. Of course, Connery was also a sexy spectacle himself, the camera often following his unclad and muscular body even when there was a competing female onscreen. But while Bond may seem to offer a lot to the female spectator, even if only in terms of beefcake, one can only enjoy him from outside the world of the film. There's no one within the Bond films with whom a self-respecting female spectator can identify, and quite a lot that the feminist spectator has to willfully ignore to enjoy herself.

In fact, far from serving as a point of female identification, the "Bond Girl" has not endeared Bond to his female audience; she's a male fantasy, not a female one. In *The James Bond Dossier*, Kingsley Amis discusses Bond's appeal as a fantasy figure: "We don't want to have Bond to dinner or go golfing with Bond or talk to Bond. We want to be Bond."[1] He also says that when the Bond girl appears, "You smile appreciatively and nudge your neighbor and lean forward."[2] But neither the "we" who wants to be Bond nor the "you" who leans forward appears to be female. Female fans are typically more likely to complain to their neighbors about what they call the "Babes" or "Bimbos of the Week" (BOTW): that is, female characters who appear once in an ongoing series and are never heard from again. In slash fandom, the BOTW trope is typically taken as evidence of the hero's latent queerness, as his relationship to other men (particularly his partner, if any: e.g., Spock, Kuryakin, Watson, Hutch) is much more important than his relationship to women. Bond, having no male partner, has proved harder to queer, and so fandom has been given no easy way of rescuing him from his apparent misogyny and casual disregard of women over the course of the franchise.

How refreshing, then, for female fans to meet Judi Dench's delightfully genderswapped M in *Goldeneye* (1995), and to hear her take down Pierce Brosnan's Bond: "I think you're a sexist, misogynist dinosaur; a relic of the Cold War." *Goldeneye* took a page from fanfiction by changing the gender of a primary character, and, as fans have long known, to change a character's gender is to change the parameters of the universe: of what can be said or done or felt in it. Judi Dench's M spoke for a generation when she told James Bond his charms were wasted on her. This seemed to have cleared the air between Bond and his female fan base, and both M and the women she represents have become noticeably fonder of Bond in subsequent films.

By the time of the 2006 reboot *Casino Royale* starring Daniel Craig, the gender politics of the series were catching up with the feminist attitudes of fandom, and consequently, Craig's Bond films appeal more to women. According to Lisa Funnell, Craig's Bond differs from his predecessors by being presented as "youthful, spectacular, and feminized relative to the gaze."[3] In this, she argues, he more resembles the younger and slimmer male action heroes of the 1990s, a category which includes not only such figures as Keanu Reeves's Neo and Leonardo DiCaprio's Jack Dawson but also women such as Linda Hamilton's Sarah Connor and Angelina Jolie's Lara Croft. Funnell further argues that Craig's Bond, who twice rises out of the sea in apparent homage to Ursula Andress's iconic scene in the first Bond film, *Doctor No* (1962), actually "replaces the Bond Girl . . . as the locus of visual spectacle";[4] in other words, that Bond and the Bond girl have been merged into a single figure, which she calls "the Bond–Bond Girl hybrid." James Bond himself is now the primary (and passive) object of the gaze.

With both a genderswapped M and hybridized, feminized young Bond, these new films caught the attention of female media fans like none before. In rebooting the Bond mythology, the Craig films also significantly alter the nature of M and Bond's relationship. In the Brosnan films (*Goldeneye, Tomorrow Never Dies, The World Is Not Enough, Die Another Day*), Judi Dench's M was presented as only the latest in a line of Ms that an already-established Bond has worked for (and the first female M; the character was based on Stella Rimington, the first female head of MI5). We get the sense that Brosnan's Bond vaguely resents her, at least at first; she is an upstart, a potentially dislikable replacement. But in *Casino Royale*, rebooting the series into the present day means that Dench's M is an early and important influence on Bond and his career; in fact, it is she who promotes him to oo status. This Bond is essentially created by female power.

This provides a golden opportunity for fanfiction writer astolat, who wrote "Queen of Spades" within a week of *Casino Royale*'s U.S. release. In "Queen of Spades," a young and sexy Bond is mentored by the older and wiser M, who makes him a better man and a better agent by both disciplining and seducing him. This conflation of teaching and seduction has a noble lineage, going back at least as far as Plato's *Symposium*. Similarly, in "Queen of Spades," the elder M becomes the object of Bond's erotic infatuation and teaches him a thing or two about inspiring lust in others. It's worth noting that age—sometimes assumed to nullify a woman's sex appeal (though not a man's)—not only does not diminish M's sexiness in astolat's story but is explicitly framed as an asset. "I will admit that it's something of an unfair advantage, being postmenopausal," M tells Bond after their first sexual encounter, which leaves Bond flattened. "I might even feel guilty if you hadn't asked for it quite so insistently." This may strike readers accustomed to heterosexist tropes as odd, but of course older women do have sex (maybe even better sex for being sexually experienced), and, as women and gay men already know, there's nothing odd about being drawn to a powerful and charismatic older partner. It's only in a sexist culture with a glass ceiling that the older partner is rarely female: no one questions the stereotype of an older male boss and young female employee. But astolat exploits M and Bond's new relationship in the films to show Bond having an experience that many men still don't have, even today: he is a young guy working for a powerful, and powerfully attractive, older woman. In "Queen of Spades" we see Bond work to impress her, maybe even to become worthy of her.

While the films show Dench's M as tough and charismatic, astolat goes further and shows us that M is *sexy*. There is nothing maternal about this M; rather, astolat makes M's steel gray, middle-aged body an object of desire, despite the fact that older women are rarely cast as sexual protagonists, even in fanfiction. The fact that M's erotic power is unexpected—by Bond, by the reader—is part of what makes the story work. M's sexuality is *weaponized*: the fact that we can't immediately see it is part of what makes it dangerous, and enviable, especially in a world of spies and undercover operations. This is the opposite of female objectification: M's sexuality, far from being obvious to the spectator's gaze, comes out like a switchblade. In fact, M is so in control of her sexuality that Bond—James Bond, the notorious womanizer!—begins to worry if his own appeal is only skin deep. In "Queen of Spades," it's the male Bond, not the female M, who's anxious: astolat's M is entirely comfortable with her sexuality, despite being, as the story tells us, forty years older and forty pounds heavier than the conventional Hollywood sex object, and menopausal to boot. These details aren't handwaved, either; astolat explicitly reminds us of Dench's current age and shape, and they help rather than hurt her depiction of M's sex appeal.

We see the young Bond differently after reading this story, too: we may see him as a character whose charms may be too obvious, whose appeal is too broadly on the surface, and whose job it is to be our on-screen sex object. The traditionally phallic Bond—so often pictured holding his gun—is so destabilized by this relationship to M that he—and the reader—begin to think of being older as a desirable state. In astolat's universe, an older woman has so much power that she is what everyone else in the universe wants to be. Of course, this is what real power does: it sets itself up as an ideal. In "Queen of Spades," the ideal is age and experience, sexual and otherwise: getting older gives one a self-control that youth and prettiness—now symbolized by Bond himself—do not have. We now want Bond to grow up to be M: to be as confident, as wise, as shameless, as powerful in his sexuality as she is. M has picked Bond as a protégé because he is *like her*, because he is prepared to use his brains and his body like a woman does.

As a result, the reader of "Queen of Spades" has at least two points of identification. She may identify with Bond, who is experiencing problems typically associated with women but really of the young more generally; he is the ingénue, the beautiful young thing being groomed for a big career. Or she may identify with M, or rather, aspire to be M someday, as Bond himself does. This idea is his salvation: M will save him from himself, and from the worst excesses of the Bond universe.

While the films later took a more clichéd turn by turning M into a mother figure,[5] astolat gives us a much more provocative notion: a Bond who both desires M and wants to grow up to *be* her—and he will if he's lucky and works hard. When was the last time you wanted to be an older woman? When was the last time you read something that drove you to imagine desiring and inhabiting a postmenopausal female body? This is a radical reimagining of female sexual power, and what better place for it than in a James Bond story? Meet M: the first Bond Woman.

Suggested Further Reading

Like Sherlock Holmes, James Bond immediately inspired a wave of fanworks not only from amateurs but from other professional writers. Just as Ronald Knox, Dorothy Sayers, and others played "the Great Game" as Sherlockians, Kingsley Amis played his version in *The James Bond Dossier*, in which he used textual evidence to investigate Bond's habits and psychology (including a valiant attempt to determine exactly which brands and exactly how much alcohol Bond drinks). Similarly, under the pseudonym of I*n Fl*ming, the *Harvard Lampoon* published the 1963 "parody" novel *Alligator*, which was in fact a full-length fanwork staring J*mes B*nd. Umberto Eco, a self-described Bondologist, coedited *The Bond Affair* in 1966 and wrote a widely reprinted essay about narrative structures in Fleming's novels.

As a "cult" writer and a genre writer, Fleming was more the subject of pop journalism and homages of this sort (which is not to dismiss them; see, for example, Paul Johnson's 1958 article "Sex Snobbery and Sadism" in the *New Statesman*) rather than formal literary criticism by professors in university presses, though this has changed in recent years. A number of essay collections—*The James Bond Phenomenon: A Critical Reader* (Manchester University Press, 2003), *Revisioning 007: James Bond and "Casino Royale"* (Wallflower, 2010), *The Cultures of James Bond* (2011, Wissenschaftlicher Verlag Trier), *For His Eyes Only: The Women of James Bond* (Wallflower, 2015), and Claire Hines's recent *Fan Phenomena: James Bond* (Intellect, 2015)—testify to the surge of scholarly interest and diversity of approaches to the Bond character and his transmedia world, including fan responses. That said, journalism continues to make important and incisive contributions to Bond and Bond fandom; probably the piece I find most useful in teaching Bond to students is Sophia McDougall's 2013 article "The Rape of James Bond: On Sexual Assault, and 'Realism' in Popular Culture," in (again) the *New Statesman*, which responds to the sexual threats to Craig's Bond in *Skyfall*. McDougall, like astolat and many other female fans, explicitly recognizes a vulnerability in Craig's Bond that serves as an important critique to other representations of masculinity in pop culture. "Is it realistic that James Bond has never been raped?" McDougall asks. "How many times has he found himself utterly at the mercy of men who want to hurt, degrade and humiliate him before killing him?" In *Skyfall*, the villain unbuttons Bond's shirt and touches his thigh. McDougall notes, "That scene is, to coin a phrase, not about sex, it's about power. And it is the most literal way I have ever seen a male hero (and the ultra-masculine Bond at that) treated like a female character." Craig's Bond is open to many kinds of audience identification.

Queen of Spades

astolat

The high-floor apartment was elegant and scrupulously clean, full of comfortable minimalist furniture and interesting art, with a spectacular view over the Thames at night. *Love the new place*, he added, and left the dossier on the coffee table.

As he put his hand on the knob he hesitated, instinct waking, and looked over: she was watching him from the bedroom door, in a long patterned-silk dressing gown with her arms folded across her chest. He quirked her his most charming smile. "Sorry, didn't mean to wake you."

"Rietzmann?" she said.

"No longer a problem," he said.

"Good." Her unamused gaze didn't waver.

He pointed at the door. "I'll see myself out, shall I?"

"Do. And Bond," M added, as he paused in the doorway to hear her out, "the next time you do something like this will be once too many."

She turned and vanished back into the bedroom. He was laughing softly to himself as he pulled the door shut behind him.

He'd seen three M's before this one come and go, while he'd been working his way up the ranks. Or down, he supposed, depending on your perspective. The first two, he'd still been in training, too low on the totem pole to know who they were officially, but he'd known anyway. Of course, everyone knew the old man with his seamed face and the dark brown scar like a sickle under the ear, who'd finally died a year after James had joined the service.

After him came the placeholder bureaucrat, cautious as a mouse and as imaginative; easy to recognize by the cold resentment he drew from the eyes of all the new instructors who suddenly took up work in the training facility: lean hard men who taught economy of words and movement by example, who gave no praise and brutal correction and spent their free time sparring against each other, dropping the few holds they kept barred with the students. James watched them for half a year before he climbed into the ring for the first time. He had to be carried out, but three weeks later he went back in, and no one was beating him best of three by the time the bureaucrat left, after a tenure of less than three years and one change of government.

It was more of a challenge picking out the successor, the thin-lipped accountant who wasn't, arriving daily at 9:00 a.m. and leaving again at 5:00 p.m. on the dot, carrying his narrow black briefcase back and forth through the car park, anonymous in the midst of all the rest of the day's staff; it had taken James three months before he'd worked out that there was one more office worker in the security videos and the staff roster than there were matching desks in the building. He left an unsigned note on the accountant's windscreen saying *Promote me.* The next morning there was a packet slid under the door of his flat with plane tickets to Budapest, and his first real assignment in the field.

This M had been a surprise. "Some bint out of the East German division," one of the others had muttered to him, as he went in for his first meeting; he'd expected the politically correct choice of some front-office politician, someone whose main qualification was that she could look the part on camera or in front of an inquiry board, and on first glance she'd met expectations. He'd smiled at her just a little unprofessionally, gave her a little of what made women turn their heads to look after him. Only a little: he wanted double-oh status, but he wasn't hungry enough for the promotion to endure the purgatory of bedding his supervisor, if that wouldn't likely have backfired in any case.

"If you're trying to seduce me, you're doing a damned poor job of it," she said. "If you're trying to impress me, all the worse." Then she'd packed him off to Kyrgyzstan. After two dreary weeks sitting at a post watching nothing more exciting than some low-level drug deals, he'd slipped the traces and gone skiing in the Tien Shan mountains. He went back to London and walked into her office with a portfolio of a dozen contacts he'd established in the smuggling rings that took the drugs back and forth into China. He perched on the edge of her desk and leaned over to hand it to her, with a smile as thoroughly unprofessional as he could manage.

"Better," was all she said. Six months later she'd handed him the dossier with his first two kills.

That had put the lasting stamp on their relationship, a scrabble for dominance as vicious as any sparring match he'd ever faced in the ring, and one he had no intention of losing. He crossed more lines than he needed to and took himself further out into the cold, all for the pleasure of seeing her forced to accept him back on his own terms when he came back successful. He needled and pushed and flirted his way through every contact to watch her eyes narrow and her lips draw tight, an acknowledgment that she needed him, that he was worth putting up with nearly anything, that he was restrained only by himself.

She had rarely resorted to ultimatums before, though, and only of the modest and specific variety when she did: *Walk out of my office now and you needn't come back ever*, or *Bring him back alive unless you plan to spend the rest of your career at the academy*.

Perhaps he had been pushing the boundaries more than usual lately. Seven years at the double-oh level now, and he was on the wrong side of all the odds, kills stacking up in his file like poker chips. In Rietzmann's dark hotel room, the job done, he'd jerked his gun back up at a deadly stranger with a spatter of blood on his cheek like a flower and his eyes flat and empty as a poured-out bowl, and pulled the trigger on shattering glass before he even realized that he was looking in the mirror. Perhaps he'd even wanted one of those little tugs on the leash, to remind him there was one, even if only by his own sufferance. But now she'd thrown him a gauntlet direct, and he could no more back down than he could fly.

He caught the next plane to Rio. The first night he slept on the beach; the rest of the week he slept in the seaside villa of the beautiful dark-eyed Selina, until her husband unexpectedly returned home and he had to drop out the window at two in the morning. He stopped in at the first club he found still open, smoky and full of tall, muscled men in black leather and tight jeans. Alexandro bought him a drink at the bar and took him back to a penthouse with a spectacular harbor view from the king-size bed where they wrestled pleasurably for position; at dawn James wrapped it up and took him, and spent that second week enjoying the spoils of victory.

He spotted the operative sent to find him instead of the other way around, and left a chiding note in the man's hotel room on his way to the airport. He sauntered into M's office tanned bronze and came around to the far side of her desk. "Did you miss me so badly, then?" he asked, heavy-lidded, his voice rough with two weeks of sex and sea air.

She had been reading a file. She took off her glasses and set them on the desk and looked up at him. "Tell me something, 007. What sort of job do you think they hired female agents for in the service when I joined? Or did you think I was a secretary?"

"Why, M, should you kiss and tell like this?" he said, delighted, already taking off forty pounds and an equal measure of years to put her in an elaborate evening gown on the arm of some Eastern-bloc politician; it was as good as an invitation to cross any number of fresh lines. She had good cheekbones, if her face was a little round: he could envision her something of a charming gamine, he thought, with a slim neck and good breasts; too short to ever have had much in the way of legs, though. He leaned over her, offensively close, and murmured, "I'm sure you were irresistible."

She met his mocking gaze, very calm, her own eyes clear, and from one moment to the next, something changed. He couldn't have named it, beyond a collection of gestures: one eyebrow rising in a narrow elegant arch, a tilt to the corner of her mouth, her chin lifting towards him a little; inconsequential details that meant nothing, changed nothing, but the air between them went suddenly electric, as easily as though she had thrown a switch. He was leaning towards her before he realized it.

He clenched every muscle to halt his movement, a tremendous effort; she was smiling, faintly, and he wanted to close that space on a level beneath conscious thought. She left him pierced on the hook a straining, drawn-taut moment. Then she looked away and the spell abruptly broke; he was off the desk and two feet away, breathing hard.

She picked up her glasses and put them back on. Taking up the file again, she said, without looking up, "Now go away, 007. I'm busy."

He woke in the middle of the night sweating and erect, the sheets tangled close around his body, plastered to his thighs. He didn't remember what he'd been dreaming about.

There were seventy-eight targets listed in her file: diplomats and government officials, generals and bishops, businessmen and kings. There was a marked lack of detail, little more than dates and brief notes: *successfully acquired plans for GTB missile, contained situation in Shanghai, diverted funds to Argentina.* There were six kills, all of them labeled *attributed to natural causes.* Another five marked *killed in retribution.*

For all his well-justified reputation, he had never had to work very hard at seduction; all he asked from a woman was to enjoy her and be enjoyed in return. Any woman who didn't want to accept that offer—temporary coy refusal aside—was a woman he didn't want anyway. Harder to imagine men betraying country, principle, self-interest, just for sex; to die for a woman they had to realize, at some point, was their enemy. Men like these, wealthy and powerful, a parade of beautiful women theirs for the taking.

He practiced in hotel bars, on women traveling for business: older ones in crisp suits, tired and annoyed, in no mood for fun and games, with wedding bands and briefcases and something to lose. He put himself at a table in rumpled and oversized clothing and his jaw two days unshaven, allowed himself one held glance only, and counted coup for everyone who came over and offered to buy him a drink. He worked it on supermodels and actresses in the London clubs, women who had bodyguards to keep men away and stayed in the VIP sections high above the floor. He could have arranged to get in easily enough; instead he lured them out to him from across the room, and to make it more difficult he took points off if he caught anyone he didn't intend to.

He didn't make it easy afterwards, either. He took them all, rich women and beautiful ones, to small ugly rooms with narrow beds, where he barely spoke with them, so he couldn't rely on charm and had to work out what they wanted without help. It was strange coming to it as work rather than pleasure, and going away alert, alive, with the satisfaction of a job well done instead of drowsy satiation.

After the first month he began to catch a glimpse of the necessary state, a certainty in his own skin like the limitless confidence he carried into a fight, beyond the arrogance that came naturally to him and on into something almost workmanlike: a simple practical belief that he could satisfy any imaginable desire better than any other man alive, and the trick of conveying as much, with nothing more than a look, and that if a woman didn't try him when she had the chance, she would regret it all her life.

He'd been at it three months when he was called in for a fresh assignment, something complicated, an assassination in Venezuela that had to look like the work of a German arms dealer. He shaved twice, with and against the grain, filed his nails short and smooth, and chose his clothes carefully: a suit perfectly cut to run just a little snug around the biceps and the thighs, crisp white shirt with French cuffs and unobtrusive links, the tie a shade of blue that brought out his eyes.

In the car park he closed his eyes and drew three slow, precise breaths before he got out of the car. Three women got onto the lift on the canteen floor, talking animatedly; they were silent by the next floor up. "Your stop?"

he said, smiling at them with impersonal charm when the lift reached their floor, and they jumped and went out.

M's assistant, a young man, stuttered a little when James walked into the outer office, and showed him in without asking first. She was standing at the side of the desk, talking on the phone: a plain soft gray suit, simple jewelry, her short cap of pale hair neat rather than stylish, her computer open on the desk. She waved him in without interrupting.

He took the armchair opposite the desk and watched her finish the call, his fingers loosely curled around the carved ends of the chair's wooden arms, his legs spread a little and planted. She was speaking crisp French to someone in Marseilles who was trying to run a mobile phone trace past third-generation encryption. That meant Prather had lost his target, James mentally filled in: he liked to keep tabs on the other double-ohs and their assignments, not a little bit of competition involved.

"Prather should never have made double-oh," he said, when she hung up.

He rather expected her to tell him to mind his own business; instead she gave him a sharp look and said, "Why not?"

He'd meant it seriously enough: he'd always known Prather was a second stringer, but he'd never pinned down a reason into words. "He can't go off the map," James said finally. "He'll follow a straight plan even if something more important's gone sideways."

She leaned back against the desk and raised an eyebrow. "His service record is a damn sight cleaner than yours, you know."

"Proving my point," he said, and stood up fluidly. "And you know it," he added softly, "or I'd be in Marseilles, and he'd be—here." He braced one hand against the desk and gave her a double-barreled smile, letting that perfect certainty take root in him.

She shut her eyes a moment, and he pressed the advantage and leaned in to murmur into her ear, "Admit it, M, you do like me best."

She laughed, and it ran like liquid fire into his veins. "Do I?" she said, turning to him, her mouth curving and her eyes alight, and in a single devastating look told him that of all the women in the world, she was the most utterly desirable; that she could fulfill hungers he didn't know he had, and if he didn't want her, he was a fool. But more than that—more than any of that, her look said she wanted him, with perfect frankness and no shame at all; that she was already imagining what she would do with him, how she would—

He was kissing her, savagely, furious; because in a moment she would put her hand on him and push him away, and he hated her for it already, because even knowing, he couldn't stop himself. Her mouth tasted faintly of mint and coffee, and the silk of her suit was crumpling under his hands. She touched his shoulder, and in one desperate final gambit, he went to his knees before her and looked up, gave her back the very hunger she'd created and said hoarsely, "Let me. *Let me.*"

He slid his hands onto her thighs, up beneath the hem of her flared silk skirt, offering himself up, and she shuddered. "Get on with it, then," she said, unsteadily, and put her hands on his head while he thrust her skirt up and out of the way. He tore the stockings and got his mouth on her skin, kissing her thighs while he pulled the little folding blade out of the heel of his shoe and sliced away the silk underwear.

He brought her off, only knowing he'd done it by the clench of her muscles under his hands, and it only made him more wild; he was up and laying her back over the wide desk, and she helped him open his belt, her hand gripping his neck tightly while he took her. "Dear boy," she said, almost tender, after he came, the one saving grace that her own voice wobbled.

"Damn you," he said, panting. She was stroking his head gently, and he liked it.

She laughed and reached over to press the intercom. "Villiers, clear the rest of my day, please," she said into it, quite normally, and then she took him over to the couch and showed him that she hadn't been lying at all.

"I will admit that it's something of an unfair advantage, being postmenopausal," she said, pressing her hair neat in the mirror. "I might even feel guilty if you hadn't asked for it quite so insistently."

"Christ," he muttered, shoving his shirt back into his trousers.

She sat down behind her desk, her suit only a little disordered, and looked up at him over her clasped hands. "James," she said, and he expected something necessary and usual: *this can't ever happen again* or *I don't usually fuck my subordinates,* but instead she said, "You're the best agent that I have."

He raised his eyebrows, lightly, and tried to sound amused more than surprised or, God help him, pleased; he wasn't going to become a damned lapdog, ready to wag his tail or lick her hand for petting and scraps of praise. "Surely there's a 'but' in there somewhere."

"But you're loyal to an idea of yourself instead of to the service," she said.

"You think I'm going to go rogue?"

She waved that away with an impatient shake of her head. "The point is, you can torture a criminal to death and still tell yourself you're a hero. But when you're on your knees sucking the cock of a mass-murdering dictator with the blood of half a dozen innocents on your hands, the only way to come out of it whole is if you're part of something larger than yourself."

"Speaking from experience," he said nastily, gone cold.

But she only looked at him unshaken. "Yes." After a moment, she added, "I don't cherry-pick the most violent and dangerous assignments for you just because you're the best. I do it because their directness gives you a shot at surviving with your sense of yourself intact. But this work won't let you preserve it, not forever, no matter how good you are. And when it's gone, I don't know what you'll have left."

He was still involuntarily relaxed, his body unwound and loose from the sex. Her words hit like a narrow, very sharp knife, slid right between the ribs: less pain than the recognition of a wound in the vitals, loaded with death and inevitability. All the pieces of himself he'd had stripped away, the things he didn't think about: Rietzmann on his knees sobbing and broken; his little girl lying in a limp heap on the floor where she'd run out into the exchange of fire; mechanically blowing Rietzmann's brains out over her dead body.

"If you want my resignation," James said, in that dark, warm, blood-stained hotel room, the heavy weight of the silenced gun dangling from his hand.

"Don't be stupid," M said sharply, and pulled him back into her bright-lit office, full of clean straight lines and pale colors, cream and gray. "I want you to stop fucking around. I don't care in the least if you go running off to Brazil for a month, am I a damned time-card puncher? What I mind is that you're doing it to make the point that you're a loose cannon. You aren't, but if you insist on believing you are, then it's very nearly as bad." Her voice gentled. "For the service and for you."

He'd put back on his clothes, his jacket, but he felt more naked than he'd been on the couch beneath her, thighs and back straining, nothing but sweat covering his skin.

"Perhaps you're wrong. Perhaps I really am."

"Then you're fit only to be used until you break," she said, coolly brutal. "And if that's so, I *will* use you. You needn't fear being thrown out. I've done far worse things than help a man to his own destruction."

"In that case, what difference does it make? You can't suppose I'm likely to last much longer."

"Not all double-ohs die in the field," M said. "Some of us even get promoted. But you can't do my job without a real commitment to the service."

"Lucky I haven't your job, then," he said, flippantly, and stared when she just looked back at him. Then he gave a short bark of laughter. "You're hardly serious."

"I do plan to retire eventually," she said dryly.

"And if I've been a good boy, perhaps I'll get to be a letter instead of a number?" he said mockingly, but against his will the idea was already settling itself into the back of his head, something to move towards that wasn't a grave.

And she saw it, damn her; saw it and smiled. "If you play your cards right." She picked up a dossier lying on the side of her desk under a paperweight, placed strategically so it hadn't got knocked off, earlier. She held it out to him. "So stop being an ass."

He was unable to keep his mouth from curving, even at his own expense. "Yes, ma'am." He crossed the room and reached over the desk to take the dossier, pausing with it held midair between them. "M, did you arrange all this on purpose?"

She tilted her head, serene. "What do you think, Bond?"

"I think you're a damned dangerous woman," he said, and leaned over to kiss her one last time.

The Wizard's Tales

Title: Never Is a Promise (2011)
Author: Yahtzee
Fandom: Harry Potter
Rating: Teen-and-up audiences, het (Harry/Hermione, Hermione/Ron)
Additional tags: epilogue compliant, unresolved sexual tension, unrequited love, friendship

Title: Scars (2013)
Author: Suitesamba
Fandom: Harry Potter
Rating: Teen-and-up audiences, slash (Harry/Snape)
Additional tags: canonical character death (not H/S)

Title: Once upon a Time (2010)
Author: busaikko
Fandom: Harry Potter
Rating: General audiences
Additional tags: transgender, trans character, postcanon

Introduction

One of the problems with the idea of a fanfiction reader is that there is absolutely no way any one story could possibly "represent" a particular fandom or its works, not just because fandom tells so many wonderful and diverse types of stories, but because the key pleasure of fandom is multiplicity: different versions, alternate paths, endless supplements that respond to each other: *but what if?* In fandom, you can have your cake and eat it; you can have things not just *both* ways, but *every way.* Mainstream commercial works aim for consistency in sequels and series: new stories are set in the same universe and pick up where the previous story left off. But fanworks are like an Etch A Sketch: draw a picture, shake it up, start again with no constraints. Best of all, each story can be complete in itself: tell an entire story, have a real ending. And then you can have another. And another.

This infinite and joyful variety is true of all fandoms but is particularly visible in Harry Potter, where just listing the pairings fans have written (Harry/Ginny, Harry/Ron, Harry/Hermione, Harry/Draco . . .) would take all the space (Lupin/Black, Lupin/Tonks, Lupin/James, Lupin/Lilly . . .) allotted for this introduction (Dumbledore/Grimwald, Bellatrix/Narcissa, Hermione/Snape, Harry/Giant Squid . . . seriously, I could just keep going, there are hundreds). Fans have fleshed out every corner of the Harry Potter universe, as the entry in Fanlore explains:

> There are stories about Harry's parents' generation at school or during the first war with Voldemort, the survivors of the war, Harry and his peers at school, Harry and his peers as adults, and the next generation of characters who are briefly mentioned in the epilogue of the seventh novel. Still older generations have been explored in stories: Dumbledore, Voldemort, Grindlewald, and some of the Hogwarts teachers. Founders Fic plays with the original Hogwarts founders (Godric Gryffindor, Helga Hufflepuff, Rowena Ravenclaw, and Salazar Slytherin), who were alive during the Middle Ages.[1]

As diverse as this is, it doesn't scratch the surface, because it doesn't take into account all the alternate universes and realities: for example, stories in which Voldemort adopts Harry and takes over the world, or in which Hermione is sorted into Slytherin, or in which Snape is the conductor of a symphony orchestra and Harry plays the violin.

That being said, I want to at least gesture toward some of that variety, and so I have included three stories here, each of which takes place in Harry Potter's future. Fans love inventing new stories for Harry, which is why so many were disappointed with "The Epilogue," also known as "Nineteen Years Later," the much-reviled last chapter of *Harry Potter and the Deathly Hallows.* (Fans, wittily, referred to the ending of the series as Potterdämmerung, a pun on Wagner's apocalyptic opera *Götterdämmer-*

ung.) Rowling's epilogue not only foreclosed so many of the exciting futures that fans had imagined for the characters (Harry and Draco become Auror partners and fight crime! Hermione becomes Minister of Magic! Snape turns out to be Harry's father! The generation that returns from the war fuels a decadent Wizarding Jazz Age!) but also told a very conventional story: married to their high school sweethearts, with kids.

In fact, before "The Epilogue," fans used to mock fanfiction writers who wrote the sort of ending that Rowling gave the characters: consider Clam Chowder's parody ending, written in 2005, years before the publication of *Deathly Hallows*, and quoted at Fanlore:

> "PEOPLE are MILLING about. It is roughly TWENTY years since the END of the SERIES. Absolutely NOTHING has changed ANYWHERE." Harry's children are named James and Lily, Draco has "given all of [his] children weird, incomprehensible Latin names," and ". . . To COMPLETE the ENSEMBLE—a GARGANTUAN CLUSTER of WEASLEYS arrive." Lupin, speaking for the author, says, "How it is that you all had children at the exact same time?"[2]

Some fans hate Rowling's epilogue so much that they have invented an entire category of fiction especially to deny it: EWE, or "Epilogue? What Epilogue?" These writers simply ignore the epilogue and tell whatever stories they want; other fanfiction writers work within (or around) the constraints of the epilogue.

Yahtzee's story, "Never Is a Promise," is one of these. Tagged "Epilogue Compliant," it takes place after Rowling's epilogue and shows us a Harry and Ginny who are now divorced, at least partly because Harry's been carrying a torch for Hermione. It's Ginny who ends the marriage; being married to Harry, she says, was like "taking care of someone else's dog." Where Rowling's epilogue arguably puts the characters in emotional stasis ("Absolutely NOTHING has changed ANYWHERE"), "Never Is a Promise" gives them recognizably thirty-something problems: a newly single Harry tries to rebuild his life while single-parenting his kids and negotiating a complicated extended family of Weasleys, including Ron, his ex-brother-in-law and Hermione's husband.

Yahtzee gives Harry and Hermione the opportunity to work out their feelings for each other by weaving her story in, around, and after the events of the novels, transforming Rowling's story without contradicting it. So in Harry's memory, Ron looms large; he is central to Harry's life.

Ron sitting beside him on the Hogwarts Express with Scabbers in his cage—rubbing Harry's shoulder the one time Harry broke down about the divorce in front of him—borne aloft on the shoulders of students chanting "Weasley is our king"—proudly nestling baby Hugo in Harry's arms for the first time—crying as they heard Hermione scream in pain when they were imprisoned by Bellatrix Lestrange

But there are new events (the baby, the divorce) nestled within familiar ones. Yahtzee also takes advantage of opportunities presented by Rowling's text, imagining a scenario in which Harry and Hermione sleep together during their time alone in *Deathly Hallows*, an event suggested by the vision Voldemort sends to Ron to torture him with jealousy. In "Never Is a Promise," the lack of resolution in Harry and Hermione's relationship causes problems for the characters down the road, just as it upset millions of Harry/Hermione shippers, many of whom were bitterly disappointed by the nineteenth-century ending of having Harry marry his best friend's sister.[3] "Never Is a Promise" thus gives closure to characters and fans alike.

In "Scars," Suitesamba gives Harry a future very different from the one the books project for him. We know this story is not epilogue compliant from the first line, in which we learn that Snape survived the final battle, though Voldemort's snake Nagini has practically torn his throat out. Snape has terrible scars, but he's not the only one:

> Hermione has a scar on her face, long and thin and narrow. Ron has scars on his upper arms, from the brains in the Ministry of Magic when he was sixteen. The scar on Harry's hand has been there for eight years now. Bill's face has been marred for seven, George's for six.

The scars aren't all physical, either: all the surviving characters are struggling to cope in a postwar world of loss and devastation. Like many fans, Suitesamba takes the Second Wizarding War seriously, and gives the characters consequences in line with those experienced by the survivors of other wars of the twentieth century: anger, grief, shell shock, post-traumatic stress disorder, a desire to break out of previous patterns of behavior.

Suitesamba imagines Harry as a disaffected twenty-something war veteran awkwardly moving between jobs and relationships. He finally decides to open up an apothecary shop ("living up to the abilities that Horace Slughorn thought he had, learning the nuances of Potion making") to sell potions and remedies to the wounded. His goal is to develop a scar cream that will heal those who were injured in the war. This brings him into renewed contact with Snape, scarred man and potions master extraordinaire.

Eventually, Harry and Snape fall in love and start a relationship. Harry/Snape is one of the more popular slash pairings in fandom,[4] as it rereads the paradoxical, canonical caring/hateful relationship between Snape and Harry as evidence of strong feelings between them that might become other strong feelings;[5] there is also the terrible intimacy that comes with having shared someone's memories,[6] the way Harry shares Snape's at the end of *Deathly Hollows*. Snape's death in the books means that Harry and Snape never have to remake their relationship in the light of this new and extremely personal knowledge of each other, but fans stage that encounter again and again.

By letting Snape live and putting him in a relationship with Harry, Suitesamba rejects the ending of Rowling's story. Even more importantly, she writes a story in which *Harry* explicitly imagines and rejects the life in that ending: in that way, Suitesamba makes Rowling's epilogue stand in for all the social expectations that queer people confront and reject when they choose the lives they want rather than the ones other people have scripted for them.

> He not an Auror. He is an entrepreneur, a Potions expert, about to become a Professor. He is not married to Ginny Weasley, not living in a cottage in Godric's Hollow with a son (James) and a daughter (Lily). He does not play professional Quidditch.

Within the story, Harry evokes and rejects the life imagined for him in the epilogue: he is not a sportsman, he is not suburban, he is not straight. His life has not turned out the way he, or anyone else, imagined. He is not even the same person that he was as a child: he can no longer talk to snakes, and his famous lightning-shaped scar is fading. But change, while disorienting, is also shown to be healing: Harry and Snape, working together as a couple, successfully develop the scar cream that heals them and their war-ravaged friends. A meaningful and happy life for Harry turns out to be one that is not epilogue compliant.

The last of these three stories, busaikko's "Once upon a Time," does something else typical of fanfiction: it puts the narrative focus on a minor character, in this case, Harry's cousin Dudley Dursley. Fanfiction often brings background characters to the foreground; in *Textual Poachers*,

Henry Jenkins calls this "refocalization" and notes that fans tend to favor "women and minorities, who receive limited screen time."[7] In "Once upon a Time," busaikko complicates the characterization of Dudley, whom Rowling draws in broad strokes as the love child of Augustus Gloop and Veruca Salt: spoiled, greedy, selfish, and mean. In contrast, busaikko's Dudley has a believable interior life: he struggles with painful desires, and with the fear that if he were ever discovered to be a "freak like Harry, there'd be no more love, ever."

This Dudley has grown up to be an unhappy adult with "five suits in the closet, one for each day of the week." He has also grown to be extremely fat. But Dudley's suits represent not only his unsatisfying corporate work but also the straitjacket of his male gender identity: in this sweet and painful story, we discover that Dudley is transgender and dreams of wearing pleated tweed skirts and pastel twinsets. He overeats not because he is simply greedy and awful, but because he is trying to crush "the inside Dudley," the part of himself that is different. Like Suitesamba's epilogue-defiant war veteran Harry, busaikko's Dudley struggles to develop a comfortable adult identity, especially since he has learned from his parents that "freaks" will be shoved into the closet under the stairs.

Here, the Dursleys' fairy-tale cruelty toward Harry is taken seriously as abuse, not only of Harry, but of Dudley, who learns by example that difference will not be tolerated. To become who he needs to be, Dudley reaches out to his wizard cousin, who meets him in a coffee shop and easily accepts his transvestism, explaining, almost offhandedly, that with a godfather who's a dog and a friend who's a werewolf, he's "used to people changing." Harry will help Dudley find a wizard who does "medical transfiguration"—busaikko understands that the wizarding world offers possibilities for transformation that would be truly magical to those, like Dudley, who feel trapped in their bodies and lives.

If "Once upon a Time," is a fairy tale, it's not the kind that features melodramatic heroes and villains, but the kind that reveals complexity under the surface of the world: a frog might be a prince (or a princess), a beast conceals the man inside. Similarly, writers like Yahtzee, Suitesamba, and busaikko have worked their own transformative magic, weaving their handcrafted and infinitely various stories on the loom of the Harry Potter universe.

Suggested Further Reading

Harry Potter as a fandom and a phenomenon has a huge critical literature that crosses many disciplines: in particular, Harry Potter has been studied by scholars of children's and youth literature, youth engagement and activism, literacy and pedagogy, and library studies. As Andrew Blake points out in his invaluable *The Irresistible Rise of Harry Potter* (Verso, 2002), among the things that made Rowling's books popular was that they were published amid what people believed was a literacy crisis, for boys in particular—and boys not only read Harry Potter, but the library is framed within the book as a significant resource for fighting evil. But scholars have written about Harry from every possible direction: philosophy and religious studies; gender, race, and class; law and legal issues; mythology; sociology; you name it. Cornelia Remi, aka Viola Owlfeather, compiles what has been referred to as "an insanely complete Harry Potter bibliography."

Works dealing with Harry Potter fanfiction specifically include Ika Willis's "Keeping Promises to Queer Children: Making Space (for Mary Sue) at Hogwarts," (2006) and Catherine Tosenberg's "Homosexuality at the Online Hogwarts: Harry Potter Slash Fanfiction" (2008). Vera Cuntz-Leng (2014) has written on twincest in Harry Potter fanfic; Mary Ingram (2014) has written on m-preg, or male pregnancy Potter fic. Anne Kustritz's 2014 "Domesticating Hermione: The Emergence of Genre and Community from WIKTT's Feminist Romance Debates" discusses the Hermione/Snape fiction produced on the listserv "When I Kissed the Teacher," and shows the community working out and through the conflicting ideologies around Hermione and Snape as a romance pairing. Darlene Rose Hampton (2015) has written about Harry Potter slash as a form of queer performance, and Erin Horajova (2015) has written about britpicking (asking British fans to edit fanfiction for accurate UK language and cultural practice) as a fanfiction practice. For insider perspectives on participating in Harry Potter fandom and fanfiction writing, see Jamison's *Fic*, which has a section called "Megafandoms: Harry Potter and *Twilight*."

Never Is a Promise

Yahtzee

He'd had no idea. Had Harry suspected for one instant that Ron didn't know, hadn't always known, it would never have come up. But they were both flying blind.

"I suppose you'll be getting out there again," Ron said as they took a pint together in a Muggle pub. (Harry preferred those pubs, by and large—he found it easier to relax when nobody recognized him.) "Dating."

"Oh, God." Harry made a joke of it, but the misery in his voice was sincere. "That's going to be—not fun. Starting over."

Sometimes he thought half the reason his marriage to Ginny had lasted as long as it had was because he'd dreaded this very prospect. They'd always been a volatile match, with passionate highs but incredibly deep lows. By the time Lily had been born, Harry had already known he was more emotionally connected to his wife's family than to his wife, but had still been trying to convince himself it would work out. By the time Albus had gone off to Hogwarts, Ginny had taken a flat of her own—but he'd still thought they might make another attempt at patching things up.

By the time Albus became the first eleven-year-old Seeker since his father—and the first ever for the Slytherin team—they'd signed the papers that made Harry's wedding ring fizzle around his finger and fall into so much gold dust.

It was better now; he and Ginny got on well enough as friends, it turned out. Neither of them had asked anybody in the Weasley family to take sides, and last month at Christmas Harry had received his annual fuzzy knitted jumper (orange this time). As rough as this had been on the children, the divorce hadn't come as a shock. Everyone was going to get through this, Harry thought, and ultimately be happier than before. But that was just patching up the life he'd already had. Rebuilding—creating a new life—that still felt very far away.

Ron looked as awkward as a former brother-in-law might when he said, "Don't suppose you want me and Hermione to fix you up with someone?"

The thought of it made Harry want to groan. "Please, don't."

"Figured." Ron took a deep drink. "I suggested it to Hermione the other day. The look she got on her face!"

Harry half-smiled as he stared down at his glass. "I can imagine."

"Still, it's not like you're going to need much help."

"How do you figure?"

Ron gave him a look. "Bloody hell, Harry, you're—Harry Potter."

"Sort of old news."

"You're on the fifty-galleon note!"

"What do you want me to do, wave money around?"

"Don't knock it. Could work, you know."

"Not with the kind of women I'd want to date."

"Getting picky now, are we?"

"Shut it." Harry had started laughing, and the Muggle Guinness was having its effect, which meant he was off his guard.

Ron said, "Guess you really never availed yourself of any, you know, groupies."

"Groupies?"

"You know you could've done. Or did you and you just never told me?" They'd never talked much about sex, which Harry figured was a natural effect of marrying your best friend's sister. "You and Gin didn't tie the knot for a few years. Back when you were footloose and fancy free, you never used that celebrity thing, gave it a go?"

He might have said anything in response to Ron's joking around. He might have pointed out that most women found his fame intimidating rather than titillating; being known for killing a notorious dark wizard wasn't quite the same as being a pop star. He might have made a joke in return, made up some fantastical four-way with the Weird Sisters to make Ron laugh. He might have asked whether it was true that Cho and her Muggle husband had split up, and if so how long ago, and should he consider calling her?

Instead Harry shrugged and said, "I've only ever been to bed with two women in my whole life. Hermione and Ginny, that's it. And I'm thirty-six years old. The thought of starting over from scratch—it's terrifying."

Silence.

Harry realized he and Ron had never actually talked about it, though there had been times during Voldemort's fall that he'd thought he felt the weight of it between them like a physical force. Obviously this hadn't been the time to open the subject for discussion. Glancing down at the table, Harry said, "Sorry. Awkward. Shouldn't have brought it up."

Ron's voice squeaked the way it used to when he was a boy as he said, ". . . Hermione?"

"Um—yeah?" Harry looked up to see that Ron looked almost white. The truth hit him in a flash of almost blinding shock. "Oh, my God. She never told you."

They stared at one another in silence for a few seconds. Ron's breaths came quicker and quicker, as if his body was trying to decide between tears and rage but couldn't quite do it. "My best friend slept with my wife."

"Whoa. It was twenty years ago, Ron. Before you were married. Before you were dating. I always believed—I was just sure Hermione must've told you. I swear, I thought you knew."

"Before we were dating?" Ron sat up straighter, and his hands were clenched so tightly around his glass that his knuckles were white. "You mean, it was you. You're the first one she had sex with."

How had he not known? Harry couldn't make his mind bridge the gap between what he'd believed and reality. "Who did you think it was? Did you and Hermione seriously not talk about this, ever?"

"No! I thought it must've been Victor Krum!"

"Victor Krum?" It was so absurd that Harry wanted to laugh, though that had more to do with nerves than any actual humor. "Ron, come on, don't get upset."

Unsurprisingly, Ron ignored this. "And you never told Ginny."

"Of course I told Ginny. I told her almost as soon as we were back together. She always understood. Ask her, if you don't believe me."

"So everyone knew but me. Everyone! Bloody hell." Ron's anger was getting the better of his pain. "Before we were dating, you said. Do you mean—back at Hogwarts, or was it—was it after I left?"

No need for Ron to elaborate: Harry knew precisely when he meant. For a few seconds, he felt the chill of the moors in December, saw the bleak gray sky overhead and felt the hollow of hunger in his belly. Hermione stood next to him, waiting and waiting for Ron to return to them, before she whisked them away beyond any following. To be safe from Voldemort, they thought they had to leave Ron behind forever. That had felt so real— the division between what they wanted and what would be.

"Yes," Harry said. "It was after you left. Just one night, that's all—"

"Just one night!" Ron shot back. "Do you hear yourself? You slept with Hermione, my wife, and she never once shared that with me in twenty bloody years and you want to act like it's no big deal?"

"We were lonely and scared." The darkness of the tent, the desperate pounding of his heart in his chest, Hermione leaning her head against his shoulder as he tentatively put his arm around her: Harry hadn't thought about it in years, hadn't let himself think about it, and was shocked to find the memory so vivid. "You remember how it was. Expecting to die any day, just about any second, and Hermione and I—that's all we had, each other."

"Because I left, you mean." Ron grabbed his coat from the hooks at the end of the booth. "Waited a while to throw that in my face, didn't you, Harry?"

"I've never done that, and you know it. Come on, mate; don't make this more than it is."

As Ron rose and tugged his coat on, he said, "If it was no big deal, then why didn't she tell me?"

Harry couldn't give Ron an answer he didn't have. After another moment's pained silence, Ron turned and stormed out of the pub. Bells on the door jangled as he left.

For a few seconds, Harry could only rest his head in his hand. The overwhelming combination of remorse and astonishment—he could imagine it was similar to the last thoughts of people who died tripping over unexploded ordnance from the London Blitz thirty years after the fact.

Pulling himself together, he tugged on his own coat and stepped out onto the street. A nearby winding lane almost too narrow for traffic seemed likely to be quiet, so Harry walked along it as he reached into his pocket. There was no owlery anywhere close by in this Muggle neighborhood, nor a fireplace connected to the Floo network. Thank goodness the Wizarding World had adapted to the twenty-first century and he could use the Web.

And of course he had a live charge, because he always took good care of Zipporah.

Harry pulled his Gossamer 80X from his pocket; the silver frame shone in the light from the streetlamps, just bright enough to reveal Zipporah's eight legs working away as she spun. When the filaments were complete, the Web glowed, and Harry said, "Call Hermione."

Another glow, as his breath fogged the cold night air, and then Hermione's face appeared on the screen. Her hair was a mess, and an ink stain marred one cheek: Of course, she had a bill in revision at the Ministry. The warm smile she gave him broke his heart. "Hullo! Are you two still out and about?"

"No. Hermione, I'm sorry. I've messed up."

Her smile dimmed only slightly. "Is Ron drunk?"

"Not when I saw him last." Though it was anyone's guess what condition Ron would be in when the night was through. Harry took a deep breath. "We were talking, and somehow we got on the subject, and—I never knew you hadn't told him. About us. You know."

Hermione's eyes widened. It felt as if he had wounded her; Harry hated that feeling. She whispered, "Oh, Harry, you didn't."

"He's upset. I mean, really upset. I told him how it was, but he isn't in a mood to listen. I thought you should be prepared before he heads home."

"Damn it. *Damn* it. How did you end up talking about—no. It doesn't matter. Oh, Ron. If only he'd call." Hermione bit her lip. They both knew that Ron, loathing spiders as he did, wouldn't hear of carrying a Gossamer in his pocket. "What did he say?"

"He was kind of all over the place. Mostly I think he was convinced that it had to be more than I was letting on, because you'd never told him." Harry felt as if he shouldn't ask the rest, but the question came out anyway: "Hermione—why didn't you?"

She didn't respond, and for a moment it was difficult to face her, even through a Gossamer screen. Unspoken words seemed to fill all the space between the warm home she sat in and the cold silent street where he stood.

When Hermione finally spoke, she didn't answer him. She said only, "Thanks for calling. I'll let you know how things go."

"Look after him. He's in bad shape." Remembering Ron's pained face lanced Harry even more sharply than the actual moment had; then, he'd been numbed by astonishment, but now nothing stood between him and the fact that he'd brutally hurt one of his best friends in the world.

"Of course I will."

"I'm sorry." For telling Ron. For not finding out what she had and hadn't told Ron. For turning to her on a rainy, mournful night twenty years ago.

"I'll let you know," was all she said before the screen went dim.

As he always did, Harry tapped the feeder tube to reward Zipporah for a good connection. While the spider scurried for her snack, he slipped his Gossamer back into his pocket. Although he had no reason to continue down this street, no real idea where it led, he kept walking. Lily was sleeping over at a friend's, and home was the last place he wanted to be. Harry needed some time to think.

Some time with his memories.

They'd been so bloody scared; that was the thing that stood out most so many years later. Scared of dying, scared of capture, scared they'd never see anyone else they loved again, scared that when the end came there would be no chance for goodbyes. And scared of one another, in some ways.

How raw he'd felt the first time Hermione had seen him naked.

How her entire body shook as he settled over her on the cot.

If it happened for any one reason, it happened because the terror of having sex for the first time was at least something different to be frightened of.

But once they were past that . . . Harry forgot about the war, Voldemort, everyone who had already died. For the minutes they spent locked in each other's embrace, he forgot anything but their frantic kisses, the half-hurting, half-happy sound Hermione made as he pushed into her, and the unbelievable, ecstatic heat of being inside a woman for the first time. It all happened so fast—absurdly fast, but he was just a boy and excited beyond control—and yet he could never forget how good and right it had felt to lay the world aside.

Though that part of it he might have done better to forget.

The next morning he received an owl from Hermione; her shaky handwriting belied the calm phrases. *Had a thundering row* and *no doubt the firewhisky* and *he'll see reason* and *don't come around for a bit.* It was as if he and Ron had had an especially bitter argument about the Chudley Cannons' latest trade.

But maybe she was right. Maybe in the end it didn't add up to more than that. It shouldn't. A quarter of an hour in a bed so long ago shouldn't undermine a friendship well into its third decade.

Harry tried to put it aside and threw himself into his work. The Aurors were busy with a new cursing mechanism that worked at a distance; it was surprising the number of witches and wizards who didn't think a curse really counted if they weren't in the room when it was thrown. He went in early, took work home, did research on his lunch breaks. And yet he still felt the weight of every day that crawled on without Ron or Hermione getting in touch.

When the weekend came, he left the office in plenty of time to get Lily ready for her weekend at her mum's. Packing a lime-and-lilac knapsack with three days' worth of clothes and a My Little Centaur took his mind off his troubles well enough. By the time Ginny arrived, he was feeling nearly cheerful.

"Here's my girl!" Ginny wrapped her arms around Lily and rocked her back and forth. "I've got us tickets to the Muggle ballet, just like you wanted." As Lily squealed in excitement, Harry and Ginny's eyes met for the shared joke; Harry knew full well that Ginny would just about as soon watch paint dry as the ballet, but seeing their daughter happy made it worthwhile.

"Oh, wait!" Lily cried. "Then I want my sequined headband to go with my dress."

"Run up and get it." Harry swatted her gently on the shoulder as she bounded for the stairs. To Ginny he said, "Heroic of you."

"Well, you took on coaching Baby Brooms Quidditch. I figured I'd spot you one." Her eyes assessed him, suddenly cool. This change in temperature was all too familiar. But her voice remained even. "I hear you're in deep trouble."

"Ron told you." When she nodded, Harry continued, "And you explained, right? That you'd always known?"

"Of course I did. Only made him madder. Then Mum stepped in—"

"Good Lord." Harry didn't like the idea of Mrs. Weasley knowing about his sex life, though he was aware mothers and daughters did talk. Worse by far was the thought of her trying to referee this mess.

"Well, I confided in her about you and Hermione way back when, and he's furious because absolutely everybody knew but him. Mum keeps telling him exactly what I told her. You two were just alone too long. You both needed somebody and you didn't have anyone else. Didn't mean a thing beyond that." This ought to have been good news. But something about the way Ginny said it put Harry on guard. She studied him more intently than she had in a very long time; it was as if he were blinking in a spotlight's glare. "Don't worry. I didn't say what I really thought."

At least half the reason their marriage had failed was because Harry never could resist taking the bait. "What's that supposed to mean?"

She tucked a lock of her fiery hair behind one ear. "Hermione's always the one you talk to first. Always was. Before me, before Ron."

"We're *friends*. Best friends."

"You always hug her a little longer. You always laugh at her jokes, and she's not that funny, you know. Everything she does is 'brilliant,' or 'clever,' or 'marvelous.' The look you got in your eyes when you spoke about all that time alone with Hermione way back when—I told myself someday you'd look at me like that. I waited and waited. Finally I stopped waiting."

Do you honestly think I never loved you? That wasn't true, wasn't anywhere close to true. But saying it wasn't going to help the situation. "You're imagining things."

"I'm not. I've spent the last twenty years of my life feeling like I've been—like I've been taking care of someone else's dog. He likes you and he wags his tail for you but the minute you leave the door open too long, he's going to break for home, and he'll never look back." Ginny breathed out sharply. "I know you didn't cheat on me. I know Hermione would never. And I'm not telling my brother a word of this; it would only hurt him more. But if you honestly think there's nothing to what I'm saying, ask yourself why Hermione never said a word. To her husband, the person she loves the most in the world. Ask yourself."

"This is ridiculous," Harry said, even as his mind started turning her words over and over, seeking reason, seeing patterns.

Ginny shrugged. "Didn't expect you to start listening to me now." Then she breathed out, frustrated no longer with him but with herself. "I'm doing that thing the counselor said not to do. Stirring it up. I'm sorry."

Harry found himself concentrating too hard on the knapsack, double-checking the zippers and pockets. "The entire situation's been blown out of proportion."

"You've been good about it, really. You've never said a word. And with us—it's as much my fault as yours. I let you pretend. You wouldn't have been able to convince yourself if I hadn't helped you do it." Ginny's voice was soft with something it took him a moment to recognize as pity. "I just hate that we wasted so much of each other's time."

"It wasn't a waste," Harry said, looking down at their daughter's knapsack in his hands. He'd charmed silver stars onto the straps.

"No. I guess it wasn't."

Then Lily's feet pounded on the stairs as she came back down, and by the time she dashed back into the room with her headband, both her parents had smiles on their faces for her.

They'd been so shy the next morning, even though they'd awakened naked in each other's arms. Harry had wrapped their blanket around Hermione, sacrificing his privacy for hers, and she'd given him an uncertain little smile that pierced him through.

And yet once they were dressed again, everything went back to normal, except better than normal. The danger remained. The fear still hung over them. But just that one night when he'd been able to lay the world aside had given him back his strength when he needed it most.

This was where the gratitude began: Harry always knew Hermione didn't care for him that way, that she had her heart set on Ron. So when they'd had sex, she'd been giving him something precious and irreplaceable—all because he needed that sense of connection.

At first he felt terribly guilty about it, almost as if he might have bullied her, which was absurd; it was Hermione who had whispered the words, had first slipped out of her shirt. Harry found himself watching her very carefully. Did she regret what she'd done? Was her mood any better than it had been before? Could they still talk as they had before?

Paying closer attention led to other things, too. Like Harry noticing just how much Hermione did for him, and stepping in to do some of those tasks himself—and even to look after her, sometimes. He began making the tea and straightening the tent. Feeling grateful to her, remembering passion for her, turned out to be a sort of kindling for a fire that had been built slowly, over a very long time, but had until then lacked a spark. Her fussier moods began to gently amuse him. Her courage in standing by his side amazed Harry all over again. Sometimes he found himself watching her from across the tent while she slept.

By the time he'd begun to realize just how much had changed that night, Ron returned. Harry was so glad to see his other best friend—and so preoccupied by the desperate battles they were fighting—that he didn't get around to really examining how he felt about Ron and Hermione. He didn't even realize it might have been a good idea to say something to Hermione until it was far too late to speak, and so he pushed it aside.

Forever, he'd thought.

But forever is a long time.

A week turned into two weeks, which turned into a month. Harry hadn't gone so long without seeing Ron and Hermione since they were all children. He and Hermione exchanged a few owls, with him always asking how things were, and her always replying that they were tense, to give it more time.

Their notes became stilted, too tactful, and far-between; it was as if the playful owls they'd always exchanged a few times a week had somehow been transmogrified into evidence of a crime, and now they were afraid of getting caught.

This meant he had to find other ways to fill his free hours. He met up with Seamus Finnegan for a meal one evening; another weekend he went to Hogsmeade to have dinner with James and then spend half the night sitting up with Neville, telling old stories as if they were new, and getting roaring drunk. Nothing like waking up hung over in the Shrieking Shack to remind you how young you weren't. As he did every few years or so, he got together with Dudley—this was always awkward, never really satisfying, and yet Harry liked that they didn't give it up. One Saturday when he was truly at wits' end, he decided to accept the invitation he'd been dutifully sent to meet up with the Slytherin Quidditch team parents' booster organization. Honestly, it had been worth it just to see their faces when he walked into the Serpent Club. Draco had been the stiffest of them all, at least until the conversation turned to pro teams, and it turned out he and Harry agreed that the last Puddlemere United win was utter rubbish, that the referee must have been bought, and their mutual denouncing of everyone involved was so enjoyable that they kept it up even after the meeting ended and even walked each other to the nearest Floo station before they'd noticed it.

In the unlikely event that any of these people knew of the situation Harry, Ron, and Hermione were in, none of them let on. Finally, he learned the big news from Lily.

"Be careful." Harry's hands hovered only a few inches away from the cheese grater. "Are you sure you wouldn't rather have me handle it?"

"I can do it," she insisted. As she started rubbing the mozzarella across the grater, he forced himself to pull back a bit, but her movements were unpracticed and jerky. He couldn't quite shake the thought of tiny hands being grated atop their pizza.

"Even strokes. All right." He took a deep breath. "Hey, after dinner, we should get you packed for Gran and Gramps' house this weekend."

"Okay." Lily continued scrubbing the cheese into the grater, keeping a good grip on it. Her rounded face was set in determination. "I want to take my tent."

That surprised him. His daughter, unlike her earthier parents or either of her elder brothers, preferred fancy to plain, ceremony to casualness, and indoors to out. "Your tent? It's cold for camping."

"We can *spell* it, Dad, come *on*."

"I know, I know."

"Besides, it's going to be crowded. Dominique and Louis are coming to visit from Beauxbatons, and Mum's staying most of the weekend, Hugo too, and now that Uncle Ron's living there it's like there's not even anyplace to sit. So I thought I could camp out in the tent. Gran would help me make it cozy, and maybe I could have a picnic."

"Mmmm." Harry kept his voice very calm. "Uncle Ron's staying at the Burrow?"

"Yeah." Lily's hands stilled. "Dad—are Uncle Ron and Aunt Hermione getting a divorce too?"

"I don't think so."

"But that's how it started with you and Mum. With her always going to the Burrow."

"It's nothing to do with the Burrow." Harry took the cheese and grater from his daughter and put his hands on her shoulders. "Are you upset about it?"

"No," she said, then promptly put her arms around his neck and pressed her face against his shoulder, the way she had done when she needed comfort ever since she was a baby. Harry rocked her back and forth, stroking her hair, feeling like hell. If only there were some enchantment that could keep adult problems from affecting children. If only Lily could be sealed off in some happier place, kept safe from such stupid things.

He found himself thinking of Albus Dumbledore, and the way he'd let Harry have the run of Hogwarts those first few years. The House Cup for Gryffindor: It had been a small token to a boy he'd believed to be destined for a young and terrible death. Trying to imagine how Dumbledore must have felt then, looking down at a Harry only two years older than Lily was now, brought a lump to his throat.

Harry finally said, "Does Uncle Ron seem—well, all right to you?"

"Yeah." Lily let go and pushed her hair back from her face, a sign she was calming down. "He says he'll help me de-gnome the garden. He makes up such funny names for them!"

Ron hadn't let any of this change how he felt toward Lily. Harry would have expected no less, but he was on the verge of getting emotional in front of his daughter, which wouldn't do. "See? You'll have fun this weekend. Come on, let's get this pizza in the oven."

After dinner, packing for the Burrow, and a full chapter of *The Horse and His Boy*, Harry got Lily into bed. He went downstairs, poured himself a glass of wine, and grabbed a piece of paper. He wrote only, *Ron moved out?* Then he strapped it to Otho's leg and let his owl fly out into the night.

Otho returned before the wine was finished. The return letter said, *I don't understand what's going on much better than you do. Can we talk? Maybe lunch Saturday at one of your Muggle places.*

Harry thought of somewhere and jotted the address down as he stroked Otho's feathers as a reward for a late night's hard work. His heart seemed to be beating very fast.

He'd chosen a café in Marylebone, one that seemed to be half conservatory, with its broad glass wall and endless plants and flowers in every corner. Harry had wandered into it one day about a year ago with some fellow Aurors and always remembered it as a relaxing sort of place.

As he sat at a corner table, waiting for Hermione, he wondered if he hadn't chosen it for the enormous windows—to prove they had nothing to hide.

Prove to whom?

Then Hermione walked in, the cream-colored trench coat she wore made appropriate for the February chill by the addition of a thick, sea-green scarf wrapped around her neck. Harry couldn't help smiling as she came closer. "Well, this is new."

"Oh, right." Her fingers went to her short-short hair, now sleek around her face. "You wouldn't have seen me since. What do you think? The kids hate it."

"You look beautiful." Which was entirely the kind of thing he would have said to her at any time, but it felt different now. Their eyes met, then didn't, as he rose to greet her. Her usual kiss ghosted against his cheek.

They made small talk as they ordered salad, soup, and wine. Clouds filtered the sunlight, so everything seemed to be the same pale washed gray except the deep blue of his sweater and the green of her scarf. Only when it was obvious the waitress would leave them alone for a bit did Harry finally say, "Is Ron still at the Burrow?"

"For now." Hermione stared down at her soup, face pale and drawn. It reminded him of how she'd so often looked that terrible winter on the moors.

"I can't believe he'd move out just because—well, just because of that."

"It's not just that. Since Rose went to school, we've found ourselves . . . I don't know. Bickering. I mean, more than usual."

Harry laughed, though the joke wasn't that funny. Then he remembered Ginny's stinging words, and the smile fell from his face.

Hermione continued, "Too much time on our hands to worry about trivial things, I suppose. It's been tense. But nothing I thought we couldn't work through."

Not just because of him, then. Harry took a deeper drink of his wine than was probably advisable. "I wish you'd told me it had got this bad."

"I didn't think it had. Then Ron found out about us, and everything boiled over, and you were the person I couldn't talk to." She was blinking quickly; her fingers toyed with her scarf, nervous energy with nowhere to go. "But you were the only person I wanted to talk to."

The one question that dwarfed all the others rose again, and Harry didn't even try to hold it back: "Why didn't you ever tell him?"

"There never seemed to be a good time."

"That's not an answer."

"I suppose it's not." Hermione looked at him then almost defiantly. It was as if she was daring him to push harder. Wanting him to.

Harry looked across the table at her, misty and gray. He wanted to comfort her. He wanted to get farther away from her. And he understood for the first time that you couldn't get over something if you didn't admit there was something to get over.

He'd never admitted that he needed to get over Hermione. So he never had.

How could twenty years feel like both a lifetime and a split second at once? Harry could hardly imagine that he'd lived all this time on one path, on one track he'd taken, and yet this parallel track had been beside him the whole while. Jumping over was possible. Switching tracks. Doing everything differently, embracing something he'd tried to hide so well that he'd nearly hidden it from himself. And there was joy there, real joy waiting for them both, maybe passion too—

Also there was Lily's worried little face, afraid the adults she loved most were all abandoning each other. Molly knitting her ex-son-in-law an orange jumper with as much care as she gave the ones she made for her children. Albus and Rose as toddlers with their toy brooms, taking lessons from Ginny on how to fly. Ron sitting beside him on the Hogwarts Express with Scabbers in his cage—rubbing Harry's shoulder the one time Harry broke down about the divorce in front of him—borne aloft on the shoulders of students chanting "Weasley is our king"—proudly nestling baby Hugo in Harry's arms for the first time—crying as they heard Hermione scream in pain when they were imprisoned by Bellatrix Lestrange—always, at the darkest and brightest moments of Harry's life, always Ron.

And always Hermione too, so inexpressibly precious to him, and yet so hurt now, so wounded. Whatever she felt or didn't—whatever reason she had for never sharing this truth with her husband—it didn't matter.

She never asked to jump tracks. She loved the life she had. This situation, with everything turned upside down—it was something Harry did to her, accidentally and unknowingly, but his work all the same.

Once Harry made it up to her by fixing cups of tea, and tidying the tent. Maybe he could do better this time.

He smiled gently. "I'll talk to Ron."

"I'm not sure that's a good idea," Hermione said. "He's been an absolute bear ever since."

"Listen, if he gets mad enough at me, maybe he'll forget to be mad at you too."

"It doesn't work like that. Honestly, Harry, you ought to know better by now." Her scolding tone was so familiar; next, Harry thought, she'd ask him if he still hadn't read *Hogwarts: A History*. He couldn't resist a smile.

"We'll put this right, Hermione. You'll see."

"I hope so." She leaned back slightly in her chair. Everything about her was more relaxed now; the danger had passed, and they both knew it. But Harry suspected the wistfulness in her eyes was reflected in his own.

He'd never walk down that other path, but he'd never forget where it might have led.

Two nights later, Harry went to a pub he'd been steering clear of for a while now. They had the latest Chudley Cannons game on the Wizarding Wireless, which was why Harry suspected he'd strike pay dirt.

He did. Ron was sitting by himself in a corner booth, so intent on the match and the chips and ale in front of him that he didn't notice Harry coming up until Harry smacked him alongside the head. "Oi!" Ron yelped, just like his thirteen-year-old self, until his eyes widened at the sight of Harry.

"You're being an enormous git." Harry slid into the opposite bench. "Don't you think it's about time you knocked it off?"

"Nobody asked you—"

"Since when did we start waiting for invitations before we gave each other advice? Listen to me—git. Enormous. You. Stop it. Hermione says you've been off your head about this."

"Oh, so you and Hermione are talking now? Meeting up behind my back?"

"Meeting up for lunch, and talking via owl, the exact same way we have since we were all first-years at Hogwarts. Don't go turning it into a big deal now." Advice for both of them, really.

It was obvious that Ron had been caught off guard by Harry's arrival, so much so that he was struggling to find his anger—as though he'd misplaced it somewhere. "If it's no big deal, then why didn't Hermione ever tell me about it?"

Any real curiosity Harry had about that question was in the process of being forgotten. "Oh, I don't know, maybe because she thought you'd overreact like some stupid wanker? No idea where she got that from. Honestly, Ron, if you're carrying on like this two decades later—two decades, mind, more than half our lives—what would you have done if she had told you way back when? Broken it off with her, most likely. With me too. And I don't know about you, but I don't like the way our lives would have looked without each other in them."

Ron stared down at his chips for a moment. His expression was more sad than anything else, and Harry wondered if he'd been too harsh. Usually that was the best way to get through to any Weasley, but he could overdo it, as his divorce from Ginny proved.

Finally Ron said, "Do you know what the worst part is?"

"Tell me."

"That stuff Voldemort showed me. When he was trying to get me not to destroy the horcrux." Ron dabbed one of his chips disconsolately in the catsup. "I always thought it was rot. But it was true, wasn't it?"

Harry could only shrug and admit it. "That's a big part of why I thought you always knew."

"I thought it was just some bad dream he was trying to show me. You two in love."

"We were never in love. So that part really was just a bad dream."

Leaning back in his booth, Ron stared at the ceiling. Over the speakers, the crowd cheered madly as the Holyrood Harpies scored yet another goal on the hapless Cannons. "It's been weird lately for me and Hermione. Not just about you."

"You have to adjust when the kids go off to school. It can be done."

"You and Ginny didn't make it."

"I think it's going to be different for you and Hermione. If you don't turn this into something more than it is."

"Bit late for that." Ron groaned. "Hermione's furious."

"She's worried. That's all. Get together with her for dinner. You'll set things right."

It wasn't that simple, of course, but Harry could feel the path being laid. Ron was already calming down, already telling Harry his troubles again. Soon it would all be as if it had never happened.

They listened to the rest of the game together, speaking of nothing more substantial than the piss-poor performance by the Cannons, who were ultimately routed by the Harpies 17-0. Harry walked Ron to the Floo, took the Muggle bus home, and after some consideration, decided not to ring Hermione up on the Gossamer. Ron would be in touch with her soon enough. When he got home, he reached into his wallet and took out the number he'd gotten last week—Cho's Gossamer. Apparently she was indeed divorced from her Muggle husband, for almost a year now. The time wasn't right yet to call her, Harry thought, but he thought that day might come soon.

Scars

Suitesamba

Harry Potter does not love Severus Snape for surviving.

There is a certain kind of respect—cautious, kept at a distance—once he knows the truth, but he is not ready at Snape's bedside with an apology when the Headmaster opens his eyes on Friday, the fifteenth of May, to a Voldemort-free world.

Harry Potter is seventeen years old. He is tired. He fights the unevenness of his emotions. Oppressing sadness wars with soul-lifting euphoria. The weight of his obligations has shifted. With Prophecy fulfilled, with Voldemort dead, he looks around, observes the living, and counts his losses. He balances them in his mind, against the counterweight of a world without Voldemort.

Snape wants to see him.

Ginny is not there to calm him. He is not sure there will be a Ginny for him. She is working out her anger, and weighing him, he knows, against a new Neville.

He doesn't blame her. He likes the new Neville too.

Hermione and Ron are not there. They have gone together to Australia, to put the pieces of Hermione's past back together.

It is Friday, the second of June.

Snape is Snape, but a Snape Harry has never before seen. The hospital pajamas are not black. His pale face, turned toward him as he walks across the floor, bleeds into the white pillow. He is less imposing on this horizontal plane, and Harry is cautious, not afraid.

Madam Pomfrey stands at the foot of Snape's bed.

"Five minutes, Headmaster."

She bustles away and Harry moves one step closer. He stands at the side of the bed, positions himself so that Snape does not have to move his head to see him. The bandages on the neck are heavy and thick, keeping Snape's head at an angle that must be uncomfortable.

Snape uses up an entire minute staring at him. When he speaks, it is without preamble or introduction of any sort. His voice is . . . compromised. Yet he leaves Harry with no doubt as to who is in charge at Hogwarts.

"You may stay here. You may return and complete your N.E.W.T.s." He emphasizes the word "may." His black eyes are fixed on Harry's face. "But you *should* move on. You have outgrown Hogwarts, Mr. Potter. If the Ministry requires N.E.W.T.s, you will contact Professor McGonagall. She will arrange tutoring."

Harry nods. He can't think what to say in return. Until this very second, he had not realized he would need permission to *stay*.

"I will need your decision by your birthday, Mr. Potter."

Harry nods again. He wonders—briefly—how Snape knows his birthday. Then remembers the Prophecy.

They stare at each other another minute. Harry shifts his weight.

"I . . ." He should not open his mouth until his thoughts are fully formed. Snape frowns.

"Professor McGonagall put the Pensieve away. Your memories are still in it." Harry moistens his very dry lips. The next word is more difficult even than he had thought it would be. He says it very softly. "Thanks."

Snape acknowledges the word with ten seconds of silence. Then—

"Robes, Mr. Potter. While you are at Hogwarts, you will wear your student robes. This is a school, not a tent in a forest."

Harry stares at Snape. Then he nods, once, a jerky, nonfluid motion.

He is gone from Hogwarts by the fifteenth of July, but until he leaves, he wears his Gryffindor robes.

Snape has given Harry a gift. Robes. A first push toward a return to normalcy.

A greater gift. A second push. Out the door.

And leaving Hogwarts? Being thrown into the deep water, learning to swim. He may not have had a real childhood, and he may have grown up in his year on the run, but he has not ever made his own decisions. Not really.

Horcruxes or hallows?

Was there ever really a choice?

Working with George is therapeutic.

In August, Diagon Alley comes alive again. Ollivander is back, and Fortescue, and Weasley's Wizard Wheezes. Quality Quidditch Supplies discounts the old model Firebolts, and Harry stops and looks through the window whenever he passes. He is not a tall man, but is a head taller than the crowds of children pressing against the glass.

Ginny goes back to Hogwarts. Hermione arranges for N.E.W.T. tutoring. Ron is accepted into the Auror's Corps and receives private tutoring there.

Neville returns to Hogwarts. To Ginny.

Harry lives with George, in the rooms over the shop. Ron lives with them. There are two beds in Harry's room, and he finds that he sleeps much better on the infrequent nights when there is quiet snoring to rock him to sleep. Ron, disappointed that Harry did not join up with him, nevertheless sees how this arrangement works. He spends most of his nights with Hermione, but Molly likes that he is living with George and Harry, watching over the brokenness, helping to knit the family back together.

Ron needs watching too. They're all good at watching each other.

Harry, at eighteen, waters down the Firewhisky, cleans the Floo when George throws all the kitchen plates, one after the other, against its bricks one Sunday morning. He meets George at the door some nights, slips ten galleons into his companion's hand. She leaves without complaint, earning her fee without delivering the goods, and Harry lies in bed with George, and holds him while he weeps.

He helps George brew, and cannot help but think of Snape, and the Half-blood Prince's book, and the secrets he learned from it. But thoughts of Snape are passing. He sees him once, a Monday in early January, at Gringotts. He's just made the shop's deposit, and is heading toward the doors when Snape enters.

Snape slows when he sees him. Gives him a thorough visual inspection. Nods. Says "Good day, Mr. Potter."

Harry has been giving the Headmaster his own inspection. He looks as he has ever looked, except that his hair is pulled back and tied at the nape of his neck. His face is somehow sallower for it.

Harry responds with a nod. "Good morning, Headmaster."

At the door, he turns to watch Snape's progress to the window. His robes are billowing.

Harry smiles as he walks down the stairs toward Diagon Alley.

At nineteen, Harry Potter is still trying to make sense of the war.

Fred's loss is still keen in George. Fred's ghost Harry sees every day. He has learned to live with it.

He is still angry at Remus. At his selfishness and cowardice. He knows this is not fair.

But Tonks was the Auror. Tonks was the real fighter, despite Remus' abilities. Someone should have stayed with Teddy. Someone named Remus. Someone should not have left Teddy an orphan.

Hermione tells him that Voldemort left Teddy an orphan, just as Voldemort left him—Harry—an orphan. Just as Voldemort is responsible for Fred's death, and Lavender's, and Colin's.

Hermione is right, except that she's wrong. *One* of them should have stayed with Teddy. He forgives Tonks but does not forgive Remus. It's not fair, and he knows it, but he looks at Andromeda when she visits and Teddy toddles over to the Pygmy Puffs and nearly squeezes one to death before Harry swoops in, saves the purple Puff and lifts Teddy to his hip. Andromeda has lost her husband and her daughter. Bellatrix is dead. Narcissa is self-exiled in France. Teddy is more than a consolation prize but there are many long years between now and when Teddy can care for her as she cares for him, as she cared for Ted and Tonks.

Remus should be here with Teddy so Andromeda can grieve.

He is not angry at Sirius. Sirius' death is a wound scabbed over, half-healed. He wonders if Sirius ever knew him, if he ever saw more than James in him. And this, too, he knows, is not fair. Sirius was damaged, by James' and Lily's deaths, by Peter's betrayal, by Azkaban. There was never enough time to know him.

And it was Remus that had kept him from going after Sirius. Remus who had anchored him to this life, but who had left his own child only . . .

Not even memories.

In hours spent in the shop, brewing with George, manning the counter, stocking the shelves, he contemplates death. He makes peace with it, and moves on. Unbelievably, impossibly, he suggests to George that they expand their business and open a small apothecary, that they sell a limited number of specialty potions. He is living up to the abilities that Horace Slughorn thought he had, learning the nuances of Potion making. He reads everything he can, amuses the hell out of Ron and Hermione. But they support him. They always do.

Ron wonders if Harry will sell Felix Felicis. He has exams coming up and could use some luck. Harry shakes his head. Liquid Luck in potion form is cheating at life. Harry reminds Ron of the Quidditch match, the placebo effect, and tells Ron to study for the exams. He volunteers to practice dueling with Ron, and is inordinately pleased when Ron bests him in three out of five matches.

Liquid Luck.

Liquid Luck did not bring him to Snape on the floor of the Shrieking Shack. It did not win him Snape's memories. It did not save Snape's life. There was no Liquid Luck when they rode the dragon out of Gringotts, or when Ron pulled him from the pond in the Forest of Dean.

George and Harry improve Dreamless Sleep. Dreams are not the problem—nightmares are the problem. A potion to keep nightmares at bay, to allow what pleasant dreams may come.

While Harry works alone in the lab while George mans the shop, he ponders the death of Albus Dumbledore.

Harry doesn't remember his father. He had never had a grandfather. Until he came to Hogwarts, he didn't understand love in any tangible way. He knows Dumbledore had loved him, just as surely as he knows that Dumbledore used him. He has forgiven him that. Moved on.

But he wonders about Snape. About the Snape and the Dumbledore in Snape's memories. He wonders if he would have killed Dumbledore if Dumbledore had asked him to.

And he remembers the cave, the lake. The potion and the locket.

And he wonders about Snape again.

And what he had said there, at the end, to Voldemort.

Dumbledore's men.

He looks down into the cauldron, sees himself reflected there on the shimmering surface, messy hair lank and greasy in the fumes.

And understands.

Fleur's sister Gabrielle moves to London to study, and Harry meets her again at his birthday party at the Burrow. He is twenty-one, she is eighteen. She is his first girlfriend—his first relationship—after Ginny. She is beautiful and young and unbroken. She makes him smile, and laugh.

Hermione doesn't like her, nor does Ginny, nor does Molly. Perhaps it is not Gabrielle that they dislike, but Harry when he is with her. Robes pressed, boots polished, hair sculpted and gelled, just so. When they are together, he is always touching her. Hand on the small of her back, on her knee when they are sitting together, knuckles grazing her cheek in affection.

He falls for her. Hard.

Falls harder when she leaves him nearly two years later.

He throws himself back into his research. The Restful Slumber potion is selling well, and now Harry is obsessed with making a cream that will fade scars, make them disappear.

Because everyone has scars.

There are scar creams available already, but they work well only when on scars not yet set, months old, not years. They fade older scars, but do almost nothing with scars from hexes, curses, magical objects.

Hermione has a scar on her face, long and thin and narrow. Ron has scars on his upper arms, from the brains in the Ministry of Magic when he was sixteen. The scar on Harry's hand has been there for eight years now. Bill's face has been marred for seven, George's for six.

In the five years it takes to perfect the potion, Harry has one girlfriend and two boyfriends. The boyfriends surprise him. The first is Paul, a friend of Bill and Fleur's. They meet at Louis's christening, play against each other as Seekers in the pickup Quidditch match that follows at the Burrow, and leave together in the evening to find a quiet pub.

George and Angelina have married now, and Harry has his own flat in London. His first kiss with a man is in this flat, just inside the front door, Paul's lips on his, Paul's knee between his thighs, Paul's hands in Harry's hair. His next boyfriend is much younger, only twenty, and Harry realizes that he wants his men older, and he doesn't need the excitement and noise of the clubs. He'd rather share a pint in a quiet pub and return to the privacy of his flat and do all sorts of imaginative things without the prying eyes of the public on him.

When Harry is twenty-eight years old, the potion is finally perfected. The scar on his hand is gone. The skin on Ron's upper arms is once again smooth. Bill's face is not scar free, but the scars have faded significantly. Harry is still working on perfecting the Potion to treat the scars left from the teeth and claws of magical creatures.

He is surprised—though he should not have been—when Severus Snape walks into their shop. It is Saturday, the sixth of September, 2008.

Harry is sitting on a stool behind the counter. He is reading *Potions Quarterly*. It is the slowest Saturday of the year, the Saturday after classes start at Hogwarts. It is indeed possible that Severus Snape knows this and has chosen the day of his visit deliberately.

He coughs to get Harry's attention.

Harry looks up. Later, he would watch Severus' memory of his face in Dumbledore's Pensieve. He knows he looks gobsmacked. Scared. Embarrassed.

He has not thought about Snape very much in some years—has not dreamed of him since they perfected the Restful Slumber Potion. He saw him in May, at the ten-year anniversary memorial. But there had been hundreds of people and no time to catch up—and no desire to, really, on either of their parts.

Harry scrambles to his feet. Snape's eyes follow the Potions journal as it falls to the floor. He lifts his eyes and fastens them on Harry's face.

Harry remains frozen, transfixed by the hand that is approaching him slowly. The hand that pushes back his fringe, the thumb that traces over his scar.

Snape drops his hand and steps back. He cannot completely bury a look of disappointment. The counter is still between them and Harry, understanding, steps forward until his belly is pressing against the wood.

"No—Snape—Headmaster. You don't understand. I haven't tried it on that one. I'm not . . ." He falters here. He has not yet explained this to his friends, to the Weasleys, to the customers who have asked. He tells Snape what he has told the rest. "I'm not ready yet."

"Not ready?" Snape is scoffing.

"I've always had it," answers Harry, trying to explain, not understanding why it is important now. "I've never *not* had it, not that I can remember, anyway. It makes me remember."

"You want to remember?" Snape sounds haughty, but he has stepped back up to the counter.

"No. No—I want to be sure is all. Once it's gone—if I miss it, I mean—I'm not going to ask anyone to launch an unforgiveable at me to get it back."

Snape stares at him. The corner of his mouth quirks upward. He appears to be trying to pull it back down into a frown.

Harry looks pointedly at the high collar that hides what Harry imagines to be gruesome scars from Nagini's bite. He has seen that flesh laid open. He knows how ripped, how shredded, that neck once was. He no longer dreams of it. Not with the Restful Slumber potion.

"I think it will help," he says quietly. "It may take some time. Bill's been using it for more than a year already."

He is on his knees behind the counter, spinning the lock of a strongbox. He reaches in and hands Snape something quite unexpected.

A piece of parchment.

Snape stares at it. Realization dawns. Harry sees it when it happens. Snape is surprised. Shocked. He holds onto the parchment. "This . . ."

Harry squares his shoulders. "The formula," he says. He looks up and there is an odd expression on his face, a strange light in his eye. "It's been a while, Professor, but if I'm right, you'll prefer to brew it yourself."

Snape is past surprised, past shocked. He is angry. He shakes his fist, parchment clenched in it, in front of Harry's face.

"Do you know what I could do with this?" he hisses.

Harry stares at him. He nods.

"If it takes away those scars, I don't care what else you do with it. If it doesn't—well, if it doesn't, I'd like to know."

"Professional curiosity?" Snape bites out.

Harry shrugs. "Mostly," he responds.

But he is lying.

And so it begins.

Snape returns in mid-October. Not to the shop, but to Harry's flat in London. It is a Sunday morning, eleven o'clock. Harry doesn't ask how he found the address.

Snape enters the flat, glances around with feigned disinterest. There are photos of his godchildren on the mantel, a Muggle telly, a wizarding chess set on the sofa table, but mostly there are books. There are so many books that Snape should feel totally at ease, but Harry knows that the opposite is true. That he has not imagined Harry Potter living in a library.

Snape faces Harry. Without leave, he begins to unfasten the buttons on his high collar. He pulls it aside and stands there while Harry stares at him.

The scars are worse than any he has seen. They are ropey on the edges, and thick and discolored everywhere else. Harry's mouth falls open. He looks at Snape, an apology ready on his lips.

Snape shakes his head, holds up a hand.

"They are better," he says in that altered voice. "They are *much* better." He is all business now. He drops, without invitation, onto the loveseat and pushes a pile of books to the side as he spreads several pieces of parchment out onto the table. He moves the stack as if he is accustomed to moving piles of books whenever he sits at a table. "I have already tried substituting logspur membranes for the aloe extract, and have increased the pumice . . ."

Harry sits on the end of the couch, perpendicular to Snape. He leans over and looks at the parchment, points to something, asks a question. Snape answers. Harry grabs a pen—a Muggle ballpoint—and scribbles something. Snape grabs the pen out of his hand and reaches for a pair of pencils lying side by side on the table.

They are at it for an hour.

Before Snape leaves, he begins to button his collar.

Harry stops him.

"May I?" He nods at the scars. He doesn't have to explain. Snape knows what Harry is asking, and why.

Snape drops his hands to his sides. Harry reaches out and feels Snape's neck.

There is no electric shock, no spark of desire.

But there is . . . something.

Harry feels the skin, rough and pitted. His fingers graze over the Adam's apple. Beneath them, he feels the pulse of Snape's heart.

He drops his hand.

Snape has a heart.

By the time Harry's twenty-ninth birthday comes, Severus' scars are visible still, but the ridges are gone. The formula has been perfected, with Snape's help, for Bill. He smiles for photographs again.

Harry and Severus are in love.

Harry is in love with Severus, and Severus is in love with Harry, but they do not acknowledge their feelings. Oddly, each thinks the other is off-limits. Too young, too old, too male. They remain partners of a different sense, heads buried in journals and ingredients and cauldrons.

Because they are working together on an article for *Potions Quarterly*, Severus spends every Sunday afternoon at Harry's. He arrives on August 2 but Harry does not answer the door. This has never happened before, so he lets himself in.

Harry is in bed, spiking fever, shivering. He is dehydrated. The room smells stale. It is too warm for Severus, too cold for Harry. Harry is barely lucid. His teeth are chattering.

It should not be the most natural thing in the world for Severus to care for him, but it is. Antinausea, fever-reducer, fluids. He changes sheets and pajamas, presses a cold cloth to Harry's head. Wakes him every two hours to force more fluids down him, to help him use the loo, to check his fever.

By late evening, when Harry's fever has finally broken, when he is weak but clear-minded, he reaches for Severus' robes as he turns to leave his bedside. No one could care for another like that unless . . . unless . . .

"Stay?" he asks.

Severus stays.

It is the New Year.

Severus is sitting at Harry's new desk, reading glasses perched low on his nose. He is reviewing a contract and Harry is arguing with him.

"I had no idea! I'm an idiot! Really, Severus, you had no right!"

"You forget that I did not do this on purpose, Harry."

"I know. It was . . ." He falters, staring at Severus' dark eyes as they regard him from just above the lenses.

"Fortuitous?" suggests Severus.

"You might say that," says Harry with a sigh.

"We can stop now. We know what's causing it. I imagine it will stay exactly as it is."

"I don't know." Harry walks over to the mirror beside the door and pushes his fringe away, staring at the barely there scar.

"If it defines you so much, what were you six months ago that you are not today?"

Severus' voice is matter-of-fact. He is not looking at Harry.

Harry stares in the mirror. In the reflection, Severus continues to read the contract, to jot notes on it, corrections.

Harry drops his fringe and turns.

He walks over to the desk, pushes the parchment and books out of the way, and slides between Severus' knees, half sitting on the desk. He leans forward and down, placing warm, open-mouthed kisses over Severus' neck, against the almost-not-there scars.

"Alone," he answers. "Six months ago, I was alone."

"You'll hardly be alone in another week," quips Severus. "You will have so much company, in fact . . ."

"I'm beginning to question my sanity in accepting this job." Harry fastens his lips just below Severus' ear and Severus shudders, pulls his chin up, and kisses him. His hands cup the sides of Harry's head. His fingers work into his hair. They sigh into each other's mouths. Severus pulls back, raises his hand, traces the faint outline of Harry's scar with his thumb.

For four months now, Severus has made a nightly ritual of doing this, of tracing Harry's scar with his thumb.

The same hand, the same thumb, that he uses to apply his scar cream every night when he gets into bed.

The lightning-shaped scar is almost gone now.

Harry can no longer speak to snakes—that power vanished with the Horcrux. He is not an Auror. He is an entrepreneur, a Potions expert, about to become a Professor. He is not married to Ginny Weasley, not living in a cottage in Godric's Hollow with a son (James) and a daughter (Lily). He does not play professional Quidditch.

He is not naked and frozen in the bottom of a pond in the Forest of Dean. He is not lying dead at Narcissa Malfoy's feet.

Severus will turn fifty in five days. He is still Headmaster. He is not in Azkaban. He is not exiled in France with the Malfoys. He is not lying dead in a pool of blood in the Shrieking Shack.

He had not expected to live fifty years, much less close out those first fifty with a companion, a lover.

Harry stands. Steps closer to Severus so that Severus' head is pressed into his chest. Harry's arms go around him. Severus inhales, works his own arms around Harry. "I'm glad you kicked me out after the Battle," Harry says.

Severus turns his head so he can speak, but keeps it pressed against Harry. "I did not *kick you out*. I *recommended* that you leave. For your own good, I might add."

Harry is ignoring him. "It made coming back all the better," he says. "Now come on, let's go tell Dumbledore that Lucius Malfoy's been elected Minister of Magic."

"You'll give him a coronary. It was bad enough when you told him that the Ministry had eliminated Hufflepuff House."

"He can't have a coronary—he's a painting," protests Harry. He is pulling Severus by the hand toward the door. "Let's just snog in front of him again. Gets him all hot and bothered."

"You've spent far too much time with George Weasley," grumbles Severus.

Harry laughs. "And not nearly enough time with you."

Their voices recede down the corridor.

"No. I am far too old to slide down the banister."

"This may be the last time you can do it before you turn fifty, Severus. The students are coming back tomorrow."

A long pause. A laugh. The corridors of Hogwarts have not heard this laugh in a long, long while.

"Fine. Just this once."

Once upon a Time

busaikko

Dudley's got five suits in the closet, one for each day of the week, and three chins like a ladder up from necktie to scowl, and a solid German car for driving to the corporate headquarters of Consolidated Demolitions, Ltd., every morning at half past seven. Dudley sits with thighs pushing knees wide apart, and drips sweat climbing the stairs, and when the receptionist snipes under her breath *It's not like you can eat yourself happy* Dudley throws such a wobbler that the next day she applies for a transfer to the department of breaking big things into little things with hammers.

She starts Dudley thinking about happiness, though, which leads to thinking about unhappiness. Once upon a time, Dudley had the pleasures of life sucked out by an invisible creeping horror. Knowing that evil really existed, waiting just around the corner from normal life, made it hard to go back to school. After that, Dudley was afraid of being put in the cupboard under the stairs, afraid of dirty old clothes and sharp words and birthdays with no presents or cake, of being laughed at by friends. It's an unpleasant shock to trace the roots of those fears down into the childhood certainty that if ever Dudley were a freak like Harry, there'd be no more love, ever.

Life was so much simpler when unhappiness was cured by bashing someone with a stick or having a go at foreigners or odd-looking people. As soon as school finishes, Dudley gets a job, a flat in London, and learns to laugh too loudly at other people's jokes over plates of greasy food and rounds of overpriced drinks. Dudley's not particularly happy being one of the lads, though. Happiness comes mostly in the recurring dream of being Aunt Marge.

The image that comes to mind is always of Aunt Marge blown up like a balloon, big and round, floating up out of her chair in her expanded tweeds. Dudley keeps getting bigger, year by year, but somehow the inside Dudley is being crushed smaller instead of rising into the sky. It would be fine if that inside Dudley just smalled itself out of existence, but it's always there, unhappy, daydreaming about balloons and huge sturdy skirts.

Dudley's twenty-four when things go sideways all of a sudden. Walking into Jean-Claude's for the usual junior corporate haircut, shave, and head massage, Dudley is full-frontally assaulted by a gilt-framed mirror and turns on one heel and walks out. Each step gets lighter and lighter until Dudley's standing in a dressing room with armfuls of clothes: pleated tweed skirts on the left, and pastel twinsets on the right.

And the clothes are absolutely perfectly right, but it's the man Dudley sees wearing them that's all wrong. Aunt Marge has a moustache, Dudley thinks, sullen the way it felt when a new toy lost its shine, but Aunt Marge also has something intangible that Dudley doesn't and all of a sudden it's what Dudley wants more than anything.

Dudley is very, very good at wanting things, and has a talent for yelling and stomping and being unpleasant until they are obtained. But there's only so much that Dudley can do, even with double strands of very nice imitation pearls and little clips to hold back the hair that Jean-Claude no longer cuts. Dudley's twenty-six and gets funny looks from the men in the office, who don't mention when they're going out for drinks anymore. Mum and Dad think it's time to get married and settle down with a nice girl in a nice house before Dudley turns (Mum lowers her voice to say it) *metrosexual*.

Dudley twirls in the dream, slowly rising, round and glorious and— here's a new thought—full of magic.

That's what Dudley's been overlooking; there *is* someone who can help, he just needs to be found.

It takes a week of badgering shop assistants in some of London's dodgiest New Age and occult supply shops to find one girl who admits to knowing who Harry Potter is, and Dudley nearly yells at her just to have the satisfaction of bullying someone whose hourly wage probably isn't enough to buy a can of tinned tomatoes. Instead, Dudley hands her a note in an envelope sealed with glue and tape and staples, and a handful of banknotes that she accepts with baffled amusement.

Fifteen minutes later Harry rings Dudley's mobile, and at half-past six they're sitting down with large mugs of foamy coffee in a shop the size of Dudley's walk-in closet.

"Looking good," Dudley says heartily, because that's how all conversations start, before moving into a discussion of sport. Harry is still short, but he's muscular, and he wears a grubby hooded sweatshirt and jeans as if clothing doesn't matter to him. Dudley expected him to be more openly freakish.

Harry laughs and gives his coffee a stern look. It stops steaming, and Harry shares a grin with Dudley before he takes a gulp. "I haven't slept through a night since the baby was born, and I know I look it."

A baby is completely blindsiding news, implying things about Harry that Dudley would never have thought possible. Mum would be crushed that Harry turned out to be the normal one, after all. "Oh," Dudley says, not heartily at all. "Boy or girl?"

"Boy," Harry says offhand, and then gives Dudley the sort of look that goes straight through all the largeness to the crushed-down Dudley inside. "You're looking remarkably like Aunt Marge."

"Do you really think so?" Dudley says. The skirt's pleated and heather-colored, and the green sweater matches the knee-high stockings, and Dudley's never worn these clothes outside of the flat and is nervous enough that it's hard to suppress overloud jovial anecdotes about shopping. Dudley sips the coffee instead.

"Well," Harry says hastily. "A younger version, of course. With less moustache."

"I thought you'd laugh," Dudley says.

Harry shrugs. "My godfather could turn into a dog, my father into a stag, my godson's a . . . well, I guess the Muggle word is *shapeshifter*, and his dad was a werewolf. I'm used to people changing." He pauses, and stirs sugar into his coffee absently. "I'm also used to people dying, and it makes family feel . . . important. So yeah," Harry says, and slaps his hands on the tabletop lightly. "You ready to go, then? I'm an Auror, that's like a policeman, so I'm not the kind of wizard you want to see. You're looking for someone who does medical transfiguration. I do have connections."

"Oh," Dudley says again. Harry's talking gibberish, but it's easy enough to nod along. "I can get you a good deal at the company I work for," Dudley says. "If you ever want anything really large smashed down until it's in tiny pieces."

Harry stares blankly for a moment, and then gives one sharp nod. "I'll keep that in mind," he says, standing and starting for the door.

"I will be coming back, won't I?" Dudley asks.

Harry gets to the door first and holds it open. "If you want to," Harry says as Dudley walks through. "Up to you." Outside on the pavement, Harry takes Dudley's arm. "The magical world's pretty brilliant, though."

It takes Dudley a moment to realize that as they walk they're climbing up through the air as though there were invisible stairs. Looking down, everyone's oblivious; looking up, Dudley sees more stars than London's skies have ever shown.

"I'm taking a shortcut," Harry says, apologetically, and Dudley feels the skirt snap in the wind.

"I dreamed of this," Dudley says, letting the weight of fear and unhappiness fall away, expanding into the sky.

And they lived, happily, ever after.

The Companions' Tale

Title: The Pond Continuum (2013)
Author: kaydee falls
Fandom: *Doctor Who* (2005, Eleventh Doctor)
Rating: Teen-and-up Audiences (gen, F/M)
Additional tags: 5 + 1 Things, Five Things, postseason / series
    7, moving on, life after the Doctor, chance meetings

Introduction

Doctor Who has been a popular fandom from its debut in 1963 through today, during which time it has run almost continuously, with new episodes
debuting between 1963 and 1989 (Classic *Who*) and then again from 2005
to now (sometimes called "new *Who*"). *Doctor Who* is the story of an alien,
known only as "the Doctor," who travels through space and time in a ship
called the TARDIS, usually joined by one or more companions. One of
the central conceits of the show is that the Doctor can regenerate twelve
times; this, in addition to a rotating cast of companions, has allowed the
story to stay fresh over half a century. When I was a kid, my Doctors
were Four (Tom Baker) and Five (Peter Davidson); today's fans are more
likely to have grown up with Doctors Ten (David Tennant) and Eleven
(Matt Smith). As I write this, the current Doctor is Twelve, played by Peter Capaldi—himself a *Doctor Who* superfan as a teenager. In fact, *Doctor
Who* was revived in 2005 by a group of creators who were themselves fans:
Russell T. Davies, David Tennant, Mark Gatiss, and others who worked
on the show first came to it as fans. And the show they made feels a lot
like professionally made fanfiction; for instance, in new *Who*, the Doctor

is more sexual than he used to be, and the show also introduced Captain Jack Harkness, one of television's first openly bisexual characters. These new creators understood some (though not all) of the ways in which the Doctor had entered his audience's fantasies.

While over its long run, the show has itself taken advantage of many of the narrative possibilities that time travel offers—in episodes like *The Three Doctors* (1972) and *The Five Doctors* (1983), for example, the Doctor teams up with different versions of himself—the practicalities of television production mean that stories where one set of time travelers crosses paths with another are more likely to happen in fiction, where you don't have to worry about actor schedules or availability. Actors also age, and sometimes die, so it's much easier to have characters from different seasons of *Doctor Who* meet each other on the page than on the screen. *Doctor Who* has told many complicated time travel stories in its extended universe of novels, short stories, audiobooks, comic books, and video games, but fans also continue to tell the stories that the authorized creators haven't, wouldn't, didn't, or couldn't tell.

"The Pond Continuum," by kaydee falls, is one of those stories, and one that repays the dedicated viewer of post-2005 *Doctor Who*. The story takes place after the episode "The Angels Take Manhattan" (2012), at the end of which then-companions Amy Pond and her husband Rory Williams leave the Eleventh Doctor and are stranded on Earth in the 1930s. (The episode marked the popular couple's departure from the series.) "The Pond Continuum" is a "Five Things" story—technically a 5 + 1 (see the introduction to "The Super Man's Tale" for more about "Five Things" stories)—summarized by the author as "Five people who have never heard of the Ponds (but might have met them anyway), and one who has." In the story, kaydee falls takes advantage of the fact that we learn in canon that Amy and Rory both live into their eighties (we see their tombstones at the end of "The Angels Take Manhattan") and that consequently, they're both going to live through much of the twentieth century[1]—which also happens to be the time and place in which most other *Doctor Who* episodes are set. This allows kaydee falls not only to give us a postcanon story—what happens to Amy and Rory after the episode? What are their lives like as they grow old together in this strange way?—but also to have their lives intersect those of other notable Doctor Who characters from across the series.

Despite the fact that the Doctor travels through all of space and time, he seems to like Earth—twentieth-century Earth, in fact—the best, and so Earth is disproportionately represented as the site of his adventures, and people from Earth are disproportionately represented among his companions. This is, of course, also just practical—it's easier (and cheaper) to set an episode on Earth than to represent an alien race or planet—but it also means that there are plenty of episodes set during Amy and Rory's new lifetimes, and so kaydee falls sets up a delightful game of "Spot the Character!" even as she tells us how Amy and Rory developed and grew after they left the Doctor. Fanfiction often gives us new perspectives on beloved characters, and this story lets us see these characters from a different angle than we normally do; we may also recognize these episodes, but we've never seen them from this direction. In "The Pond Continuum" we meet Martha Jones, Captain Jack Harkness, Rose Tyler, the Ninth Doctor, Sarah Jane Smith, and, as the +1 bonus, a character that Amy and Rory actually *have* met before: Canton Delaware III. The story is constructed as a series of vignettes, in historical order as Amy and Rory would have lived them; to wit:

"New York City, 1930." Amy and Rory are sent back not to New York in 1938, as "The Angels Take Manhattan" leads us to expect, but slightly earlier, in 1930: or at the end of the two-part arc "Daleks in Manhattan" and "Evolution of the Daleks" (2007). Amy and Rory find themselves in the aftermath of that story, which is set in a Hooverville in Central Park from which the evil alien Daleks are kidnapping poor and homeless people to experiment on. The young doctor that we meet in the story is Martha Jones, a medical student and one of the show's few black companions. When Rory asks her what happened, she laughs and says, "You wouldn't believe me if I told you." But of course, Rory Williams is one of the few people who actually *would* believe her. This first vignette also sets up the larger arc of the story: that Amy and Rory will have to live through a twentieth century whose major fixed points they know already: "The Great Depression and World War II and then the Korean War and Vietnam and the Gulf: all of her twentieth century history lessons, and why is it Amy can only remember the wars?"

"London, 1941." Traveling through time "on the slow path," Amy and Rory end up in wartime London, the scene of one of the most memorable new *Who* stories, the two-parter "The Empty Child" and "The Doctor Dances" (2005). In those episodes, the Ninth Doctor and Rose find themselves being haunted by mutated zombie children in gas masks who are looking for their mother (this is the "mysterious illness" being treated at Albion hospital); in the end, all of the children are healed and saved ("Everybody lives, Rose!" the Doctor cries out joyously. "Just this once, everybody lives!"), which is why the hospital is empty and the head physician is in such high spirits. The episode is also notable for introducing the character Captain Jack Harkness, a fifty-first-century charmer who flirts with both the Doctor and Rose in this episode (and kisses both of them in another). The idea of Captain Jack as a man who is always up for a happy threesome is therefore more or less canonical, and kaydee falls takes advantage of this to have Amy and Rory invite Jack into their bed. This also tells us a lot about Amy and Rory's marriage: Rory is secure enough that he's happy to see his wife "laughing and flirting outrageously." Like Captain Jack, whose fifty-first-century sexuality challenges simple binaries, Rory and Amy are both utterly devoted and casually polyamorous.

"London, 1953." *Doctor Who* canon tells us that Amy is a journalist; in this third vignette, Amy's career is doing sufficiently well that she is sent to cover the coronation of Elizabeth II—an event that is the subject of "The Idiot's Lantern" (2006), an episode written by Mark Gatiss, later one of the creators of the BBC's *Sherlock*. In that episode, Rose and the Tenth Doctor battle a villain who is selling cheap television sets and who plans to use them to literally consume the minds of millions and millions of viewers. (Elizabeth's coronation was the first to be televised, and was in fact the first major television event for what was then a relatively new medium.) Here Amy Pond briefly interviews Rose Tyler about the significance of television—a fact that Amy knows is culturally important because of course, she's from the future, from the age of television. We also get a glimpse of Ten in his iconic pinstriped suit.

"Barcelona, 1966." In "Rose" (2005), the very first episode of new *Who*, the Ninth Doctor and Rose meet and have an adventure, but at the end of the episode, Rose decides not to become his new companion. The Doctor tries to cajole her into adventuring with him in the TARDIS: "This box isn't just a London Hopper, you know. It goes anywhere in the Universe, free of charge," but Rose turns him down. The TARDIS dematerializes, to our (and Rose's) disappointment, but reappears what seems like a moment later. The Doctor pops out and adds: "By the way, did I mention it also travels in time?" and grinning, Rose runs to join him. kaydee falls's fourth vignette takes place in the moment between the disappearance and reappearance of the TARDIS—in the interim, she imagines Nine going to Barcelona and meeting Rory, who gives him the idea of how to tempt Rose along. (But why Barcelona, I hear you cry? Well, in "The Parting of the Ways" [2005], the episode where Nine regenerates into Ten, a tearful Nine says, "Rose Tyler, I was going to take you to so many places. Barcelona. Not the city Barcelona, the planet Barcelona. You'd love it. Fantastic place," and then the first words of Ten, the new doctor, are "Hello! Ooh, new teeth. That's weird. So where was I? Oh, that's right. Barcelona!" and then he sets the TARDIS's coordinates to take her there.)

"London, 1972." Sarah Jane Smith is arguably the most popular companion in the history of the series, so much so that she was the first companion to get her own spinoff shows (first 1981's *K-9 and Company* and then *The Sarah Jane Adventures* from 2007 to 2011). Sarah Jane traveled with the Third and Fourth Doctors from 1973 to 1976, a time when feminism was having a renewed impact on popular culture. The character was portrayed as a plucky investigative journalist and a self-identified feminist, a woman trying to make it in a man's world. In this vignette, Amy—a later companion, but by now an older woman and a senior journalist—meets the young Sarah Jane at journalism school. One of the consequences of time travel is that Amy's now lived most of her life in a time before "women's lib," and kaydee falls here shows us Sarah Jane pushing her way through male students to talk to this rare female mentor.

"Washington, D.C., 1969." In this last vignette, the +1, an elderly Amy and Rory seek out Canton Delaware III, a character they met previously on their adventures with the Doctor. Amy and Rory first meet Canton Delaware in the present day as an old man, but they later go back to the 1960s and meet him again: he is an ex-FBI agent who helps and befriends them. We learn that Delaware had been forced to resign from the FBI because they disapproved of his personal life. The Eleventh Doctor complains about this to no less than Richard Nixon, arguing that "Canton just wants to get married," and that he shouldn't be thrown out of the FBI just because of whom he loves. Nixon assures him that "something can be arranged" before discovering exactly who Canton's love is:

PRESIDENT RICHARD NIXON: This person you want to marry—black?
CANTON DELAWARE: Yes.
PRESIDENT RICHARD NIXON: I know what people think of me, but perhaps I'm a bit more liberal than . . .
CANTON DELAWARE: *He* is.
PRESIDENT RICHARD NIXON: . . . I think the Moon is far enough for now, don't you?
CANTON DELAWARE: I figured it might be.

Having the rumpled, middle-aged law enforcement character turn out to be both queer and in an interracial relationship undermined the cliché of the "middle-aged cop" and instantly rocketed Delaware up the list of favorite characters. (It also didn't hurt that the character was played by

Mark Sheppard, an actor who has appeared on many shows popular with fans, including *Supernatural, White Collar, Leverage, Battlestar Galactica, Firefly*, and others.)

This last vignette is the first one that's not told from Amy's or Rory's perspective; rather, it's told from Delaware's. He is processing the events of "The Day of the Moon" (2011), in which he and the Doctor defeat an enemy called The Silence on the day of the moon landing, when he sees "an unfamiliar older man and woman, maybe in their sixties or seventies," standing outside his door. He's shocked to discover it's Amy and Rory— for him, it's only been a day, but for them it's been forty or fifty years. Again, we see kaydee falls creating a new story in the interstices of an old one—Amy and Rory have had a whole world of adventures before Canton Delaware's had breakfast—and in this way, all fanfiction is like time travel. A world of stories can be told between one narrative moment and the next.

Suggested Further Reading

Like other long-lived fandoms, *Doctor Who* has attracted much serious critical attention both as a storyverse and as a fandom; notable books include Henry Jenkins and John Tulloch's 1995 *Watching "Doctor Who" and "Star Trek"* (Routledge) and Matt Hills's *Triumph of a Time Lord: Regenerating "Doctor Who" in the Twenty-First Century* (I. B. Taurus, 2010). And like other rebooted and recurring transmedia fandoms (*Sherlock* and *Lord of the Rings* both come to mind), *Doctor Who* fandom has experienced some amount of conflict between old-school Whovians and younger, internet-era media fans who only know the "new *Who*," a conflict Laura Hadas discusses in her 2009 article "The Web Planet: How the Changing Internet Divided *Doctor Who* Fan Fiction Writers." There are also many essay collections dealing with *Who* fandom and fanfic, including Paul Booth's 2013 *Fan Phenomenon: "Doctor Who,"* Gillian I. Leitch's 2013 anthology, *"Doctor Who" in Time and Space: Essays on Themes, Characters, History and Fandom, 1963—2012* and the two "popular" essay collections from Mad Norwegian Press, *Chicks Dig Time Lords* (2010) and *Queers Dig Time Lords* (2013), which articulate specifically subcultural fan responses to the *Doctor Who* text. Krystal Fogel's 2015 essay, "It's Bigger on the Inside: Fandom, Social Media, and *Doctor Who*," shows the continuing interest of fans and scholars alike as *Who* fandom continues to grow.

The Pond Continuum

kaydee falls

1. New York City, 1930

When Amy blinks, the cemetery around her becomes a chilly autumn night in Central Park. Or she thinks it's Central Park. It's some sort of park, okay, and there's a brisk wind toying with her hair, and the air smells of that weird uncertain mixture of earth and iron and cement and garbage and soot that's somehow uniquely New York in any century. And most importantly of all, Rory's already wrapped his arms around her so tightly she thinks they must still be falling, falling, falling.

He chants her name in a voice like gravel, and she can't breathe through her tears with his arms like a vise around her ribs.

Once they sort themselves out—and let's be real, here, it takes a hell of a lot of sorting—they get smart enough to hunt down a copy of the evening paper to check the date. *Saturday, November 1st 1930*, the New York Record proclaims.

"Huh," Amy says. "I thought we were supposed to end up in 1938 for good."

"Guess the angel didn't want to get too predictable," Rory says sourly. "Just in case there was any hope of the Doctor tracking us down again."

There wasn't, Amy doesn't say. *There never will be again.* The words get caught in her throat like a sob, and from the terrible look in his eyes, Rory already knows.

"I expect we'll see 1938 again soon enough anyway," Rory plows on ahead. "On the slow path."

1938 follows 1937 and 1936 before it, after all. They'll get there. They have to. They have no other choice. The Great Depression and World War II and then the Korean War and Vietnam and the Gulf; all of her twentieth-century history lessons, and why is it Amy can only remember the wars?

Right, mustn't allow herself to dwell on it. There must be good things to look forward to, too. Brighter stars. Rosie the Riveter and the Greatest Generation and Madison Avenue and Sputnik and the Beatles on Ed Sullivan. *Okay*, she tells herself firmly. *We can do this.*

First, though, they need shelter for the night, and period-appropriate clothing, and food, and money. Right at the start of the bloody Depression. Right.

"Right," Rory says resolutely. "We're not the only people who've had to start from scratch."

They find a tent village in the middle of the park, with fires in trash bins and a few weary men standing watch with rifles, but there's also a muscular woman ladling out thin soup into tin cups beneath a hand-painted sign that proclaims HOOVERVILLE in jagged letters. Amy and Rory exchange looks and then shuffle to the back of the queue. There's no shame in it, Amy reminds herself. They have no psychic paper to pave their way; no access to the Doctor's stash of random alien currencies. No TARDIS wardrobe, which Amy will mourn until the end of her days. So they'll make do as best they can.

A very pretty blonde woman barrels out of one of the tents. "Hey, anybody know where we can get some more clean water?" she demands of the group at large, her New York accent so thick that Amy can barely make out the word *water*. She looks out of place here, somehow different even in this particularly diverse sampling of humanity. "The doctor says boiled if you can."

Amy's ears prick right up at that, and she exchanges a quick glance with Rory. He shakes his head ever so slightly. Not *their* Doctor, of course not. But . . . still.

"Someone injured?" Rory asks, pitching his voice to be heard over the low mutterings of the group. "Only I'm a—medic. I mean, I can help."

Probably only Amy caught the hitch in his voice, when he almost called himself a nurse before remembering *when* they were and how odd a male nurse would be. They don't want to be too memorable, not now, not like this. They can't hop into a blue box and fly away when the pointed stares get to be too much to handle.

"*Someone?*" the blonde woman echoes, tone disbelieving. "Oh, honey, you must've missed all the excitement. We got lotsa someones hurt here. Yeah, sure, I bet she could use the help."

Amy follows them, her hand caught tight in Rory's, because she might never let him out of her sight again. And she can help, too. Though they probably don't have any defibrillators in Hooverville.

After showing them into the tent, the blonde goes off again in search of water. There are a number of injured men on cots—*recently* injured, even Amy can tell. Maybe that has something to do with the armed sentries they'd seen stalking the edges of the tent city.

The doctor inside is . . . not what either of them expected. She's young, for starters, about their age if that, and she's black. And female. Maybe 1930 in New York City is more progressive than Amy would've expected. She also feels clearly *off* in this place, like the blonde but different, in a way Amy can't quite put her finger on.

"You're a medic?" the doctor asks, pushing her hair back out of her face wearily. Her accent is pure London, another surprise. "Thank goodness, I can't tend them all at once and Tallulah . . . well, she tries, but. Here." She passes Rory an armful of bandages and steers them toward one of the younger men—hardly more than a boy—with awful burns across his face. The tent is haphazardly lit with kerosene lamps. Between the darkness and this young doctor's obvious exhaustion, it's no great wonder that she doesn't notice anything particularly strange about Amy or Rory.

Rory sets immediately to work, murmuring curt, simple instructions that Amy follows as best she can. "What happened to them?" he asks the doctor, keeping his tone pitched low and soothing for the wounded men's benefit.

The doctor laughs, short and strained. "You wouldn't believe me if I told you."

"Yeah, try us," Amy says under her breath, but the other woman doesn't hear. Satisfied with Rory's skill, she ducks out of their tent to go tend to some more injured men across the way. Their paths only cross a handful of times over the course of the long night, when the doctor checks in on their progress or Rory sends Amy out to scrounge for more supplies.

They never are introduced properly—though Amy overhears the blonde woman call the doctor *Martha* once—and it's only much later, when dawn starts creeping its way fitfully across the gray sky, that Amy realizes what felt so off about her.

Her clothes. Jeans and a leather jacket, and nothing remotely 1930 about them at all.

But when Amy goes to look for Martha in the morning, she's nowhere to be found.

2. London, 1941

The thing is, Rory's got a bit of an immortality complex. It's not that he thinks he's going to live forever. But he read the inscription on his own gravestone. That's a fixed point in time if there ever was one, and that says he's going to live to be eighty-two years old.

He's not exactly sure when that'll be—even before the angels, he and Amy had already spent long, fruitless hours debating how to factor in time traveling when calculating their actual, linear ages—but they've faked themselves identification papers now, and that'll probably be the age the undertaker counts in the end. So he's not going to die until around 1980, and that foreknowledge sometimes makes him . . . reckless. Just a bit.

Plus, he's died so many times at this point that he has trouble believing it'll ever actually stick.

It also doesn't help that he's lived through the entire twentieth-century once before already, and then some. He still doesn't think about that much—the Centurion's memories remain buried in the deepest recesses of his mind, rarely accessed—but sometimes he wakes up in the middle of the night in a cold sweat, scared half out of his mind that something might've happened to the Pandorica while he slept, grasping for a sword that isn't there.

Anyway, point is, there's no way in hell Rory's going to cool his heels in New York while London burns. Rory wants to punch some Nazis in the face. Or help evacuate some museums during air raids, at the very least. He has a unique skill set.

Amy, of course, is right there with him. She breezily reminds him that only one of them has advised Winston Churchill in his war room, thank you very much, and she's quite certain he'll be requesting her assistance again just as soon as he's made aware of her availability. And then her voice takes on a harder edge as she points out that just because he won't *die* in the Blitz doesn't mean he can't be maimed or crippled or live out the rest of his eighty-two years locked up in a mental ward, and she's seriously considering putting him there herself to keep him from doing anything stupid.

So they spend the Blitz dodging bombs and helping the war wounded in London hospitals. Rory might as well be a doctor himself at this point, and Amy's becoming a pretty decent field medic, though she spends most of her spare time writing cracking articles about the quiet war waged on the home front. In New York, she'd freelanced for several magazines, writing mostly travel and lifestyle pieces. Looks like she's gunning for a Pulitzer by war's end.

Rory's the one who hears rumors of a mysterious illness at Albion Hospital. In another life, he'd have set Amy on the trail and they'd both be up to their ears in trouble by nightfall. But this is real life, now. It has to be. There are far too many people in his own hospital who need him; he can't just drop everything and go haring off after adventure. And anyway, it might not be anything at all.

Besides, he's got a date with Amy at the local after his shift tonight, and there's no way he's missing out on that. This pub's become a particular favorite of the RAF lads of late, and Amy's always had a fondness for men in uniform. Best not chance it.

Sure enough, Rory arrives to find his wife holding court with a circle of admiring officers, each at least a decade her junior. It's a sight he wouldn't miss for the world. Rory left jealousy behind years ago; he trusts Amy completely. He *loves* seeing her like this, vibrant and beautiful as she was when they first married lord knows how many years ago (or ahead), laughing and flirting outrageously. She catches his eye across the smoky room and her lips curve into a crooked, heated smile that's all for him, only ever for him. God, he loves this woman.

Most of the men are scared off by the approach of the husband, more fools they; one handsome fellow braves it out, shifting easily to include Rory into the conversation. "I usually hate to hear that a beautiful woman is spoken for," he says, in a too-charming American accent, "but in this case, hell, who could blame her?"

Rory rolls his eyes and ignores the heat rising to his face. "Flattery will get you nowhere."

"On the contrary," the officer says with a wink. "I'm an easily acquired taste."

"He does grow on you," Amy agrees, linking her arm with Rory's. "Not unlike a fungus."

The officer's laugh is honest and full-throated. Rory can't help but be charmed. There's something strangely familiar about the man, itching at a dark, closed-off corner of Rory's mind. "Sorry," Rory says. "I didn't quite catch your name."

"Well, if it wasn't love at first sight, I'm always happy to walk by again."

The officer extends a hand, flashing a blindingly white smile. "Captain Jack Harkness."

The missing piece slots into Rory's memory—a pub not terribly unlike this one, during another Blitz, plastic flesh just as pliant and sensitive as real human skin, a few brief hours of distraction and companionship against a backdrop of war while the Pandorica rested unwaking in a not-yet-destroyed museum. That was a different Rory and a different Captain, though. It has nothing to do with the here and now.

It's an altogether pleasant evening, and though it's been a while since Rory and Amy invited anyone else into their bed, they certainly haven't forgotten the delightful mechanics of the act. The Captain's even more, ah, "open-minded" than they expected; a man well ahead of his time, they privately decide afterward. Someone like Jack would be far better suited to the stars.

A few days later, Rory realizes he'd never followed up on the rumors out of Albion Hospital. He heads across London early one morning before his shift, just to see what's what. But there's nothing amiss at Albion—in fact, they have no patients whatsoever at this time, and their head physician is in curiously high spirits for a man whose city remains under siege.

3. London, 1953

For once, Amy is willing to overlook being thought English instead of Scottish. If it means her editor will give her the plum assignment of covering the coronation, then pip pip cheerio it is. The queen-to-be won't ever quite measure up to Liz 10, but she's going to be a tough old bird, and Amy fully intends to see her reign start off right.

"So remind me why we're not enjoying the spectacle outside Westminster like everyone else?" Rory demands, looking around the slightly shabby suburban street celebration with some skepticism. Ugh, Amy's clearly still far too jetlagged for that much alliteration.

"Because every other fashion reporter on the planet will be writing the same exact story about the coronation. What sort of hat the Queen Mum is wearing, how lovely the young Queen looks, how many men in the honor guard, yadda yadda yadda. I'm not interested in pomp and circumstance." Amy strokes her notepad lovingly. "I want to know how the British *people* are celebrating the coronation."

She'd been shortlisted for a Pulitzer for her reporting of the Blitz, and it wasn't because she'd written about how many bombs the Germans had dropped or the speeches Churchill had given to rally the troops. She'd focused on the stories of ordinary Londoners adjusting to life at war, given voice to the everyman—and woman, of course. She wasn't about to sell out now.

Rory regards her fondly. "All right, then, what's it to be? The many qualities of home-brewed English lemonade?"

"The television revolution," Amy says. "Bringing the spectacle right into people's sitting rooms."

"You don't sometimes think that you're technically sort of cheating—"

"Not a chance, kiddo," Amy says airily. "Let's remember whose slightly advanced insights are paying the rent on our fabulous Gramercy Park townhouse, Mr. Miracle of Modern Medicine."

It's not that they're changing history by knowing it all already. In fact, they've been extraordinarily cautious. But Amy's certainly not the only one in this relationship who uses a bit of foreknowledge to get ahead in the workplace.

"So why here, in particular?" Rory asks, helping himself to a glass of lemonade from one of the tables set up along the street. He passes another glass to Amy.

It's a touch too sweet for her tastes, but she doesn't mind. "Apparently this neighborhood's got the highest rate of television ownership of all England. Magpie Electricals," she adds, nodding to a darkened storefront. "That shop singlehandedly placed a new TV in every sitting room on this street, just for the Coronation."

"How patriotic of them."

Amy gives him a wink and then saunters over toward the nearest clump of neighbors, pulling her notepad and specs out of her handbag. One thing she's rather fond of in the 1950s is the fashion—she can hardly bemoan the need for reading glasses when they come with adorable cat eye frames. She thinks they make her look clever and insightful, as befitting her advanced age. She turns fifty-five this year—well, give or take. Her hair's as much gray as red these days, but strangely enough, she doesn't mind. She's earned the gray hairs, every one.

"Excuse me, ladies," she says, joining a cluster of housewives of varying ages. "Amelia Williams, *New Yorker* magazine. Mind if I ask you a few questions about the festivities?"

The housewives preen a bit, pleased by the attention, though one older woman sniffs a bit at Amy's Scottish accent, undiluted even by twenty years living in the States. Still, they're quite happy to chatter away about how lovely the young queen looked and how brilliant it was to be able to see all that magnificence right from their very homes—though she notices that they all shy away from the topic of the televisions themselves, or the shop that sold them, with uneasy glances exchanged behind smiling masks.

One woman remains mostly silent, keeping herself somewhat apart from the rest of the group, though she'd been chatting happily enough with them before Amy's arrival. She's younger than the others, probably someone's unmarried daughter or niece; her pink poodle skirt is noticeably brighter than the average housewife's attire.

"And what do you think of Mr. Magpie's generous contributions to the event?" Amy asks her, with her warmest, most inviting smile.

The girl catches her tongue between her teeth, humor sparkling in her wide brown eyes. "Oh, I couldn't really say," she replies. She has the air of knowing a great joke that she's not quite willing to share. "It's certainly electrified the neighborhood."

"Rose!" someone calls, and the girl turns. A tall young man in a pin-striped suit is waving at her impatiently across the crowd.

"Sorry," Rose tells Amy, not sounding sorry at all. "I've got to run, yeah? Best of luck with the article, I'll be sure to look it up." She flashes an impish grin and darts off.

As the afternoon goes on, Amy realizes that none of the other house-wives had known Rose at all, nor had the faintest idea who she was or where she'd come from. And she never gets a satisfactory explanation about Magpie Electricals or their television sets. The elusive Mr. Magpie himself never returns to his shop at all.

4. Barcelona, 1966

For all that they maintain a lovely townhouse in New York, Rory thinks they spend less time actually at home these days than they ever did during their years with the Doctor. Retirement definitely has its perks. For example, the perk of sitting on a sun-drenched beach in Spain, surrounded by young people in flimsy swimwear (*Thank god for the sexual revolution*, he said once, and Amy swatted him and called him a dirty old man; one thing led to another, which really just proved her point, but she certainly wasn't complaining afterward), while his still-gorgeous wife frolics in the surf in a truly ridiculous floppy hat.

It's a very good day.

Once Amy's done splashing about, she's going to demand a cold drink. Rory knows her well. Might as well fetch one now and avoid the whinge-ing.

Fuck, *standing*. Standing is one of those things that really isn't a perk of getting old.

There's a man with a cart of drinks and ices further up the beach; Rory buys a couple of Cokes and pops one open there, enjoying it. Something will change in the chemical formula somewhere down the line, he suspects, because these taste better than he remembers from his youth in the future.

And there's a sentence he's become far too used to thinking.

"*Barcelona*," someone grumbles beside him. "It had to be sodding Barcelona, didn't it?"

Rory doesn't know why he engages the man, who clearly wasn't speaking to anyone in particular. Maybe because it's nice to hear another British accent every now and again, especially in an unexpected place. "What were you expecting?" Rory asks lightly. "Leicester Square?"

The man snorts. "Could do, if I'd a mind to it."

Rory gives him a quick look over. "You're clearly not of a mind for the beach, are you, in that get-up. Aren't you roasting?"

The stranger looks oddly offended at that, straightening the lapels of his beat-up leather jacket as though it were a tuxedo. "Don't know what you're on about. Better than sunblock, this. Keeps my delicate skin lily-pale."

He cracks a hint of a grin, and Rory laughs. "Right. Whatever floats your boat. At least get yourself a cold drink, will you? Sunstroke's no joke. Trust me, I'm a doctor." Well, close enough, anyway. And retired. But still.

The man's smile twists into something sharp-edged and bitter. "Aren't we all?" he mutters, as though to himself.

There's something weary about his manner, and angry, and sad. He's a couple of decades younger than Rory, at best guess, but he somehow seems much older. After a moment's consideration, Rory hands him the second bottle of Coke. "Here. Drink this. Don't want to dehydrate in this heat." At the stranger's quirked eyebrow, he adds, "My wife would only wind up stealing mine, anyway. She claims they taste better that way."

"Cokes?"

"Beverages of any kind," Rory says, long-suffering. "Soft drinks, booze, tea, you name it. She nicks my jumpers sometimes, too. She's down there," he adds, gesturing at the waves. "The madwoman in the floppy hat."

The other man passes the bottle from one hand to the other without actually drinking from it. "You're here on . . ." He grimaces in distaste. ". . . *holiday*, then?"

"Here, there, and everywhere," Rory agrees cheerfully. Shit, have the Beatles recorded that single yet? No matter. "Not many places we haven't traveled, us."

The man gives him a look that clearly says he very much doubts that. Well, Rory supposes they must look a couple of daft old bats to him. But then his gaze shifts, becomes intent. "If there was anywhere you could go," he says, all at once, "I mean *anywhere*, anywhere at all, not just Spain or Tokyo or Timbuk-bloody-tu, somewhere completely new and fantastic like you'd never imagined before—where would you go? Where would you take her?"

Home, Rory thinks at once, but of course he can't say that. He's not even sure quite what the word means anymore. He thinks about it for maybe too long of a moment, really considers the question, wondering what the man wants to hear.

He looks down the beach to Amy, who's digging her feet deep into the wet sand at the waterline like a child at play, giggling when the waves suck the sand around her toes. She glances over at him and smiles. She's pushing seventy now, and she can still make his breath catch in his throat with nothing more than a glance.

"I'd take her back to the moment when we first met," he says quietly. "Just . . . just so that we'd both know. Promise her that everything would be all right in the end. That it'd all be worth it. Because it was."

He tears his gaze away from his wife. The other man is still staring at him. Suddenly he grins, the smile cracking his face open, his eyes lit with a manic fire that's all at once familiar in the utterly unfamiliar face. "You're absolutely brilliant, you are!" he tells Rory, delighted. "Of course! Time! How did I never mention it travels in *time!*"

He shoves the unopened bottle back into Rory's hands. Rory grabs at it before it drops to the sand, his pulse suddenly racing. "You—"

"And *then*, maybe," the man goes on, still grinning like Christmas has come early, "Barcelona!"

He whirls around and is gone, dashing up the beach and away, and for one agonizing second, Rory nearly tears off after him. But then he glances back over his shoulder, and sees Amy walking across the sand toward him, her expression quizzical beneath that absurd hat, and he feels rooted to the spot.

Those days are long gone now. Besides, they're doing rather well for themselves, all things considered.

"Rory?" she calls. "Something wrong? Who was that bloke?"
"No one," he lies, managing a smile. "Here. I got you a Coke."

5. London, 1972

Amy will never write a full autobiography; there are too many stories she'll never be able to tell. But after nearly four decades of a public career in journalism, not to mention a Pulitzer (at long last!), she's managed to pull together a very creditable collection of memoirs. It helps that she's always known where and when best to position herself in search of the very best stories. She knows better than to try to meddle with history (*fixed points,* the Doctor whispers in her ear); she can only let the twentieth century unfold before her, in all its chaotic glory, and record as much of it as she possibly can.

The book sales have given her a nice little bump on the lecture circuit. When she's offered the opportunity to do a guest lecture at the London School of Journalism, she jumps at the chance. She's rather missed London these past few years.

Afterward, the usual cluster of bright young things gather around her podium, asking questions. Mostly male, of course, and while she certainly enjoys the eye candy, she's secretly thrilled to notice a few female faces among the throng. It's been a dreadfully slow process, living through Women's Lib on the slow path, but the times, they are a-changing. About damn time.

Even if the boys are the ones with all the questions, while their female counterparts still hang back around the edges and rarely get a word in edgewise.

One young woman today is more determined than most, and she actually manages to push her way to the front after the first ten minutes or so. She's younger than most of the other students, scarcely twenty, face still rounded with the lingering traces of childhood, her eyes bright beneath the dark fringe of her hair. Having shoved her way this far, she seems suddenly shy, mustering the courage to speak. Amy gives her an encouraging smile.

"Hello," the girl says in a rush. "Oh, my goodness, you're really Amelia Williams, aren't you?"

Amy barely manages not to snort with laughter. "I am indeed," she agrees, and the girl's face reddens.

"I mean—it's amazing, what you've done. What you've written. I used to clip your articles and hang them on my wall." She blushes even deeper, but forges on. "It's—your stories. I mean, they're not stories, they're *true*, but the way you write them—"

"I'll let you in on a secret," Amy tells her, leaning forward conspiratorially, and the girl leans in as well. "All stories are true. Even the ones you made up for yourself as a child, every last one of them." She smiles. "It might not sound like the best advice for good journalism, but really, what are we doing if not finding the truth and weaving it into words?"

"Oh," the girl says softly. "I hadn't thought of it that way."

When she doesn't say anything further, Amy prompts her. "Did you have anything in particular you wanted to ask, or . . . ?"

She bites her lip. "I only wanted to—that is, may I ask you to sign my book? Or your book, I mean. My copy of it. Only it would mean ever so much to me—"

"Of course," Amy says, suppressing a grin. She gestures imperiously and the girl passes the book over, eyes alight. It's a slightly worn copy, spine broken and pages dog-eared, clearly in the possession of a person who loves the words inside far more than she values the physical shell. Amy flips it open to the dedication page (*To the raggedy man who pointed me at the stars*) and twirls her fountain pen between her (not quite arthritic yet, thank you Rory) fingers. "To whom shall I make it out?"

"Oh!" the girl says. "To me. Sarah. That is, Sarah Jane Smith."

"Sarah Jane Smith," Amy echoes, writing it out. Such an ordinary name for such a bright-eyed young woman. Still, there's a kind of music in it, one that's all her own. "Shall I look for your name on the byline of tomorrow's papers?"

Sarah colors again at that, her cheeks tinting a light rose. "Perhaps not tomorrow," she says. Then her chin tilts up defiantly. "But the day after that, certainly!"

Amy laughs. *To Sarah Jane Smith*, she writes. *May all the stars be someday within your grasp.*

Looking at the young woman, Amy feels the strangest certainty that someday, they will be.

+1. Washington, D.C., 1969

It's been a hell of a long week. Hell, it's been a long several *months*, if he's going to be honest with himself. And if there's one thing Canton always tries to be, it's honest. Gotten him into all kinds of trouble, too.

Did he really admit to the goddamn President of the United States that he wanted to marry another man?

In the cozy sunlight of a Saturday morning at home, it all seems unreal, somehow. The Doctor, the Silence, tally marks on pale skin, wondering what was lurking just behind his back. He can't even remember what it was for. Can he?

He hears the shower running, and pulls on his robe, wandering out to the kitchen instead. Sam promised him pancakes this morning. Good thing, too, 'cause Canton can't cook worth a damn, and he's just about sick to death of cold coffees and greasy diner food. It's good to be home, and to know that he'll be staying here for a while.

Of course, that's when the damn doorbell rings.

"Seriously?" Canton asks the empty room. The dark, paranoid corner of his brain whispers that he really shouldn't have spoken so freely to the President, that he and Sam are breaking the law every damn day (twice or three times, actually, if they're lucky), that the Secret Service or the feds or the cops are here to arrest them both.

But that's not all that likely, and anyway, nothing he can do about it now if they are.

When the doorbell chimes again, he sighs and goes to answer it. Ten o'clock on a Saturday morning, for chrissakes. It's practically indecent.

A glance through the curtains on the front window reveals an unfamiliar older man and woman, maybe in their sixties or seventies, well-dressed, waiting patiently. Canton yanks open the door with a muttered curse. "If you're here to ask me if I've heard the good news, buddy, let me tell you—"

"Canton Delaware the third," the woman says, with a flourish. Her accent is . . . Scottish? "Surely you haven't forgotten us already?"

"It *has* been something like forty or fifty years," the man points out fastidiously.

"Not for him it hasn't!"

"Yes, but." The man gestures between them, with a fond sort of half-smile. "Well, look at us, Amy."

The penny drops. Canton gapes at them both. "Not—*Amy*? And Rory? But—"

"See!" Amy says triumphantly, and damn, now that he's looking properly, who else could it be? She gives him a brilliant smile, and it's as though decades fall off her face.

"But I just said goodbye to you yesterday!" Canton protests. "You were—"

"Time travelers, remember," Amy says, with a wave of her hand. "It's complicated. We've been waiting rather a long time to see you again. Now, are you really going to leave a fragile old lady like myself standing out on the front step all day?"

"Fragile, my left foot," Rory mutters. But he's grinning, too, as he links his arm in hers.

There's a story to be told here, make no mistake. And—well, what better way to spend a lazy Saturday than catching up with a couple of old friends? "Won't you come in?" Canton says with a courtly gesture, a matching grin growing on his own face.

"Don't mind if we do," Amy says airily as they step inside. "Now, first things first—Canton, aren't you ever going to introduce us to your young man?"

Canton laughs and kicks the door shut behind them.

The Detective's Tale

Title: Subliminal (2011)
Author: Speranza
Fandom: *Sherlock* (BBC)
Rating: Teen and up, slash (Sherlock/John)
Additional tags: footnotes, fun with formatting, POV Sherlock
 Holmes

Introduction

Sherlock Holmes is a product of nineteenth-century magazine culture. Born on the pages of *Beeton's Christmas Annual* and *Lippincott's Monthly Magazine*, Holmes really became popular in *The Strand*, which published a series of Holmes stories as well as *The Hound of the Baskervilles* in serial. If you were alive from 1891 to 1893, you could read a new Holmes story about once a month: "A Scandal in Bohemia" was published in July 1891; "The Red Headed League" in August 1891, "A Case of Identity" in September 1891, and so on.

If this regular production schedule seems familiar to you from television or the movies, you're right: nineteenth-century magazine culture is one of the first forms of mass media, and mass media is the matrix within which fanfiction developed. While one could certainly argue that there was fanfiction before mass culture—one could claim, for instance, that Virgil's *Aeneid* is Homer fanfic, or that the Arthurian tales are a kind of shared universe—I think it's useful to distinguish between fanfiction and these other forms of literary creativity, not because I think they're qualitatively or artistically different (I don't; they're not) but because the material and legal conditions under which they were created are different in ways that matter. The mass media give us industrialized storytelling: teams of professionals produce stories for us at a distance on a regular schedule for profit.[1] Television works this way (watch Fridays at 9:00!), as well as Hollywood movies (*Iron Man 3*), and even books are increasingly published as regular serials (*Harry Potter*, *The Hunger Games*, *Twilight*) or with the author as "brand" (one reads an Agatha Christie, a Stephen King, a James Patterson). It's not that different from making cars or computers or any other industrial product. In mass culture, there are professional producers (writers, actors, directors) and cultural consumers (whose role is the system is to buy and enjoy), but this is the system that fanfiction flouts: in fandom, the "consumer" is also an artist, who turns the industrial story into something local, idiosyncratic, personal, handmade.

It is from this perspective that Sherlock Holmes looks an awful lot like the first Western media fandom: before *Star Trek*, before *The Man from U.N.C.L.E.* The magazine culture in which Arthur Conan Doyle wrote his stories was not that different from the culture of network television (and Doyle often sounds hilariously like a disgruntled TV writer of old). Conan Doyle wrote the Holmes stories for money and published them regularly through the mass-media form of the monthly magazine. Like the Trekkies who organized the letter-writing campaign to save *Star Trek*, Holmes's fans saved him from "cancellation" by wearing black armbands after Doyle killed him in "The Final Problem." And Holmes was almost immediately taken up by other writers and artists, who drew pictures, wrote parodies, staged plays. In fact, Sherlock Holmes as we know him today is more of a collaborative product than most people realize. Doyle's Sherlock Holmes never wore a deerstalker hat or a tweed Inverness cape; the iconic image of him comes from illustrator Sidney Paget, whose drawings were published alongside Doyle's text in the *Strand*. Doyle's Sherlock Holmes never said, "Elementary!" either; that line was developed for Holmes by the playwright and actor William Gillette, who adapted Holmes for the stage in 1899 and who not only wore Paget's deerstalker but also added the famous curved briar pipe that gives Holmes his distinctive silhouette. Gillette also asked Doyle's permission to marry Holmes off to a female character in the play, prompting Doyle to cable back: "You may marry him, murder him, or do anything you like to him."

Fans of Sherlock Holmes have been doing anything they liked to him for over a century. There have been novels and stories, plays, movies, radio and television shows, comic books, board games, video games, and cartoons. Sherlock Holmes has fought the Nazis, been transported into the twenty-second century, met Sigmund Freud, worked as a private eye in Harlem, and been a mouse. As I write this, there are three active big-budget Sherlock Holmes serials going—the BBC's *Sherlock*, CBS's *Elementary*, and the blockbuster *Sherlock Holmes* movies directed by Guy Ritchie and starring Robert Downey Jr.—as well as many other adaptations, continuations, and revisions, as well as oodles of fanfiction.

The BBC's *Sherlock* series in particular has become a worldwide phenomenon, launching star Benedict Cumberbatch into international celebrity. The series sets Holmes and Watson in contemporary London and reimagines Holmes as "a high functioning sociopath" so completely plugged into the digital world that he's half-computer himself. Cumberbatch's Holmes is as sleek and modern as an iPhone, as is the show's cinematography and direction, and as Michele Tepper points out in "The Case of the Travelling Text Message," the show brilliantly integrates digital information into the televisual frame. Information important to Sherlock's work —text messages, clues, observations, and deductions—appear printed on the screen so that we in the audience can follow along, reminding us that a television is "just another screen in a multiplatform computing system," and showing us that "Sherlock views the whole world through the head-up display of his own genius."[2]

For example: in *Sherlock's* first episode, "A Study in Pink," Sherlock examines a dead woman in a pink raincoat, and we see words on the screen describing his observations: *wet* (the back of her coat), *dry* (her umbrella), *wet* (the back of her collar), *clean* (her bracelet), *clean* (her earring), *clean* (her necklace), and *dirty* (her wedding ring). This information leads Sherlock to make the following deductions, also displayed for us:

married
unhappily married
unhappily married 10+ years.

Sherlock takes the woman's wedding ring off and sees that it is *clean* on the inside even though it's *dirty* on the outside, and concludes that it was *regularly removed* and the woman was a *serial adulterer*. These words, too, appear on the screen.

In this way, *Sherlock* gives us direct access to Sherlock Holmes's thoughts: something that is rarely, if ever, done in prose versions. One of Watson's most important functions as a literary narrator is to keep us out of the detective's head, where presumably everything is obvious and elementary;

this preserves suspense and allows us to test our wits. Watson typically sees what Sherlock sees, but he can't interpret what he sees the way Sherlock does. In film and television, the camera often usurps Watson's function, dumbly showing us the story's clues without telling us what they mean. But in *Sherlock*, the creators use technology both literally and as a metaphor to give a sense of what it must be like inside the great detective's head: we get to see not just *what* Sherlock sees but *how* he sees. "What is it like in your funny little brains?" Cumberbatch's Sherlock groans. "It must be so *boring*," and *Sherlock*'s cinematography confirms this: Sherlock Holmes's brain teems with information.

The story that follows, Speranza's "Subliminal," translates *Sherlock*'s visual, digital Sherlock Holmes back into text. You might think that since *Sherlock* is itself an adaptation of Arthur Conan Doyle, translating *Sherlock* back into prose would just get you a Conan Doyle story. Not so: a translation of a translation often gets you something completely new, like putting a phrase into an online language translator and retranslating the result. You almost never get what you started with, and here, the result feels like a giddy mistranslation, almost steampunk: a digital character translated back into an analog world.

"Subliminal" is told from the point of view of the BBC's Sherlock, and Speranza uses distinctively prosaic means—punctuation and textual formatting—to show the reader how Sherlock's brain processes information. Sherlock's running observations and deductions about the case he is working are presented parenthetically and in subscript; so, for instance, Speranza introduces Sherlock's client thus:

> "Mr. (elocution lessons) Holmes?" he asks, standing (good posture) in the doorway. Sherlock ostentatiously lifts his eyes from his Blackberry, but does not otherwise move. The man (blue eyes) is wearing expensive (Fendi; SW1X; Peter Jones, David Mellor, Royal Court; fashion design; hairdressers; advertising?) glasses and (cuffs altered at least twice) a secondhand (*not* advertising, then) designer suit.

Here, as in the BBC's *Sherlock*, we are given direct access to Sherlock's unboring brain, in which we see Sherlock tapped into a running stream of subliminal information. It's too much for a normal person to process, but Speranza shows us that Sherlock hears a false note in his client's accent before he even looks at him. We also see a chain of associations and deductions spinning from the man's expensive eyeglasses: Fendi (the brand of glasses) has a flagship store located in in Chelsea, post code SW1X: from there, Sherlock mentally surfs the area around Sloane Square—Peter Jones and David Mellor are stores in the area; the Royal Court theater also is there; and Sherlock makes a provisional first guess at the man's profession: fashion design, hairdressing, or advertising. A few observations later, Sherlock changes his guess and decides (SW1X + expensive glasses - cheap shoes + elocution lessons = Royal Court) that the man must be associated with the theater, though not as an actor: he is too careless with his fingernails. The case proceeds from there.

Passages like the one above evoke both the showiness of *Sherlock*'s heads-up display as well as the original, almost magical, recitations that Holmes makes in the Doyle stories, for example,

> On the inside of your left shoe, just where the firelight strikes it, the leather is scored by six almost parallel cuts. Obviously they have been caused by someone who has very carelessly scraped round the edges of the sole in order to remove crusted mud from it. Hence, you see, my double deduction that you had been out in vile weather, and that you had a particularly malignant boot-slitting specimen of the London slavey. (Doyle, "A Scandal in Bohemia")

But not all of Sherlock's observations and deductions in "Subliminal" pertain to solving the case. Speranza also gives us a second set of observations that pertain exclusively to John Watson. In addition to being one of the first media fandoms, Sherlock Holmes was also an early slash fandom: Holmes and Watson's Victorian bromance is more or less canonical, and it's fairly easy to read their easy homosocial intimacy as anticipating or actually embodying modern homosexuality. While Sherlock and Watson have been adapted in many ways—World War II, twenty-second century, private eyes in Harlem, mice, and so on, as noted above—there has yet to be a mainstream adaptation in which Holmes and Watson are interpreted as gay, though many fans hoped that *Sherlock* would be that adaptation,[3] particularly since one of the show's creators, Mark Gatiss, is himself openly gay. So far this has not come to pass, though various characters in the world of the show have simply assumed that Sherlock and John are a gay couple, forcing John Watson, at least, to repeatedly deny it.

But in fandom, Sherlock Holmes and John Watson's love for each other has long been stipulated, though fans differ in their opinions as to how sexual their love is. (As I discuss in my essay "Sherlock as Cyborg," Sherlock/Watson is not only a slash pairing of long standing, but the character of Sherlock Holmes has also been claimed by the asexual community due to his articulated lack of interest in sex. More specifically, he is often seen as a romantic asexual: that is, someone who is not that interested in sex, but is emotionally interested—even in love with—John Watson.) In "Subliminal," Speranza shows us that one part of Sherlock's brain is tuned into John Watson at all times, and that attentiveness itself reads as sexy: Sherlock is aware of Watson's every move. Notably, however, all the information about Watson is pushed down into the story's footnotes—down below, in what one might call the story's sexual subconscious. "Subliminal" is a story that shows us the vast, chaotic stream of subliminal information that the great detective has trained himself to attend to—and it is also about his subliminal, or at least suppressed, attraction to Watson. Again we see fanfiction taking us places that we rarely get to go: here, into the buzzing, chaotic mind and repressed heart of the world's greatest detective.

Suggested Further Reading

The BBC's *Sherlock* has spurred much new interest in Holmes and historical Sherlock Holmes fandom, as well as in the new show itself. Roberta Pearson's "It's Always 1895: Sherlock Holmes in Cyberspace," first published in *Trash Aesthetics* (1997) and republished in *The Fan Fiction Studies Reader* (2014), is probably the seminal essay when it comes to Holmes and the bridge between the historical literary fandom and the fanfiction-writing media fandom that now largely exists online; Lynette Porter's *Sherlock Holmes for the 21st Century: Essays on New Adaptations* and Kristina Busse and Louisa Stein's *Sherlock and Transmedia Fandom: Essays on the BBC Series* are the two field-defining essay collections (both 2012). Ann McClellan's 2014 "Redefining Genderswap Fan Fiction: A *Sherlock* Case Study," close-reads particular stories, as does Anne Jamison's *Fic*, much of which is concerned specifically with *Sherlock* fandom and fanfic and which begins with a marvelous reading of the Sherlock fanfiction story "The Theory of Narrative Causality" by falling voices.

Subliminal

Speranza

The man arrives in the midst of foul weather. Mrs. Hudson shows him up. "Mr. (elocution lessons) Holmes?" he asks, standing (good posture) in the doorway. Sherlock ostentatiously lifts his eyes from his Blackberry, but does not otherwise move. The man (blue eyes) is wearing expensive (Fendi; SW1X; Peter Jones, David Mellor, Royal Court; fashion design; hairdressers; advertising?) glasses and (cuffs altered at least twice) a secondhand (*not* advertising, then) designer suit. His shoes (*very* interesting) are poorly made, and he has a messenger bag slung over his shoulder. He clears his throat (a shop assistant, perhaps, confined to the *back* of a counter), a trickle (Tube, no umbrella, raincoat taken from him downstairs by Mrs. Hudson) of rainwater running from his hairline (though *not* from the bag), obviously waiting to be invited into the flat. In the kitchen, John[1] looks up from his newspaper and sets down his mug of tea (SW1X + expensive glasses - cheap shoes + elocution lessons = Royal Court). Sherlock sighs, (anxious, willing to splurge on fees, discretion required) slides the Blackberry into his pocket, and rolls up to his feet.

The man comes forward at once, extending a hand (no rings, no watch, careless with his fingernails, tsk) and wearing (*not* an actor, then) a relieved expression. "Thank you so much for seeing me."

Sherlock (I haven't seen *much* of you; not yet) smiles mechanically. "Not at all,"

---

1. Nubbly gray jumper, faint purple shirt beneath; by what rubric does he dress himself? Reading the same article for the last fourteen minutes, eyes flicking up and down the far right-hand column of yesterday's *Guardian* ("Children among the Victims as Bomb Kills Nine"), which he selected over today's paper—readily available, sitting ignored on the table—which has no news of the Afghan war on its front page ("Lib Dems Humiliated in Barnsley," "Oasis to Play at Glastonbury in 2011"). Sherlock doesn't think there's much of a case here, but he's prepared to pursue the matter if it pulls John away from that damned newspaper. It does.

he says.[2] "My colleague," he says, raising his voice as he gestures carelessly toward John. "Dr. John Watson," and John stands up awkwardly[3] and smiles. He comes into the sitting room, and the man turns (oh, very interesting) to shake his hand, messenger bag swinging forward.

"Cup of tea?" John asks with his usual, boring good manners. "Or perhaps," (John's eyes have sharpened) "something stronger?" (He's *seen* something; what has he—? Hair, glasses, earring hole, shirt, tie—oh, what a wealth of information; the knot alone!— shirt: label, buttons, cuffs—) But John is still talking. "Calm your nerves," he suggests with a quick, understanding smile.

Sherlock huffs out a breath and crosses his arms (yes, fine; constriction of the pupil, tension lines at the corner of the lip, slight knotting of the shoulders; child's play; a child could do it; *emotionalism!*) as John goes to the sideboard and pours some whiskey into a tumbler. "Please. Have a seat," Sherlock says, and sinks back into his armchair. The man sets down his bag and sits opposite, gratefully accepting the whiskey from John, who then perches, casually,[4] on the desk.

"So: Mr. Markham," Sherlock says, with a flip of his hand. "Tell me about yourself. Other than that you're twenty-eight and a playwright, originally from Sheffield but currently living somewhere in the vicinity of Regent's Park, spending a year writing in residence at the Royal Court, experimenting with veganism, and are going out with a woman called, hm, Rachel, I know hardly anything about you. Why should anyone steal your laptop?"

Pleasingly Mr. A. (Alan? Alex? Doesn't matter) Markham's mouth falls open. Sherlock cuts a glance at John[5], who meets his eyes and nods almost imperceptibly, mouth curving at one corner. Markham reaches down and yanks his bag into his lap without seeming to realize he's doing it. "I'm not experimenting," he says faintly. "Animal agriculture takes a devastating toll on the—"

Sherlock ignores this. "What's on your laptop?" he inquires.

Markham clutches his bag to his chest. "My new play."

---

2. —and John is poised to get up, trying to decide whether to get up. Courtesy? Insecurity? He glances back at the paper—

3. Bracing a hand on the table as he gets up; subliminal reaction to Afghanistan?

4. Or perhaps not so casually. He's pretty sure John has slipped his revolver into his pocket when he went over to the sideboard. Still, he *seems* relaxed, though he's got one foot on the floor and he's holding himself in such a way that he could probably spring into action pretty quickly.

5. It was almost a sickness. He couldn't remember ever being so pathetically desperate for approval, not since his mother died. *She* had appreciated his deductions as if they were a magic trick, designed to amuse her. But John took them as a challenge, a superior version of the cryptic crossword.

Sherlock waves him on. "What else?"

"*Nothing* else!" Markham looks offended. "Moreover, someone's tried to *kill* me for it!"

"I find that highly unlikely," Sherlock replies.

"Twice," Markham insists, and murder, even attempted murder, is, of course, always interesting. He tilts his head to the side (scrapemarks on his shoes; grease stain on his right elbow), and considers. He decides that Markham's story, while implausible, is hardly impossible.

"All right, go on." Sherlock lets his head roll back and stares up at the faint cracks (297) in the ceiling. He steeples his fingers. "Tell me of this manuscript worth killing for."

"Well." Markham seems taken aback. "It's about a girl who works at a chippy in—"

"I retract the question." Sherlock sits up straight; John[6] has slipped out of the room. He doesn't miss a beat. "Is it at all based in reality? Biography, a newsworthy story—?"

"No."

"—rehashing a local sex scandal, perhaps? Extortion, racketeering, a political misstep?"

"*No*," Markham repeats, frustrated. "It's about the *postindustrial decline* of a warm, vibrant community, blighted by the *systematic abuse* and *underinvestment* of an alien and remote . . ." Here Sherlock stops listening. (If that stain is to be believed, the second attempt of Markham's life happened today, and the first no more than three days ago, judging from the weather and condition of those terrible shoes. He'd guess Saturday last, sometime after Markham and Rachel had dined out for their three-year anniversary. They'd spent too much on dinner, and Mr. Animal Agriculture had had fish, no doubt sustainably sourced. He'd bought her a gift from Tiffany's, she'd bought him an iPhone cover from Crumpler; he

---

6. John moves with a stealthiness that you wouldn't assume, that even *he* had not surmised. He had initially misread the clue of John's boring clothes: yes, they caused one to disregard him, but not because John was a shy, self-effacing personality cursed with the typical Englishman's utter lack of style. Rather, his sacklike garments gave him a tactical advantage: he could move about without being particularly noticed, and he could act fast, and with astonishing agility, if he needed to. Sherlock himself has taken the opposite tack, making himself as conspicuous as possible, the better to mislead; after all, someone looking for a tall, artistically dressed young man is hardly likely to register the stooped old geezer selling papers as the same person. It's simply not how the brain works.

But now he *has* noticed. He's seen the wiry strength in John's arms, in his thighs; he's seen John's cool decisiveness in action. And now that he's seen, he can't unsee it, and it seems impossible that no one else sees John for what he is. Yes, of course, human perception is notoriously faulty, and misdirection is easy if you know how, but it's as if he's got a loaded gun lying about, like he's wearing a hand grenade around his neck. An unconcealed weapon; that's what John is. It makes him shiver to think of it.

wanted to marry; she, sensibly, didn't. Still, there was nothing to indicate that Rachel actually wanted him dead, though she was a more likely suspect than—) ". . . one of the members of my writing group," Markham was insisting. "Warwick, for instance, would *kill* to have a play this good. He's been stuck on his verse drama about John Major for *years.*"

The fool! "Would you *please*—" but wait, wait, wait, it's *there*, he *has* it. Though he doesn't know what it *is* yet, only that it just zipped past, tripping all his wires and making his nerves sing. Suddenly he *must move* (scrape; stain; Oxford knot; terrible shoes; sustainable fish) and he gets up to pace (anniversary; Tiffany's; iPhone; Crumpler; proposals) pressing his fingertips to his temples. (Warwick; verse drama; John Major—wait, go back. Go back.) He slows, stops, stares with unseeing eyes. (Tiffany's. A tiny, silver pull hanging from the zip of Markham's messenger bag: T&Co. Shiny despite the run of terrible weather; only days old; a token given with compliments to the purchaser of an expensive anniversary present.) And that's it—he's fumbling his Blackberry out of his pocket, (Tiffany's; jewels; missing) and it's all right there. A minor story, a single paragraph buried deep in the paper, because in this day and age, £30,000 hardly qualifies as a heist. In fact, the take was so small that the article's last line questioned whether the gems had actually been stolen; possibly they had been misplaced. That was what had caught Sherlock's attention—the idea that, by thinking small, a thief might do quite well. Sherlock had also been impressed by the shop assistant's outrage and bewilderment, which had come across quite clearly.

The satisfied rush nearly knocks him over. "You went to Tiffany's because it's just across the square from the Royal Court. You bought Rachel a ring—"

"Bracelet," Markham says sullenly.

"No one cares, least of all her. What's important is that you were carrying a large messenger bag with several outside pockets."

Markham's face is purpling unexpectedly. "I'll have you know—"

"It was Saturday, and the store was relatively full. Among the patrons was a thief who had managed to pilfer several rings from a temporarily unobserved velvet tray. However, he either suspects that he has attracted unwanted attention or otherwise gets cold feet, and so he manages to drop the jewelry into your bag, most likely into that gaping rear pocket."

"I'll have that." The voice is a little muffled, because the man who has appeared in the doorway is wearing a latex mask of Margaret Thatcher's face, but the gun's clearly visible. Markham swallows and clutches the bag to his chest.

"Ah, Maggie, you're looking surprisingly well," Sherlock says. "Still mugging the arts, eh?"

"Cut the comedy and give me the bag," the man says.

"No," Sherlock says, almost gently.

"No," John agrees, and there's an audible click[7] as he chambers a round. He looks at Sherlock and says, "I assume you've got handcuffs around here somewhere?" in the same voice he uses to say, "Come on, now; where've you hidden the sugar?"

"Yes.[8] Hang on, I'll fetch them," he says, and it only takes a moment's rummaging through drawers before he comes up with a serviceable pair of cuffs. He tosses them over.

John snatches them out of the air with one hand. "Ta very," he says, and goes to it, pushing Margaret Thatcher face first into the wall and cuffing his hands tightly.[9]

Markham is gaping between them. Sherlock strides over to him and says, "The bag, please?" After a moment's hesitation, Markham reluctantly hands it over. Sherlock fishes about in the pocket meant to house an eco-friendly, BPA-free, stainless steel water bottle and comes out with sparkle and fire. The six rings are exquisite; four feature diamonds in various avant-garde arrangements; the fifth is a starburst; the sixth, a single square-beveled emerald. He holds them in his palm and pokes at the discreet silver-backed price tags. £6,890, £11,340, £3,350. Hardly top of the line, but together, even more than £30,000. He wonders if Tiffany's routinely writes this sort of theft off as a minor expense.

He extends his palm to Markham, who blinks at the gems in surprise. "The good news is that it wasn't your play they were after," Sherlock tells him. "The bad news, I suppose, is that it wasn't your play they were after. Still," he says, stuffing them into his pocket, "I'm sure you'll make a success. Perhaps you'd be so kind as to send us two tickets when it opens."

The next hour or so is consumed with telephone calls and visits from the police. Lestrade comes over personally to take possession of the gems

---

7. The sound gives him an erection, but that's nothing to be ashamed of surely?

8. Actually, he has several pairs of handcuffs, but he's always losing track of them, so he's glad to find some without difficulty. He's reasonably sure there's a pair in one of his shoeboxes, but he'd hated to have to have gone to the bedroom for them; it would send the wrong message (or possibly not?)

9. He wonders if the direct approach would work. What would happen if he just went up to John, pushed him back against the wall, and thrust a hand up his jumper? John would deck him in all probability. But it was far from a certainty. There had been various indications . . . But his deductions regarding John had so far only been 68 percent correct. And John had turned out to be an incalculably invaluable flatmate. He needed to act with reasonable certainty that this particular deduction would not fall into that horrifically amateurish 32 percent.

and, secondarily, Maggie, who turns out to be an enterprising young man from Battersea.

Once they're gone, John grins and stretches his arms behind his back. His nubbly gray jumper rises up, revealing the tails of his faint purple dress shirt.[10] "Well," John says, turning for the kitchen, "I call *that* a productive morning,"[11] and Sherlock puts a hand on his arm. John looks at him inquisitively and Sherlock pushes John against the wall and thrusts a hand up his jumper. And then he waits for what will happen, his body tense as a bow.

But John only says, "Yes," and then, "All right," and when Sherlock finally meets his eyes, everything's there on the surface.

---

10. Striptease of the damned, and yet his heart beats fast.

11.—and certainty is overrated, is it not? Sherlock's never cared much for poems himself, but he's fairly sure that all the best ones are always blathering on about risk, the virtues of venturing all for love and so on and so forth. Granted, these are alien feelings, but he has more than a passing familiarity with the joys of spontaneity and the perils of boredom. Moreover, he has always surmised that the anxiety famously associated with the early stages of romance—the feelings vulgarized as "butterflies in the stomach" and the like—are in fact actually indistinguishable from the pleasurable feelings of that same stage; anxiety being not a side effect of pleasure, but the very thing itself! He has further surmised that the underlying pleasure/pain is caused precisely by a vertigo-inducing lack of certainty: in one's self, in one's partner; in the potential welcomeness of one's advances. He theorizes that a lack of certainty is synonymous with excitement. Sherlock finds himself very excited.

The Demon Hunter's Tales

Title: Wolf Man's Party (2012)
Author: Mollyamory
Fandom: *Supernatural / Teen Wolf*
Rating: Teen-and-up audiences
Tags: crossover, humor, fluff, crack

Comic: Supernatural, aka The Boys in Arizona (2010)
    and Fanservice Sequel
Artist: Glockgal
Fandom: *Supernatural*

Introduction

No collection of fanfiction would be complete without a crossover—that is, a story in which characters from one universe get to meet and interact with characters from another. Even when done by professionals, the crossover is an essentially fannish genre: what else but fannish love is behind the desire for Abbott and Costello to meet Frankenstein, or to put together a team like The League of Extraordinary Gentlemen, where classic literary characters like Alan Quartermain, Mina Harker, The Invisible Man, Dr. Jekyll, and Captain Nemo team up to defend the British Empire? But fans have always told more and better crossovers than the pros, because they don't have to care about the practicalities of creative production or about copyright or other intellectual property rights. Fans want to know who would win in a fight, Captain America or Superman, and they don't care that one of these characters comes from Marvel and one comes from DC. They're still going to fantasize about that smackdown.[1] They want to know which house Leslie Knope of *Parks and Recreation* would be sorted into at Hogwarts, and have invented entire genres like Superwholock, which crosses the shows *Supernatural*, *Doctor Who*, and the BBC's *Sherlock*.

While there are some fans who will write crossovers just for the sheer challenge of it—isn't everything better if you add vampires?—others write them for the joy of seeing similar but distinct worlds mesh.[2] The story that follows, Molly's "Wolf Man's Party," is one of this kind: a crossover between *Supernatural*, a show about two brothers, Sam and Dean Winchester, who hunt demons, ghosts, monsters, and other supernatural creatures, and *Teen Wolf*, a show about a teenager who learns to deal with becoming a werewolf with the support of his friends and family (some of whom are themselves werewolves, were-coyotes, were-jaguars, banshees, or kanima, which are a kind of lizard creature that results when a werewolf bite goes wrong, which sometimes it does).

I think you can see the crossover potential already.

Molly plays the situation for its full comic effect, summarizing the story as one "in which Dean and Sam Winchester investigate reports of a high school lacrosse team in Beacon Hills, California almost entirely comprised of werewolves, and the expedient application of chocolate chips to the problem first endangers, then saves, several lives." This is a terrifyingly accurate summary of the story, but not only does Molly set up the situation in which fandom's favorite hunters go after fandom's favorite werewolves, but she also uses the crossover to showcase aspects of the various characters' idiosyncratic personalities.

So, for example, when we meet Dean Winchester, he's holding a gun on Melissa McCall, mother to eponymous teen werewolf Scott McCall; Dean is also munching a chocolate chip cookie and reflecting on his time in Purgatory. All these things are characteristic of Dean, who's clocked some hours in the underworld and who is a lusty eater, messily chomping down on some food or snack at least once an episode. Fans of Dean will also not be surprised to see him attracted to the young and sexy Melissa McCall, who, with her chocolate chip cookies and her arsenal of weapons, would be just his type. Other characters who turn up are as deftly characterized: Scott's best friend Stiles Stalinski (not a werewolf) is snarky and courageous and vaguely in love[3] with Derek Hale, the fearsome werewolf with a heart of gold who arrives midway through the story to save Scott. It's not implausible that *Supernatural*'s hunters, Sam and Dean Winchester, might have crossed paths with *Teen Wolf*'s hunting family, the Argents, and even that they might have had some embarrassing sexual encounters: Sam Winchester did in fact spend most of *Supernatural* season 6 soul-less and sleeping around. And when the angel Castiel appears at the very end of Molly's story, dottily talking about bees, that's in character too: Castiel decides at one point on the show not to intervene in human affairs anymore: "Outside today in the garden I followed a honeybee. I saw the route of flowers. It's all right there, the whole plan . . . I don't fight anymore. I watch the bees" *(Supernatural* season 7, episode 21).

A story like "Wolf Man's Party" stages a kind of multifandom cocktail party: put all these characters in a room and watch them interact in a snark-off. If the classic fanboy crossover involves fighting—Captain America versus Superman, the Hulk versus The Thing—fanfiction more typically brings characters together to battle wits or have sex, or best of all: both. As Dean observes in this story: when sex is involved, even weird things make sense.

I have also included, for your enjoyment and edification, a short comic: "Supernatural, aka The Boys in Arizona," by Glockgal. A noted fandom artist, Glockgal was inspired by The Racebending Revenge Ficathon—a 2010 challenge to "Re-write one or more white characters in the fandom(s) of your choice as chromatic/non-white/PoC" with "some acknowledgment of how the racial difference would make a difference to the story being told."[4] Glockgal's comic tells the story of a Sam and Dean who have brown skin, and consequently find it a lot harder to exist in their universe. Their story is over fast—too fast—as they are pulled over, arrested, and eventually deported.

Racebending gets its name not only as an analogy to "genderbending" but also from a fannish protest that happened around the whitewashing of *Avatar, the Last Airbender,* whose chromatic characters were cast with white actors in the live-action film. The characters of *Avatar* have special powers over the air, water, earth, and fire: that is, airbending, earthbending, firebending. Racebending, therefore, is a similar power: one that fans have:

> We want to know how a man called Sherlock Holmes in Victorian England would function if his skin was the colour of soot, or what Latino Dean and Sam Winchester would do to convince people to trust them, and if Buffy the Vampire Slayer can be Asian and still save the world (a lot).

Glockgal's racebent comic resonated strongly in fandom, and not just among fans of color. Sam and Dean Winchester canonically drive around in an old car with a trunk full of weapons. That story seems to depend on them being white—or, to flip it around, Glockgal's comic is an important reminder that *Supernatural*'s fantasy road trip isn't available to everyone. As a follow up, Glockgal produced the Fanservice Sequel, a comic directed at fans who claim race doesn't matter to them; it depicts a *Supernatural* fangirl who stops liking her favorite characters once they're not white. Here, as is so often the case in fandom, the personal becomes political, and popular culture becomes a means of tackling important cultural issues of desire and of representation.

Suggested Further Reading

Catherine Tosenberger's 2010 special issue on *Supernatural* fandom— "Saving People, Hunting Things"—in *Transformative Works and Cultures* is a good guide to the field, and includes several essays on different kinds and modes of *Supernatural* fanfiction, as well as vids, role-playing games, wikis, and other fannish works. Lynn Zubernis and Katherine Larsen have collaborated on several books on *Supernatural* and its fandom, including *Fandom at the Crossroads: Celebration, Shame, and Fan/Producer Relationships* (2012), *Fangasm: "Supernatural" Fangirls* (2013), and the essay collection *Fan Phenomena: "Supernatural"* (2014).

For more on crossovers, see Julie Flynn's 2010 essay "Dean, Mal and Snape Walk into a Bar: Lessons in Crossing Over," in Heather Urbanski's *Writing and the Digital Generation*. Natalia Samutina has an article "Fanfiction as World-Building: Transformative Reception in Crossover Writing," in *Continuum*, and Paul Booth's 2016 book *Crossing Fandoms: SuperWhoLock and the Contemporary Fan Audience* theorizes the incredibly popular triple-crossover of *Supernatural*, *Doctor Who*, and *Sherlock*.

Media fandom has also become increasingly conscious of race—and fandom's failings when it comes to race—as Glockgal's comics demonstrate. Scholars of fandom are trying to catch up too: Sarah N. Gatson and Robin Anne Reid edited a 2012 special issue, "Race and Ethnicity in Fandom," for *Transformative Works and Cultures*, and Mel Stanfill has been writing about fandom and whiteness in articles like "Doing Fandom, (Mis)doing Whiteness: Heteronormativity, Racialization, and the Discursive Construction of Fandom," (*TWC*, 2011) and "Straighten Up and Fly White: Whiteness,

Heternormativity, and the Representation of Happy Endings for Fans" in Lucy Bennett and Paul Booth's *Seeing Fans: Representations of Fandom in Media and Popular Culture* (Bloomsbury Academic, 2016). That book also gives us Rukmin Pande's "Squee from the Margins: Racial/Cultural/Ethnic Identity in Global Media Fandom." Lastly, Rebecca Wanzo recently published an important piece in *Transformative Works and Cultures*, a call to arms entitled "African American Acafandom and Other Strangers: New Genealogies of Fan Studies" (2015).

Wolf Man's Party

Mollyamory

Dean's been off his game since he got back from Purgatory. Oh, he's sharp enough, and quick enough, and he gets the job done. But things throw him off, things he knew he could have dealt with a year ago. Like how weird it is to look at humans now and understand that they're just humans—not something infinitely nastier walking around in a human-shaped meat-suit. Like watching TV late at night and losing the plot because he's thinking about how strange electricity is. Like scouting out a nest of werewolves and getting sidetracked by the smell of fresh-baked cookies.

It's not that he's going crazy, he assures himself. It's just culture shock.

"I'm usually really good at this," Dean tells the woman holding the gun on him. "A year ago, I'd just show up, pop the kid over there with a silver bullet, and be out of here before you made it downstairs." He gestures at the boy with the hand holding the half-eaten stolen cookie, *not* the hand holding his own gun. He's a little off his rails, but he hasn't gone entirely stupid.

The woman raises her gun anyway, like she's as nervous about the cookie as she is about his Glock. Her hair is tied back from her face with a blue scrunchy, and she's wearing a threadbare blue robe over a cute little pajama shorts set that shows off her long bare legs. A little old for him, Dean judges, but not by much. Maturity alone is an insufficient deterrent. Maturity plus maternal instinct and a twitchy trigger finger is a sure-fire boner-killer.

Slowly—carefully—Dean lowers the cookie. He keeps the gun trained on the werewolf. "Let's just all observe how nobody has shot anybody yet," he says. "So far, nobody's having a bad day."

"You're pointing a gun at my son," the woman says coldly. "I'd say that makes this a pretty bad day for all of us." The barrel of her shotgun bobs in warning. "Especially you."

Dean nods. "Fair enough. But in my defense . . . your kid's a werewolf."

"I *know* that. That doesn't give you the right to break into my house and threaten him!"

"O . . . kay." Dean can roll with that. "Let's define our terms. Werewolves are monsters. Monsters kill people. I'm a hunter. I hunt monsters. If you've got a monster in your house, I'm kind of morally obligated to break in and threaten it."

"Him," the werewolf's mom says grimly.

"Whatever. I got to tell you, lady, after the initial freakout, a solid 60 percent of the suburban homeowners I've met have walked away considering me one of the good guys."

"Well, probably the monsters you were hunting weren't their kids!"

The werewolf's head whips around, an incredulous, hurt look in his yellow eyes. "*Mom!*"

She cuts him a brief glance. "Sorry, Scott. But you are kind of . . ."

The werewolf—Scott—rolls his eyes, which turn from yellow to dark brown as his teenaged indignation reaches a peak. The tufts of hair on his face sink back beneath the skin, and his claws resolve themselves into raggedly bitten fingernails.

"Happy now?" he growls. But it's exactly the kind of growl Dean always got when he made Sam do the dishes, not a wolfy growl at all.

"Look," Dean says. "I've actually got a pretty enlightened outlook on the whole monster deal these days. Maybe we could all just sit down and talk. I would hate to alienate the baker of these really, really awesome cookies by ganking her pet werewolf if it's not totally necessary."

"It's really, really not necessary," Scott says. "I'm like, *completely* harmless."

"Me, too."

Dean drops the cookie, and quicker than thought his backup piece is in his hand, trained on the new kid in the door to the hall. The new kid has a mostly shaved head and a pointy face and isn't a werewolf as far as Dean knows, but it pays to be careful. Missing the cookie already, Dean wiggles his new gun at the new kid. "Who're you?"

"I'm Derek," the kid says firmly, eyes cutting over to Scott in a suspiciously meaningful way. "Scott's friend Stiles called me when he heard all the commotion downstairs, and so of course I said everybody should sit tight and not do anything stupid, because I'd be right over."

Dean frowns. "No offense," he says, "But you don't really look like the kind of guy I'd have on speed dial for ass-kicking."

"No offense," the kid says, "but you're kind of old, and it looks like you've been dining at the Tollhouse a *lot* lately. I could probably take you."

"Hey!" Dean says, glaring.

"*Stiles*," Scott says, groaning.

"Scott!" the kid who clearly isn't Derek says, clutching at his nonexistent hair. "Oh my god, what is wrong with you?"

"All right!" Mom says loudly. "Everybody calm down!"

Dean wouldn't have expected the Mom Voice to work on him, given his lack of early home training. But apparently it's an instinct, or a genetic memory or something. Like flatworms. Against his will, he finds himself calming right the fuck down.

Not, he reminds himself, that he was all that excited to start with. It's just *one werewolf*, after all. After Purgatory, one werewolf is barely enough to get him out of bed in the morning.

"I'm calm," he says, bobbing his head reassuringly. "You?"

"I was never *not* calm," the woman says.

Dean says, "I love that about you."

Scott looks from Dean (smirking) to his mother (blushing) and his eyes pop over to yellow again. "Down, boy," Dean says. "A guy can look, right?"

"Not at my *mother!*"

"Not while you're pointing a gun at my kid," she says regretfully.

The other kid, Stiles, stares at her open-mouthed. He says, "Seriously? That's how it is? No shooting Scott, but pointing a gun at me is totally cool with you? Thanks. I've only sat at your breakfast table about a *billion times* in my short and soon-to-be-terminated life, but I suppose that doesn't warrant any concern or loyalty. It's blood or nothing with you people. It's so not fair!"

Dean has spent the last five minutes or so stalling by mouthing off, buying time for Sam to finally check his text messages and get his ass over here for backup and a little light mayhem before bedtime. So when Stiles starts babbling about nothing, apparently for no reason, Dean recognizes the tactic and instantly snaps to full attention. (Two kids and a MILF only rate half his attention these days, even if one of the kids is a werewolf.)

"So this Derek guy," Dean says to Stiles. "He's really on his way over here right now, I take it?"

"Wow, genius, you cracked my clever code," Stiles says.

"About how long would you say it'll take—"

"Not very long at all," a voice says from behind Stiles in the hallway, and then there's Dean, a mom, a kid, a little werewolf, and a seriously fucking huge werewolf, all piled into one tiny kitchen.

The big werewolf is pissed. He's got bright red eyes and he's all furred out, claws unsheathed on both hands. His face is rippled and twisted into a snarl. He steps in front of Stiles and gently pushes him back with one giant—hand? Paw? Dean's not sure of the proper terminology when they stop halfway between forms, but it's a secondary problem. The primary problem is he's looking at two werewolves, an armed mom, and a smartass right now, and while he's not yet out of guns, he's definitely running short on hands to point them with.

"Okay," Dean says. "Before I start evening the odds, can I get a round of names? My internal monologue is getting a little cluttered."

"He's Derek," Stiles says. "Me, you know. That's Scott, that's Scott's mom—"

"That's not my first name, Stiles," Scott's mom snaps.

"Melissa," Stiles says. "Sorry."

"Ms. McCall," Scott growls.

"I'm Dean," Dean says politely, and jerks his head toward the kitchen door, smiling. "And that's Sam."

The kitchen door flies open, glass shattering and falling to the linoleum floor in a bright, cheery clatter. Sam crashes into the kitchen in a far less ninja-like manner than Dean had been hoping for, landing in a sprawl between the refrigerator and the center island. He's bleeding from what appears to be a small boot print on one cheek, and there's a sleek black arrow sticking out of the arm of his jacket. He pops to his feet and scrambles over to stand next to Dean, a position of solidarity that would have a lot more meaning if he weren't completely ass-kicked and unarmed.

Sam tugs at the arrow and wiggles it around. Dean grabs at Sam's arm, scanning for blood. "Are you *punctured?*"

"I'm fine," Sam says, shaking him off and giving the arrow another frustrated yank. "But this jacket was new."

A tiny girl with flying black hair launches herself through the door and into Scott's arms. He grins, spins her around, and plants a kiss on her adorable, upturned nose. "This is Allison," Scott says smugly. "My girlfriend."

"Ex-girlfriend," Allison says.

Scott, surprisingly, beams at her. She beams back. Stiles the smartass and Derek the werewolf exchange a stunningly executed, synchronized eye-roll of disgust.

"We've met," Sam mutters, carefully not looking at Dean.

Allison detaches herself from Scott and saunters over. She's wearing black leather boots, a black leather miniskirt, and a black cashmere turtleneck sweater. In one hand she's carrying a gorgeous black crossbow; a black quiver of black arrows is slung over one shoulder. She plucks Dean's guns out of his hands, takes them to the sink, drops them in, and turns on the water. Then she holds out a hand.

Sam gives the arrow a final twist, frees it from his jacket, and hands it to her. "For the record," he says, "you mostly missed."

Dean turns to Sam. "Dude. You got your ass kicked by a little goth Katniss. You suck. And you owe me guns and ammo, by the way."

"Sorry about your face," Allison says to Sam. She pats him on his non-bleeding cheek, and gives him a wicked smile. "You shouldn't leave it lying around on the ground like that."

Sam makes a noise halfway between a groan and a whimper; Dean can only assume he's imagining the abundance of joy this moment will bring his brother for years to come.

"Dean," Melissa says sweetly, "Sam. Maybe now we could discuss this problem like civilized people."

Dean raises his eyebrows. "We could if all of us *were* people." He looks pointedly at Derek, still fully fur-faced.

"Hey," Stiles says, "Werewolves are people! They're like—people, plus!"

Derek bares his teeth at Stiles. Dean is mildly alarmed, until Stiles goes red in the face and smiles at Derek. All becomes clear: *Werewolf flirting.* Of course there would be teeth involved.

"I'm sensing a lack of objectivity on your part," Dean says to Stiles. "Just a little."

"Stiles is right," Melissa confirms. "Werewolves are people. My son is people. Derek is people."

"Jackson, Erica, Boyd, and Isaac are people, too," Derek says.

Sam's eyes go wide. "There are *six* of you?"

"Seven, if you count Derek's uncle," Scott says.

Stiles shudders dramatically. "We don't."

"He's a dick," Scott says. "If you absolutely have to kill a werewolf tonight, I vote for him."

"Oh, well, if we're voting," Stiles says, and raises his hand. Allison and Scott raise their hands, too. Melissa raises the hand not currently menacing Dean and Sam with the shotgun.

Derek's fur, claws, and snarl retract. His eyes change from red to brown. Honestly, it doesn't make that much of a difference. He makes a face that could curdle milk and says, "We're not *voting*. This isn't *Survivor*."

Scott's eyes widen. "You watch *Survivor*? . . . wait. You have a *television*?"

Derek hunches his shoulders, and looks at the floor.

"I may have had an episode on one night," Stiles says. "Possibly two nights, last fall, you know, after the whole Kanima thing, but before random people started showing up in our kitchens in the middle of the night trying to kill us? There was maybe one night when Derek came over for, uh, research purposes. Maybe two nights. To collect some very important research. That I had done, for him, that you guys don't know about because—"

Derek drops his head into his hands.

"*Because*," Stiles finishes desperately, and presses his lips firmly together.

There's a brief moment of silence to memorialize the big scary werewolf's lost dignity. Then Dean clears his throat and says, "Back to the headcount?"

"Seven werewolves, two hunters," a new voice says from the demolished doorway.

"Dad!" Allison says.

"Sweetheart," the guy says. He's a lean blond guy with weird blue eyes and an extremely threatening smile. The giant crossbow he's cradling in his arms like a baby only adds to that impression.

Sam stares at the new guy in round-eyed surprise. "Chris—?" he says. "*Sam?*"

"Brad?" Dean asks the ceiling. "Janet!?"

Stiles barks out a hysterical laugh and says, "Oh, God."

Chris blushes from the roots of his hair to the neck of his stylish beige cardigan, and stares at Sam like he's seeing a ghost.

Dean's extremely familiar with the expression. He turns to Sam in horror. "Seriously?" he demands. "Could I get a list of the hunters you *didn't* bang in your *Year of Living Soullessly?*"

Allison gasps, and says, ". . . Dad?"

Chris shrugs uncomfortably, not meeting her eyes. "It was a long time ago."

"Yeah," Dean says dryly, "way back in the olden days of 2010."

"*Dad!*" Allison stares at her father, shocked, and after a moment says, "What about *Mom?*"

Now, Chris is avoiding everyone's eyes. "Your mother and I shared everything," he says carefully. "You know that."

Dean leers at Sam proudly. Allison goes pale. "That's so much worse," she says weakly, and buries her face in Scott's chest. For an ex, that kid gets a lot of play.

Melissa lays her shotgun on the table and goes to the fridge. She gets out a carton of milk, slams the door closed, and pulls six mismatched mugs and two glasses out of a cabinet. She sets them on the counter with a loud clatter.

Everyone—kids, werewolves, hunters—stares at her.

"What?" she demands, a cute line of anger forming at the center of her forehead. "I think we all know each other a little too well for shooting now, don't you?"

Derek folds himself into a chair at the table. "Whatever," he says, and yawns widely, covering his mouth at a sharp look from Melissa. Stiles takes the chair next to him.

Scott gives Stiles a weird look, then he sits down, too. Allison perches on his knee, still staring at her father with liquid, wounded eyes.

Chris says, "Coffee's fine for me. Sam?"

"Coffee's good," Sam says. He reaches across the island to shake Chris's hand. His face is completely blank, giving absolutely nothing away. "Nice to see you again." Dean rolls his eyes.

"Milk, cocoa, or coffee?" Melissa asks Dean.

He really does love her. "Does this mean I get another cookie?"

It's hard to maintain an air of badassery once somebody breaks out the milk and cookies. The Winchester ideal of home cooking usually involves a microwave at a 7-Eleven, so fresh baked cookies are an unprecedented luxury, even if they are Nestle Tollhouse. He takes way more than his share, and then steals one of Sam's for good measure. After the first time around, the plate mysteriously passes just out of his reach.

"So, you're hunters, too?" Allison says, eyeing Sam coldly. "How long have you two been doing this?"

Sam's face goes red. He doesn't answer.

"A while," Dean says. He pats Sam on the shoulder. "Sam's just never been much good at it. What about you?"

"About a year," Allison says.

"Wow, a whole year," Dean says. He looks at her dad. "You?"

Chris smiles, showing his teeth. "Longer."

Dean leans back, hooks one arm over the back of his chair, and glances casually at the werewolves. "Well, you're doing an awesome job in this neck of the woods, I can tell."

"Dean," Sam says evenly. "His name is Chris *Argent*."

Dean's eyes go wide. He looks at Allison and Chris again. "Really?"

"Not historically soft on werewolves," Sam says.

"Uh, no." Thanks to Bobby, Dean knows stories about the Argent family Sam's *still* too young to hear.

"So if we're still alive," Scott says, "it's because we don't need killing."

Dean thinks this over. After a moment he says, "Still skeptical. Everyone in this room has clearly gone native."

"It's because we're not *monsters*," Derek says darkly.

"That's what all the monsters say," Dean points out.

Stiles gulps the last of his milk, belches loudly in satisfaction, then says, "It's because Scott is Allison's boyfriend."

"Ex-boyfriend," Scott and Allison say together, and then smile at each other so hard it makes Dean's teeth hurt.

"Whatever," Stiles says, waving a hand airily. "You all know it's true."

"Oh, so it's a *sex* thing," Dean says, relaxing. He grins. "Okay, *that* makes sense."

When it's over—the bickering, the showing off, the catching up, the death threats and the exchanges of email addresses—Melissa packs hunters, werewolves, and teenagers off to their respective mansions, ruins, houses, and cars and goes to bed. It's been a long night, a *weird* night, and she's earned it. Scott follows Allison back to her house, and Stiles, looking even shiftier than usual, slinks out after Derek. The house is hers again. Mostly.

At 3:00 a.m., something wakes her from a sound, blissful sleep. She looks around her room; it's silent and empty. She waits a beat, and then a beat longer, and then the doorbell rings. She relaxes back onto the mattress and ignores it.

At 3:03 a.m., it rings again. This time, it doesn't stop. Fatalistically, she grabs her shotgun from beside the bed and goes downstairs to see who it is.

There's a crazy man on her porch. He's wearing a trench coat.

"Did I miss the party?"

Melissa stares. The crazy man has bright blue eyes, black hair, and a sweet—if completely deranged—smile. In one hand he has a plastic bag from the convenience store down the street. "I'm sorry?" she says.

"The werewolf party," he clarifies. "I brought milk."

"For the werewolves," she says slowly.

"No!" he laughs. "For the cookies!"

"Of course." Melissa fondles the gun, just out of sight behind the door frame. "You can leave it on the steps."

"I *am* late," he says. "I'm very sorry; I must seem so rude. I attempted a shortcut through Nebraska, but I was distracted by an odd pattern in the corn."

"Of course," Melissa says again, nodding. "But unfortunately the party is over, and everyone has gone home." She pauses, rethinking. "Except the extremely large and very protective werewolves. They're still here."

"Of course," the crazy man says. He smiles at her, and doesn't leave.

After a full minute of silence, he's still there, and still smiling.

"Is there something else I can help you with?" she says, thinking, *before I call the police?*

"Can you tell me where to find Dean and Sam Winchester?"

Melissa has some recent experience in this area. She isn't *new*. "Nope," she says. "Never heard of them."

"That's too bad," the man says. He sighs, and smiles again. He still doesn't leave.

"Well," Melissa says, "I'm going to go now. Good night."

"Wait!" the man says.

"Yes?"

He reaches into his pocket. "Would you like some bees?"

Melissa slams the door between them, and presses her back against it. Dean steps out of the kitchen, bare to the waist, a plate of cookies in one hand and a half-eaten cookie in the other.

It's like living in an X-rated cooking calendar, she thinks through a haze of appreciation. He'd be July, or maybe August. Definitely a summer month.

"This night sucks," she says, reaching behind her back to turn the deadbolt. She thought he'd disappeared into the night without saying goodbye, and she's very pleasantly surprised to be wrong. "There's a lunatic on my porch with a bag full of bees. He's looking for you."

"Yeah," Dean says. "That happens sometimes. What did you tell him?"

"I said you weren't here." She hooks a finger in his belt buckle and tugs. "I hope you're happy, mister."

"Oh, I plan to be very happy," he says, grinning. He lets her pull him in; there's a smear of chocolate at the corner of his mouth, and he smells like gun powder. "What about you?"

Supernatural, aka The Boys in Arizona

Glockgal

SAM AND DEAN DIDN'T HAPPEN TO HAVE THEIR PASSPORTS OR THEIR BIRTH CERTIFICATES ON THEM AND THIS WAS A CRIME IF YOU ARE BROWN IN ARIZONA.

THEY WERE THEREFORE DEPORTED TO MEXICO.

TWO HOURS LATER OLD MAN WHATISFACE DIED FROM GHOST-RELATED DEATH.

THE END.

Supernatural: Fanservice Sequel

The Billionaire Superhero's Tale

Title: When they finally come to destroy the earth (they'll have to
  go through you first) (2012)
Author: AlchemyAlice
Fandom: Batman, Iron Man, Justice League, Marvel
Rating: General audiences (Steve/Tony implied)
Additional tags: phone calls, telephones, crossover, bros!, boarding
  school, drunk dialing

Introduction

Poor Batman. Batman, aka Bruce Wayne, has become increasingly defined
by his tragic origin story.

While his parents' murder was established early on—the story is first
told in flashback in *Detective Comics* 33 (1939)—it was presented neither
as a deep psychological trauma nor as the singular event defining Bruce
Wayne's character. Rather, the random street violence that kills Thomas
and Martha Wayne gives Bruce his motivation to protect Gotham City:
their deaths are the spur to a vocation, not an emotional problem to be
overcome. Back in the Golden Age, when Bruce Wayne was merely a mil-
lionaire, he was a pretty normal person, life-as-a-secret-vigilante aside: he
had a girlfriend, an extensive (if mostly performative) social life, and was
soon to acquire a ward (the orphaned circus acrobat Dick Grayson, aka
Robin). Later, Batman helped form the Justice League and hung out with
Superman, Wonder Woman, and Aqua Man, and sometimes he had a
(larger or smaller) Bat-family that could include not only Alfred Penny-

worth but Catwoman, Batwoman, Huntress, Batgirl, Aunt Harriet, Uncle Philip, Oracle, Ace the Bat Hound, Bat-mite, and one or more Robins, depending on the year.

Not today. The character of Batman is now routinely interpreted in ways that suggest that the early, traumatic loss of his parents has left Bruce Wayne damaged: he is a loner, a paranoid-obsessive, a person who cannot connect to normal people in the normal ways. This has been the case not only in many of the comics,[1] but for at least the last two sets of movies as well as all recent video games.[2] As early as 1991, in the wake of Tim Burton's *Batman*, critic Andy Medhurst protested Batman's transformation into someone characterized by "his humorlessness, fondness for violence, and obsessive monomania,"[3] and the Bruce Wayne of Christopher Nolan's trilogy is a reclusive billionaire of such disturbing weirdness that you can't imagine him hanging out with Superman or Wonder Woman. As I write this, Zack Snyder's nihilistic *Batman vs. Superman* has kicked off a proposed DC-verse with a contest of toxic masculinity; the film begins, of course, with the death of Batman's parents. You can't imagine any rational court giving any of these guys custody of a minor;[4] Bats is an overgrown child himself.

Which may of course be the point. Burton's 1989 *Batman*, Nolan's 2006 *Batman Begins*, and Snyder's 2016 *Batman vs. Superman* are all Robin-free, and one could argue that Bruce Wayne's childhood trauma has been amplified and magnified in these films at least partly to prevent Robin from showing up in the story (on the grounds that if Bruce is this obsessed with his own mommy and daddy, he's in no position to parent anyone else). This strategy, if it is a strategy, has been so successful that I suspect that most of the younger readers of this book who only know Batman from the movies no longer strongly associate Batman with Robin at all and may never have heard the phrase "The Dynamic Duo": Batman and Robin are no longer irrevocably conjoined in the public imagination.[5] Consequently I further suspect that many of these readers might not know that Batman was one of the first fictional characters to be interpreted as homosexual, with Fredric Wertham arguing in the 1950s that Bruce Wayne and Dick Grayson seemed like "a wish dream of two homosexuals living together."[6] To be fair, even today people might talk if a rich young bachelor suddenly adopted a hot teenaged gymnast, and gay men as well as slash fans have enjoyed imagining Batman and Robin as lovers. The Sherlock Holmes stories face similar issues (see the Sherlock entry earlier in this book), but where recent Holmes adaptations have used various strategies to resist, channel, or acknowledge the homoeroticism of the Holmes-Watson relationship, filmic adaptations of Batman seem to have decided to eliminate Robin entirely or shove him into the deeper corners of the narrative.

But something besides gay subtext is lost when you drop Robin from the Batman story: perspective. You can't argue that the death of Batman's parents is the worst thing that ever happened to anybody ever when *the exact same thing* happened to Robin, who is typically depicted as a relatively sane and cheerful person. Batman's grief starts to look a little excessive, and fans have a name for this self-centered, narcissistic angst: *manpain*. Manpain refers to the sort of psychologically painful backstory (typically caused by someone's death)[7] that sets up one character's suffering as more important than anyone else's, and so justifies behavior that would be considered evil or crazy in anyone else. The modern Batman practically defines manpain, and in "Some Thoughts on Manpain," fan ThingsWithWings articulates three distinct flavors: (1) my pain is greater than anyone else's ("No one has ever felt the way that I feel, no one could possibly understand, my pain is more important than yours") because (2) the weight of the world is on my shoulders ("I have so much power, oh it is hard to have such power") and so (3) it's so hard for *me* when you get hurt, raped, or killed ("My pain is more important even than the pain of the person to whom the original injustice was done"). ThingsWithWings notes that manpain is used to build sympathy for high-status white male characters like Bruce Wayne at the expense of everyone else; in other words: *Poor Batman!* It's so *hard* being a billionaire and having to save Gotham City from itself all the time! The responsibility! The angst! It's all on poor Bruce's shoulders, isn't it?

Not in the story that follows. You can tell from the title, "When they finally come to destroy the earth (they'll have to go through you first)." That "you" is important: there's already someone else responsible for the world besides you; you're already not the only one who's important. While historically Batman's foil was (young, cheerful, punning) Robin, in AlchemyAlice's story it's (wisecracking, irreverent) Tony Stark, the Marvel superhero known as Iron Man, who serves that function. (Perhaps not coincidentally, both characters wear bright red-and-yellow outfits.) Alchemy-Alice posits a crossover universe in which rich kids Bruce Wayne and Tony Stark went to boarding school together and being a billionaire superhero doesn't make you unique. In this story, the peerless Bruce Wayne has a peer (and a foil) in Tony Stark, and ultimately, in the Avengers and the Justice League, a cohort. This punctures his manpain and brings him back into community: he is just one billionaire, one freak, among many.

Fanfiction writers tend to be interested in relationships and communities; this is why most fans still write Batman stories set within the larger DC comics-verse that includes the Bat-family and the Justice League rather than within the world of the blockbuster films. Some fans have done wonderful things with the darker Batman of the DC universe, using him to explore themes such as child abuse, sexual violence, domination, fetishism, and kink; after all, Batman wears more leather and black rubber than most people outside of an S & M club. But others, especially since the Marvel movie juggernaut leading up to *The Avengers*, have started to bring Batman and other characters from DC into the Marvelverse, which feels like a healthier, saner place. In a hilarious College Humor animated short, "The Dark Knight Meets the Avengers" (2012) a grim and obsessive Batman freaks out when the Avengers invite him out for a beer after a mission, noting that he usually just sits alone in a cave and thinks about his dead parents. "Dude," Tony replies in dismay. "That sounds . . . lonely." In reply, Batman rants, "Being a superhero isn't supposed to be fun with your friends! It's an obligation! It's a sacred mission! It's— It's— Stop playing volleyball!" and of course the Avengers *are* playing volleyball, or hanging out at the pool, or signing autographs and going to parties. This is barely an exaggeration; in Joss Whedon's film, the Avengers go out for shawarma after saving the world. Whedon, of course, is a fan auteur extraordinaire (see the *Buffy the Vampire Slayer* fiction in this book) and *The Avengers* was designed to hit fannish buttons: strong female characters, collaboration and teamwork, good-looking and slashable scientists, wit, heart. Consequently there is Avengers fic of almost every kind and featuring every conceivable pairing, including Tony/Bruce, Clint/Natasha, Thor/Loki, and Loki/everyone. (It helps that Loki canonically genderswitches and once gave birth to a horse.)[8] There are four times as many fanfiction stories featuring Tony Stark than there are featuring Bruce Wayne, and more than sixteen times the fanfiction for *The Avengers* as for the Christopher Nolan Batman trilogy.

AlchemyAlice was partly inspired to write her DC/Marvel crossover by some animated GIFs, or short sequences of captioned images, depicting Christian Bale's Batman looking horrified as Robert Downey Jr.'s Tony Stark gives a press conference announcing he is Iron Man; the caption reads "TONY YOU'RE DOING IT WRONG." Her story integrates the Nolan films with both the larger DC universe and the Marvel movieverse by creating a childhood bond between these universes' two biggest narcissists: the billionaire superheroes. In this story, Tony Stark is the only one who knows Bruce Wayne well enough to immediately guess that he's Batman, drunk-dialing him to slur, "You are one *crazy* motherfucker." Similarly, Bruce has no doubt as to who's inside the Iron Man armor: "A red-and-gold robot suit? Seriously?" Tony teaches Bruce how to act like a playboy, and Bruce helps Tony grieve for his parents, a process that is complicated by the domestic violence in Tony's family. Each ends up on a team despite himself: Tony with the Avengers, and Bruce (as he never was in the Nolan-verse) in the Justice League. They have other commonalities, too: Bruce is friends with an Amazon while Tony works with a Norse god, and they're both "bossed around" by boy scouts wearing red, white, and blue (note that Tony's a little in love with his). AlchemyAlice ends the story by giving Bruce Wayne a brief moment of peace; he finally gets to a party where he stands with Clark Kent, sees Wonder Woman talking to Black Widow and Tony talking to Captain America, and "thinks also of the Gordons at home in Gotham, and Dick on patrol, and the rest of their collective dysfunctional families." Batman has been brought back to a place where he can reflect positively on his relationships with others and see them as people who are making important contributions to fighting crime and saving the world.

Suggested Further Reading

For more about how Batman came to be such a dark knight, see Will Brooker's comprehensive *Batman Unmasked: Analyzing a Cultural Icon* (Bloomsbury Academic, 2001) and its sequel *Hunting the Dark Knight: Twenty-First Century Batman* (I. B. Tauris, 2012). Roberta Pearson and William Urreccho's *The Many Lives of the Batman* (Routledge, 1991), which features Andy Medhurst's incredibly useful queer history, "Batman, Deviance, and Camp," has gone into a second, updated edition, *The Many More Lives of the Batman* (2016), which features many new essays. Joseph Darowski has edited a collection called *Tony Stark: The Ages of Iron Man: Essays on the Armored Avenger* (McFarland, 2015).

Matthew Costello's 2013 special issue "Appropriating, Interpreting, and Transforming Comic Books" for *Transformative Works and Cultures* is a good starting point for researching comics fandom and fanfiction, and includes an essay on fridging by Suzanne Scott and one by Catherine Coker on Captain America / Iron Man slash.

When they finally come to destroy the earth (they'll have to go through you first)

AlchemyAlice

201.

Batman is on the national news for the first time, the Tumbler roaring down the highway and destroying probably more property than Bruce is entirely comfortable with, after the fact.

His private phone blares over the newscaster's commentary, and when he picks up, the first thing he hears is a slurred, "You are one *crazy* motherfucker."

"I don't know what you're talking about," Bruce says flatly.

"Of course you don't. Hey listen, I know a guy who knows a guy who says that Wayne Enterprises' carbon fiber-reinforced articulated fabrics are shit. On a totally unrelated note, there's this engineer in Stark R & D who knows about these things, and is about to be made redundant by my idiotic board of directors by the end of the month. Do you want her?"

This is how Tony Stark shows that he cares. Or at least, this is how he shows Bruce that he cares.

"Tell her to send me her CV," he says. "I'll pass it on to Lucius next time I see him."

"Good," Tony says vaguely, "Good. Okay, well. Later, alligator."

"Take it easy, Tony," Bruce says. "It's barely past six and you already sound wasted."

"You're on Gotham time. It's barely past four in L.A., which means that pregaming for happy hour is a go. But don't worry, dearest, I understand. Time for bats to get ready to leave to their caves, it's all good, whatever floats your boat—"

"Tony . . ."

"Nighty night! Don't let the bad guys bite!"

It figures that only Tony Stark would figure out Bruce Wayne's most important secret within hours of getting wind of it, all while under the influence of enough alcohol to fail a breathalyzer three times over.

Bruce hangs up, and takes comfort only in the fact that Tony is perhaps the only discreet drunk he's ever known.

700.

Tony answers his phone and immediately says, "I don't want to hear it, Wayne."

Bruce is staring at the television, his eyes glued to speed-of-sound blur of color streaking across the screen. "A red-and-gold robot suit? Seriously?"

"It's called showmanship. And the gold is totally necessary, it's an essential alloy coating—"

"You're joking."

A pause. "There's nothing funny about this," Tony says.

Since Tony's capture, Alfred has been leaving the newspaper religiously opened to the business section every morning at Bruce's breakfast table, tracking the stutter, rise, and fall of Stark Industries stock in tandem with Tony's disappearance, return, and dissolving of SI's weapons manufacture.

Bruce thinks about the weeks Tony endured, isolated and surviving, not by choice, but by force. "No," he admits, "I guess I can't say that I'm laughing."

"Yeah," Tony agrees. "Hey, where do you buy your undersuit Kevlar in bulk?"

Bruce continues to look at the screen, unseeing now, and wonders whether to celebrate Iron Man, or mourn the Tony Stark that he used to know. "I'll email you their number," he says, after a second.

It will take him years to realize that Tony has been mourning him in just the same way for more than a decade.

4.

They are little more than a couple of shrimpy kids when they're sent off, and their only similarities are that they come from wealth, they don't talk much, and they regularly fuck up the bell curve for everyone else in their classes.

In math and science, Tony is always best, Bruce second best. In the social sciences and humanities, Bruce is best, and Tony is above average, but mostly unwilling to apply himself. They don't study together. They don't compete. Tony takes to sitting down next to Bruce at lunch, but Bruce figures this is because Tony knows he can count on Bruce not to make too much conversation.

Bruce privately resents Tony in the first year, for the same reason he privately resents everyone else—because Tony has parents to come home to, not just an empty house, where every resonant step on a marble tile echoes the absence and loss that Alfred can never entirely stifle.

But then they come back from the holidays, and Tony has a split lip that he shrugs off as a skiing mishap, and his dismissal is a study in everything every policeman has ever done in front of Bruce to make him fuss less, make him want vengeance less.

Tony sits down in the cafeteria that first day back, next to Bruce as usual, his shoulders hunched like he's cold even though they're close to the kitchen's radiant heat. Bruce says quietly, "Hey."

Tony blinks at him. Then he says, "Have you done the problem set for trig yet?"

"It was pretty easy," Bruce nods.

"It was ludicrous!" Tony throws up his hands. His sleeves fall back around his forearms.

For a moment, Bruce can see the fading bruises on his wrists, in the shapes of fingers. Then Tony realizes what's happened, and the cuffs are wrenched back down over his hands.

Bruce looks at the clenched fists in Tony's lap, then up at Tony's challenging expression, and says, "When do you think they'll let us attend the upper-level classes?"

Something very subtle shifts in Tony's eyes. "I dunno," he says. "But it better be soon, because I'm bored out of my mind."

"We can play blindfold chess during, if you like," Bruce offers.

Tony ducks his head. "Yeah. That'd be cool."

After that, they're maybe not friends, but they are allies.

862.

Bruce looks carefully at the woman standing in front of his desk. At first and second glance, she looks like not much more than an inordinately pretty secretary, fiery red hair framing a soft face and well-maintained hands clasping a file folder and clipboard.

But then Bruce notices the minute scars webbed across her knuckles, and the way she finds and grounds her center of balance every time she shifts in her towering stilettos.

"You said you want to know about my experience with Tony Stark?"

"That's right," she says, her smile pleasant and neutral. "I'm putting together a profile article for *Vanity Fair*, and I was hoping to get a more intimate perspective on his early years."

"Well, I don't know what you've been reading about boarding schools recently, but Stark and I have never been *intimate*." Bruce waggles his eyebrows for good measure.

Only a small tightening of the muscles around her eyes indicates that she knows he's evading her.

"What was he like as a child? I imagine quite a handful."

"Depends," Bruce shrugs. "All children are rambunctious at times."

"I imagine his genius became apparent very early."

"I couldn't say. We didn't share many classes."

"Trigonometry, physics, BC calculus, drama, and economics, actually," she corrects, not bothering to look down at her notes.

"Goodness," Bruce says, cocking his head and smiling vacantly. "How ever did you manage to access those sealed student records? Say, what was your name again?"

"Natalie Rushman," she says, demeanor hardening by degrees. "And you're not doing him any favors."

"Tony doesn't particularly care for favors," Bruce replies, and pulls a stack of papers from his inbox. "He prefers to earn whatever praise or scorn he gets. Will that be all, Miss Rushman?"

"I should think so," she says, and turns on her heel.

(Later, Tony says to him, "Man, she was probably telling the truth. You could have told her that I'm not nearly so screwed up as everyone else thinks I am."

"Who says I think you're *not* screwed up?" Bruce retorts, and Tony hangs up on him, as usual.)

21.

Tony becomes CEO of Stark Industries at age twenty-one, and his face beams out of every major newspaper for a week and a half while everyone speculates as to what he will bring to the table, and whether he is really destined to live up to Howard Stark's memory.

Bruce calls him from a pay phone at the docks, his cheek still stinging from where Rachel slapped him, his hands burning from the asphalt.

"Hello?" Tony sounds . . . off. Bruce can't place why, though.

"It's Bruce."

"Bruce! It's been a while. What can I do for you?"

"I just . . ." Bruce stops, swallows down *I'm leaving*, and says instead, "I wanted to offer my congratulations. On the ascendancy."

There's silence for a moment, and then Tony says, a bit tightly, "Thanks. I mean, the board didn't really have a choice, did they? Dear old Dad's instructions."

Bruce exhales. "You'll show them up. You'll be fine."

"Yeah, sure." Tony pauses, and then adds, "Hey, do you want to come to New York some time? I heard you're not at Princeton anymore, so I thought maybe you'd be available."

"I can't," Bruce replies, "I'm going . . . I have some things I've got to do."

"Right," Tony says, easily enough. "Well, I've got to get through this mountain of paperwork myself, so I guess I'll talk to you later."

He rings off.

Bruce looks up at the freighter looming in front of him, half loaded. He wonders why he called Tony at all.

676.

It's a sunny, bland day when Tony goes to Afghanistan, and doesn't come back.

Bruce realizes distantly that this is probably what it felt like to Tony when Bruce first disappeared underground.

His phone goes off and displays a number he recognizes from when he'd last checked up on Tony. He picks up, and it only takes a second for him to make the connections.

"Listen, you don't know me, but I'm—"

"You're Lieutenant James Rhodes, U.S. Air Force. You were Tony's closest friend at MIT, and one of the last people to see him before he was taken," Bruce finishes. He's standing behind his chair now, gripping its back hard enough for his knuckles to turn white. The flatscreen opposite him is on silent, but the ticker tape beneath the talking heads keeps scrolling, TONY STARK TAKEN FROM CONVOY, TONY STARK MISSING.

Bruce has lost a lot of people from his childhood. He isn't going lose this one. "You want to know whether I can put the weight of Wayne Enterprises behind the military's to get him back," he says. "The answer is yes."

He hears Rhodes pause, and then snort quietly. "You know, I really didn't believe Tony when he said he'd trust Bruce Wayne with his life, but I guess I'm happy to be proven wrong in this case."

"Don't tell anyone," Bruce says.

Rhodes laughs, but the sound is thin and worried. "Jesus. You're practically two of a kind."

Bruce would normally feel vaguely insulted, but coming from Rhodes, it's a strange sort of comfort. "We'll get him back," he says.

"Yeah," Rhodes says gravely, "Yeah, we will."

130.

Seven years after Bruce disappears into the criminal underworld, and a week after reappearing, Tony shows up at Wayne Manor with a bottle of Taittinger with a tag on it that reads, *Congratulations on not being dead!*

Bruce looks at him, and then at the bottle, and says, "I guess you'd better come in."

"Good choice. You were about two seconds away from getting beaned in the head with this for letting your dearest friend think you were dead. Is your good crystal in the same place? Alfred! Can I get a bucket of ice for this? Hey, you talked to Rachel lately?"

"Master Tony, it's good to see you. If you'll adjourn to the green room, I'll bring everything there."

"No, I haven't," Bruce says, leading the way. "Why?"

"Just wondering if you're going right back to business as usual." Tony narrows his eyes. "Something's different about you, though. Have you been working out?"

"You could say that."

"Fine, don't tell me. I see how it is."

Bruce sighs. "It's good to see you, Stark."

"There we go, the friendly Bruce Wayne we know and tolerate. Ow! Fuck, you pack a punch nowadays."

"Maybe you're just soft. How's Stark Industries?"

"Booming. The board doesn't even get on my case about the hookers and blow anymore."

Bruce looks sharply at him. Tony shrugs, wide-eyed and guileless.

"I'm glad you're enjoying yourself," Bruce says finally.

Alfred comes in with an ice bucket and two champagne glasses. "Thanks, Alfred," Tony says. "Don't look at me like that, Wayne, it's not like I mean anything to the shareholders beyond being an extra special brain and a name to slap on things. I deserve my perks."

He pauses, and Bruce listens to everything that silence says. Before he can question further though, Tony adds curtly, "Besides, Obie's got my back."

"I guess I'll drink to that, then," Bruce says, relieved at least that Tony doesn't pry further about where Bruce has been all this time.

Tony never lets the conversation stray back into company talk either, though.

778.

"Hey," Tony coughs. His voice sounds wet, like he's talking through a mouthful of water. Or blood. "You ever get tired of being the one who has to make his superpowers?"

"No," Bruce replies, as he picks up his office phone to dial Rhodes. "I'm smarter than they are, so it doesn't matter."

Tony laughs, hiccuping. "'Mnot smart enough, Bruce. I'm fucking brilliant, and I can't fix it."

"Can't fix what?"

"Hah! The usual."

He hangs up.

Bruce drums his fingers on the desk, listening to Rhodes's phone ring, and wonders whether there was something he could have done, when they were younger. He fears the answer lies somewhere in the seven years that he wasn't in any position to do anything.

923.

Neither of them understands how they eventually manage to acquire *teams*.

"Fuck this, I get enough micromanagement from Pepper," Tony says. "I can't cope with SHIELD and their moto bullshit."

"You need to stop borrowing marine slang; it doesn't work for you, and Rhodes will kill you for switching allegiances," Bruce replies. "Also, you probably need the micromanagement."

"Hush, you control freak. Aren't you getting bossed around by some red-and-blue wonder too?"

He sighs. "Two years, and he's still a goddamn overgrown Boy Scout. No aspirin in the world is strong enough."

"I hear you. Sometimes I just want to mess him up a bit."

Bruce raises his eyebrows. He knows it doesn't translate down the phone lines, but Tony knows him well enough to sense it anyway.

". . . Shit. Forget I said anything."

"Sure, Stark, whatever you say."

Like he's going to forget that his oldest friend still holds his same childhood torch for Captain America, even when the Cap is back from the dead and apparently just as obnoxious as Clark.

Tony grumbles something about spandex and distracting biceps and hangs up.

Bruce sits back in his chair.

"Alfred! What would be the ramifications of hacking into SHIELD to get information on Captain America?"

"I couldn't possibly begin to speculate, Master Wayne, but no doubt it would not be appreciated by anyone involved."

265.

"Pepper's gonna kill me. Whenever I come here she thinks I'm gonna get straight up murdered," Tony confides, leaning over to Bruce in the limo while their dates giggle to each other over their champagne. His breath already smells astringent with vodka.

"Are you trashing my city, Stark?" Bruce says, eyes narrowed even as the corners of his mouth turn up.

"I'm not! Pepper definitely is, though. Don't understand why, she's a New Yorker through and through, could probably throw a top-end Gotham mob boss at her and she'd just pepper spray him into submission. Hah, Pepper with pepper."

"She sounds impressive."

"You'd love her, you know, when she's not trashing your 'hood. Younger than I am, but competent as fuck. Keeps me in line, as much as that's possible. Hey," Tony turns and squints at him, "you got someone watching your back? You know, with the—"

"Unlike you, I don't need a disciplinarian to keep me on task," Bruce interrupts dryly. Then he raises his voice, "Work hard, play hard—am I right, ladies?"

The two women raise their glasses and cheer.

Tony doesn't react though, except to cock his head slightly. "This really isn't you anymore, is it?" he says eventually.

Bruce drinks his champagne, and doesn't say anything. He knows his only real thoughts all night have been about the case file he has waiting at the manor, and the armor hanging up in the cave.

Tony says, "I guess it wasn't you to begin with, either. Silly me."

Bruce has the fleeting thought that it's kind of absurd, the way Tony can always see through Bruce's bullshit, but never his own.

688.

"Hey. I hear you helped get me out."

"I hear you brought back a souvenir."

"I'm clearly going to have strong words with Rhodey, he is a tattletale of the first degree."

There's a faint tapping over the line, like fingernails against something close by and glassy. Tony has many nervous tics, but tapping had never been one of them before.

"Try not to do anything stupid, Tony."

"Nag, nag, nag."

456.

The Joker shakes Bruce to his core, unlike anyone he's ever dealt with before.

Hours before he truly goes to ground, an enemy of the city and of the state, Tony calls him and says, "This is bullshit. This has gone too far."

"This is necessary," Bruce says, feeling like he's coming out of his own skin, pulling up all of the databases he'll need, making contingency plans, shoving himself forward into the abyss without hesitation.

"You're doing so much fucking good!"

"Oh? And what would you know about that, Stark?"

Tony hangs up. Bruce winces. He'll probably need to keep up with Tony for the sake of Wayne Enterprises. He supposes it's for the best though, that even Tony should feel alienated from the Batman.

13.

Howard and Maria Stark die on a dark rainy highway, and the first place Tony goes is Wayne Manor.

Actually, that isn't true. The first place he goes is his dorm in Boston, then the lab at MIT, then back to his dorm, rinse, repeat, for two weeks.

He doesn't leave Boston until the funeral, and then he goes to New York and watches the coffins go down into the earth; but as soon as it's over, before Obadiah can steer him towards the waiting company car, Alfred is having a silent conversation with Jarvis, and then Bruce is leading him towards a different car altogether.

Then they are out of New York, headed towards the outskirts of Gotham.

"Obie didn't look happy," Tony says quietly, two hours into the car ride.

"Mr. Stane can feel how he likes," Alfred says. "Mr. Jarvis and I have decided that you ought to get some distance from everything before beginning to take care of business affairs."

"You also making decisions for me now, Alfred?" Tony asks, biting but also curious.

"I'm happy to turn the car around if you wish," Alfred replies.

Tony looks at him, and then at Bruce. "That's okay. I'm good," he says eventually.

Then, thirty minutes and forty miles later, he whispers, "*Shit,*" and Bruce slings an arm around his shoulders, holding him tightly as he crumples down into a ball in the back seat.

Bruce's grief over his parents is something pure and elemental, the product no doubt of them being genuine, decent people, and of Bruce losing them so early and so violently. Tony's grief is a complicated, knotted up thing by comparison, almost entirely alien to Bruce.

But it is still grief. Bruce knows what to do with that.

790.

They fight for their cities, they fight for the world, they refuse to talk about things that they know other people won't really get, because other people didn't grow up the way they did, didn't love, hate, and manipulate their privilege the way they did.

Bruce puts a compound fracture in his arm taking down Killer Croc, and Tony coordinates a kidnapping with the increasingly precocious Dick Grayson, such that Bruce finds himself held hostage out in Malibu with JARVIS and a great many tablet PCs for company.

It's only Bruce's respect for the memory of Jarvis-the-man that keeps him from hacking JARVIS-the-AI and getting the hell out. Also, his arm does still hurt. Slightly.

Later in the year, Tony nearly dies (again) and Bruce flies out to New York on the pretense of a business deal while actually conspiring with Rhodes to keep the whiskey out of arm's reach.

There are SHIELD agents lurking in the penthouse, but they don't seem to know Bruce's other identity (or at least are pretending they don't), and they treat him with blank politeness.

"Wait, Stark had friends in grade school?" one of them, a compact guy with a compound bow on his back, asks. "Friends who can still stand him?"

Well, mostly with politeness.

Bruce smiles blandly. "One friend."

734.

"The truth is . . . I am Iron Man."

Bruce lets his head drop onto his desk in despair. Alfred calls him two minutes later.

"It seems we've failed to teach Master Stark the meaning of discretion."

"Unfortunately," Bruce says through gritted teeth, head still on the desk, "I don't think we could ever claim to be surprised about that."

960.

Bruce can't help himself. Let it never be said that Batman is entirely bereft of a sense of humor.

"His *brother*? Your team has some family issues to work out."

Tony's huff of exasperation is particularly static-y down the line. "Adopted brother. A frost giant, apparently. And who are you to judge? JLA is just as dysfunctional as we are."

Bruce thinks about Clark suggesting last week that he should just *push the earth out of orbit a bit* to avoid a gamma ray burst.

"It's a wonder we haven't all destroyed the world yet," he says.

There's a clang down the line; Tony must be in the workshop. "Amen, brother," he says.

941.

In between missions, Bruce gets into the habit of calling Tony to berate him about his yo-yo-ing stock prices.

Tony sees it as a favor, considering that Bruce is just important enough to merit him dropping his real responsibilities to take his calls, and Bruce finds it useful because it means that he can do reconnaissance on corporate buildings while looking like a distracted angry stockbroker.

However, the third time Bruce decides to interrupt (scoping out one of Marconi's old outfits that has since been turned into a white-collar crime mill), instead of Tony's drawl he gets a feminine voice which says evenly, "Mr. Stark is in a meeting, Mr. Wayne, so I'll save you the effort and merely pass on that, quote, you can take your truly hurtful criticism of my badass company and shove it up your ass, unquote."

Bruce pauses. "You have the authority to act as your boss's mouthpiece verbatim, Miss . . . ?"

"Potts. Virginia Potts."

"Ah, *you're* Pepper. No wonder."

"Mr. Wayne, you need to stop—"

"Miss Potts, I commend you for handling Tony for far longer than you probably deserve, but I'm afraid I'm going to have to ask you to keep me on the line until Tony's available, so that I can tell him exactly what he's doing to my portfolio."

"I don't take orders from you, Mr. Wayne."

"Do you want to hear about the macaroni incident of 1983 or not?"

There's a pause, and then, "I can get him out of the meeting in ten minutes. Spill."

Ten minutes later on the dot, Tony is on the line, and Bruce is clear to wave off the security guard and head for the elevator. "Bruce, it's not that

I mind skipping out of shareholders meetings, but if you steal my PA's loyalty again I will sick Barbara on you."

"Oracle doesn't—"

"Oracle loves me. We diss Steve Jobs and make plans for world domination together."

Well, shit. "Listen, if you wanted me to not have dirt on you, you really shouldn't have been such a stupid kid."

"At least," Tony says dramatically, "I can say I've lived."

Bruce rolls his eyes, and launches into a spitting critique of SI's management as he slips into one of the unguarded offices. Tony laughs obnoxiously over the rant in between what sounds like Pepper trying to pry his phone away and then getting into a cab.

"Hey, I heard you have a Amazonian goddess in your lineup. How's that going?"

"She has a far firmer grasp of social cues than your Norse god, so I think we'll come out ahead. How's your boyscout?"

"Rogers? He's . . . surprisingly decent."

Bruce pauses halfway through picking the lock on a filing cabinet. "Tony. You haven't."

"What?"

"You *have*." The money-laundering records are going to have to wait. "Tony."

"Nothing's going on," Tony says, a little too sharply. "Steve's a fossil, a literal fossil, like excavated from ice fossil—"

"Fossils don't actually—"

"—and he's straighter than an arrow, so it doesn't even matter."

Bruce is not the person Tony should be talking to about this. "That doesn't exactly change anything on your end, though."

"It doesn't matter," Tony repeats. "You know me, Bruce, I'd eat him alive anyway."

"From what I hear, he can take care of himself."

"Yeah, well."

Bruce swallows. "I have to finish casing this place."

"You and your broad daylight raids. Are you sure you're nocturnal? I thought Batman was supposed to be a nightmare, not a daydream."

"I take my opportunities when they come," Bruce replies. "Now let me tell you about how you're running your company into the ground."

"Fine," Tony sighs. "Honestly, I don't get half as much abuse from my board, I should just hire you to be my taskmaster."

"You have Pepper for that." He turns back to his lockpicks and eases open the file cabinet, and then launches into a diatribe about SI's projected earnings for the next quarter.

He tries not to think about Tony's wayward feelings. If he has to give Rogers the "You hurt him, I hospitalize you" talk, he's going to have to maybe reassess his life choices.

143.

What Bruce never says but Tony knows anyway, is that everything Bruce knows about playing the playboy, he learned from the years before Iron Man existed, the years of Tony's life that Tony would come to hate.

Two weeks after Tony's impromptu welcome home, Alfred brings Bruce a protein shake and says that if Bruce wants to keep up this daft boogey-man charade, then Bruce is expected, on no uncertain terms, to act as a young billionaire should, when not in costume.

So, Bruce watches the tabloids watch Tony. Tony in designer suits, tripping though expensive clubs, picking up supermodels, puking into trash cans, living hard. Bruce watches and he doesn't call or email, because he doesn't have anything to say to this Tony that he doesn't really know, and he reads the police reports of disturbing the peace and public disruption, in between highlighting the more serious crimes that he'll take his time pursuing.

Then he goes and stands in front of his bathroom mirror, and cultivates his Tony Stark smile. He shades it a little duller, a little more insipid, but the uncaring, flashy emptiness stays at its core.

Tony ribs him about it, much later, patting his cheek in condescension at a party in the Hamptons, and Bruce bats his hand away, never losing the signature smirk that they now both share and knowingly fake.

Of all the things that Tony has invented over the years, his public mask is the one Bruce respects, and hates, the most.

1000.

Eventually, they both end up at a gala in DC. Several of the Avengers are there, as are a couple of members of the JLA. Clark is hovering somewhere on the outskirts with his notepad, attempting to look like a man of balsam rather than one of steel. Bruce is still nursing three broken ribs under his tuxedo from a run-in with the Scarecrow, such that when one of his shareholders vigorously shakes his hand, he barely manages to keep his expression bland and pleasant.

He apparently doesn't do a good enough job, because when Tony greets him, loud and obnoxious, his bonhomie clap on the back looks hearty but comes down on his spine gently, barely causing him a twinge. "Playing too hard?" Tony asks, smile wide and eyes worried.

Bruce returns the smile. "You know how it is."

"That I do. Hey, have you met Steve? Steve, this is Bruce Wayne, of Wayne Enterprises. We go way back. Bruce, Steve Rogers, aka Captain America."

Steve is tall and ridiculously chiseled, and he watches Tony with a sort of confused adoration, like he doesn't know why he's in Tony's thrall, but can't be bothered to mind all that much. Huh.

Bruce is going to have to actually indulge in some proper alcohol for this.

"It's a pleasure to meet you, Mr. Wayne," Steve says earnestly. "It's always great to meet Tony's friends."

"Wow, that is such a lie," Tony says.

Steve quells him with a look. "Your *real* friends, Tony," he says, and oh, that *is* interesting.

"Pleasure's all mine, but please call me Bruce," Bruce says, shaking his hand. "And thank you for your service, Captain."

Steve nods, but his gaze is steady. "Thank you for yours, Bruce. Gotham owes you a great debt."

Bruce shoots Tony a look, and Tony shrugs. He touches Steve's forearm for slightly longer than necessary and says, "I'm gonna grab us some drinks. Coke okay for you?"

"Sure thing," Steve smiles at him, and watches him slide away through the crowd.

"So," Bruce starts, and then realizes that if he says, "What are your intentions towards Tony?" aloud, he will actually have to call Dick and ask him to come over from Gotham to punch him in the face.

"Are you the Bruce that Tony's always calling?" Steve blurts, and then his ears turn pink.

Bruce stares at him for a second, and then blinks. And then he laughs, and he's pretty sure it's the first time he's genuinely laughed as Bruce Wayne in public in a very long time.

Steve goes redder.

Bruce composes himself, and grins. "That'd be me," he says. "We used to go to school together. We've . . . watched each other grow up, I suppose."

Steve nods. Bruce decides to put him out of his misery. "I'm not seeing him, if that's what you're wondering."

"Oh! Well, I mean, it's obviously none of my business. I just—"

"It is definitely your business, and that is all I'm going to say about that," Bruce says flatly.

Tony appears at Steve's elbow, holding a coke and tumbler of scotch. Bruce snatches the tumbler out of his hands and drains it. "I've got to go and mingle," he announces, handing Tony back the empty glass over his outraged spluttering. "You two have things to talk about, I'm sure. Tony, it's great to see you, I'm really happy for you, and before you call me in a panic two weeks from now, you do deserve it, stop thinking you don't. Captain, good to meet you, we'll talk later. Have a good evening."

And with that, he walks away, towards the entrance to the ballroom.

Clark falls into step with him. "You know, I think I get it now, why everyone eavesdrops when you decide to lecture me," he says thoughtfully. "It's kind of hilarious when you're not the one it's happening to."

"Shut up, Clark," Bruce says. He glances back over his shoulder, at Diana chatting with Natalie (no, *Natasha*), at Tony and Steve, now bent together in quiet conversation. He thinks also of the Gordons at home in Gotham, and Dick on patrol, and the rest of their collective dysfunctional families.

For two guys like them, he and Tony haven't done too badly, it seems.

Tony spots him for a split second through the crowd, and mimes "I'll call you" at him with raised eyebrows.

"Of course you will," Bruce murmurs.

Clark laughs.

Not too bad at all, really.

11.

Bruce plants himself in the doorway at the Stark mansion as Tony packs, which mostly consists of heaping great piles of laundry and books into suitcases until they're fit to burst. "Look at you, all ready to go to college like a real boy," he says.

Tony flips him the bird. He's still scrawny, the mop of his hair too long. Howard and Maria are arguing downstairs, their voices muffled.

"You need any help?"

"Nah," Tony replies. "I got this." He turns and regards Bruce. "You gonna survive your last couple of years in that hellhole?"

"Obviously," Bruce shrugs. "You'll call though, right?"

"Of course. You know I've got your back."

Bruce smirks. "Pretty sure I got yours first."

Tony snorts, and quirks a smile at him. "Yeah. I guess you do."

The Stormtrooper's Tale

Title: The Story of Finn (2016)
Author: LullabyKnell
Fandom: *Star Wars VII: The Force Awakens*
Rating: Teen-and-up audiences
Additional tags: Finn is the hero of the stormtroopers, stormtrooper culture, stormtroopers are people, storytelling, rumors,
rebellion, revolution, autonomy, escape, names, families of
choice, canon-typical violence, spoilers, character study, POV
original character

Introduction

Star Wars (1977) is the fandom that formalized the split between science
fiction and fantasy fandom and what came to be called "media" fandom;
Star Trek had been a cult phenomenon, but *Star Wars* was a movement.
If you liked *Star Trek,* you were a Trekkie, but if you liked *Star Trek* and
Star Wars—and *Doctor Who*[1] and *Starsky and Hutch* and *Blake's 7* and *The
Professionals* and all the fandoms that came after, once the floodgates had
opened—well, *that* made you a media fan. Like Harry Potter twenty years
later, *Star Wars* drew enormous numbers of people into participatory fan
activities: hanging out in festive groups to see the films in the theater,
waiting on lines that ran around the block; making and wearing costumes;
joining fan clubs; buying merchandise and building models; making fan
films and writing fanfiction. Some people see *Star Wars* as a special case, as
the rare cultural text that warrants these intense levels of fannish engagement, but look askew at other fans and fan practices; this, too, happened

with Harry Potter.[2] There are people who might stand in line at the movies dressed as Darth Vader or go to a book release party costumed as a witch but think that being a Trekkie or a Whovian is weird. But in fact, many *Star Wars* fans crossed over (as did Potter fans much later) to become not just fans of one particular storyverse but *media fans* broadly speaking. *Star Wars* was thus one of the biggest and most important gateways into the larger cultures of fandom, introducing thousands to artmaking and cultural practices that became important to them, all lightsabers aside.

Star Wars is also notorious among fanfiction writers and vidders as a site of fan-producer conflict. As Henry Jenkins notes in *Textual Poachers*, "Lucasfilm originally sought to control *Star Wars* fan publications, seeing them as rivals," and later "threatened to prosecute editors who published works that violated the 'family values' associated with the original films."[3] Such works included much fanfiction, including most romance and erotica, het and slash alike. In the early days, Lucasfilm asked fans to send the studio a copy of every fanfiction zine published, which fans experienced as censorship; consequently, much *Star Wars* fanfiction went underground.[4] Lucasfilm was similarly controlling about fan video in the early days of digital remixing, offering fans a limited number of clips to work with, most of which were of spaceships and alien creatures.[5] Not exactly the parts of the films most of interest to female media fans, who tend to be interested in characterization and interpersonal relationships.

Lucasfilm's then-vice president, Jim Ward, famously warned fans away from making transformative fanworks by saying, "Fandom is about celebrating the story the way that it is." The dubiousness of that claim aside: who gets to decide what the story is? J. J. Abrams's 2015 film *Star Wars: The Force Awakens* makes a pretty good case that *Star Wars* is the story of the (increasingly dysfunctional) Skywalker clan, and fans immediately exploded into creative mode upon its release. Rey as the film's protagonist is certainly at the center of many stories, but fandom does love its pairings, and so there are stories shipping not only Rey and Finn, but Rey and Kylo Ren (notwithstanding the fact that they might well turn out to be siblings or cousins) as well as slash pairings Finn/Poe (fandom's first major slash pairing featuring two men of color) and Kylo/Hux (the almost de rigueur "trash," darkfic, or kink pairing, in this case featuring two characters from the dark side of the force; you can just imagine what they get up to up there on those star destroyers. Or maybe you can't, in which case—never mind, nothing to see here.)

But fanfic-writing fandom is also excited about the narrative possibilities offered by the *Star Wars* universe's first unmasked, and thus human-ized, stormtrooper, FN-2187, otherwise known as Finn, as played by black British actor John Boyega. While there have been important black charac-ters in the *Star Wars* universe—Lando Calrissian and Mace Windu come to mind—none had as central a role as Finn, nor one that so invited audi-ence identification. While fanfiction writers, who are often compelled to write their own genderbent or racebent stories to get diverse protagonists, rejoiced in the film's diverse casting—none of the three new central charac-ters is a white male—Finn was seen as a particular triumph. The year 2015, in addition to bringing a new *Star Wars* movie, was also the year of #os-carssowhite; that is, the year that the Oscars had to be publically shamed for not nominating a single black actor or actress. But as Anthony Lane pointed out in an article in the *New Yorker*, the combined global earnings of all *ten* of the films that starred Oscar's all-white nominees took in a little more than half of the box office takings of *Star Wars: The Force Awakens*, a film that was "fronted (at times, indeed, pretty much held together) by a young black man and a young woman."[6] Lane concludes by saying that, re-garding Hollywood's dismal record on race, "there just might be, amid the gloom, what Lucas would call a New Hope." Boyega's Finn is that hope.

Finn also gives hope to the characters in the story that follows, LullabyKnell's "The Story of Finn." The story of how I discovered this story is, in a way, the theme of the story itself. Upon asking for *Star Wars* fanfiction recommendations, I was recced a story called "Have You Heard" by peradi, whose summary is "Finn sparks a revolution."[7] In her story notes, peradi says that her story was inspired by "Tomorrow (There'll Be More of Us)" by dimircharmr,[8] a story about how the Resistance is starting to get stormtroopers defecting to them en masse. *This* story then points back to LullabyKnell's story, "The Story of Finn,"[9] which itself points back to a long Tumblr post by sunshinetrooper, which begins:

no but like
    imagine finn as the stormtrooper messiah, patron saint of rebellion

and continues:

finn must be the single most high profile former stormtrooper in the galaxy, and i mean, no matter how hard the first order will try to keep word of him from reaching the ears of their troopers, they will fail
    just imagine all these stormtroopers, people with no names, living

lives they've been taught don't belong to them, hearing the stories of finn the traitor, the defector, the rebel, the person

imagine all these people hearing about finn, the things he did, the things he chose, and realizing that they don't need to be what they've been taught, they don't need to be nameless, they don't need to be choiceless, they don't need to be less in any way at all

imagine all these people picking their own names, making their plans, making their choices, rebelling, defecting

Sunshinetrooper ultimately concludes, in all-caps:

IMAGINE FINN AND HIS DEFECTOR TROOPER BUDDIES ORGANIZING UN-
DERGROUND RAILROAD TYPE SYSTEMS FOR FREEING PEOPLE STILL EN-
SLAVED, DOING RAIDS ON TRAINING CAMPS AND FREEING CHILD TROOP-
ERS AND CRIPPLING THE ORDER'S PERSONNEL PIPELINE

This is what we mean when we say that fanfiction is written commu-
nally, collaboratively, in a network; this idea of Finn becoming a legendary figure whose story, spread from person to person, sparks a revolution
was taken up by LullabyKnell and others and has since inspired a whole
universe of stories, all of which are concerned with the impact of—not
Finn, but the *story* of Finn. In that way, "The Story of Finn" is classic fanfiction, fleshing out the part of *Star Wars: The Force Awakens* that we know
least about (the subculture of stormtroopers, who we learn are nameless:
taken from their families and raised to military service from birth without
choice). But it is also a story about race: Finn is overtly framed as a figure
of liberation, the founder of an underground railroad, with fandom collectively emphasizing the degree to which FN-2187 is an escaped slave, his
number-not-name evoking the numbers given to those who worked in
forced labor camps. In the larger genre of stormtrooper stories, names are
an important theme, as you can see from Sunshinetrooper's post (*imagine all these people picking their own names*) and tags like LullabyKnell's
"Names" and dimiricharmer's "Identity Issues." Some escaped stormtroopers take Finn's name; others choose names of their own: nonslave names.
Across these stormtrooper stories, fans draw on their knowledge of history
to tell tales of the stormtroopers' postcolonial culture. So in the end, Finn's
story is not just his own. Finn's story—having Finn be at the center of a
story—has galaxy-shaping impact and leads directly to the fall of empires.

Last but not least, "The Story of Finn" is also a meta story, a story of fandom itself; the story of our stories and the liberatory impact hearing and telling stories have had on our own lives. At the end of this first chapter of "The Story of Finn," "BeeKay's Bunkroom" (the homey BeeKay being derived from her slave name, BK-1245), the stormtroopers wonder how FN-2187 could do what he did: how he was able to break his programming, break free. "What makes *him* different?" they wonder. "Why him and not . . . just for example . . . *me?*" This is the impact that fanfiction has had among so many of us; having read it, we now think about writing it. *She did it; why not me?*

Suggested Further Reading

Will Brooker's 2002 *Using the Force: Creativity, Community and Star Wars Fans* is still the go-to academic monograph on *Star Wars* and fandom, though it does not include the most recent films. William Proctor's 2013 article in *Participations*, "Holy Crap, More *Star Wars*! More *Star Wars*? What If They're Crap? Disney, Lucasfilm, and *Star Wars* Online Fandom in the 21st Century," summarizes fandom's anxiety in the face of the third trilogy; John Borland's 2005 "*Star Wars* and the Fracas over Fan Films" and Simone Murray's "'Celebrating the Story the Way It Is': Cultural Studies, Corporate Media, and the Contested Utility of Fandom" (*Continuum*, 2004) both summarize fans' problematic relationship with Lucasfilm as a controlling corporate entity. *Finding the Force of the Star Wars Franchise: Fans, Merchandise, Critics*, is a 2006 collection of academic essays. Lastly, the 2010 documentary *The People vs. George Lucas*, supposedly interested in *Star Wars* and its fans, is useful for what it *doesn't* do and *doesn't* say; women are nearly invisible in it (only 4 out of 126 speakers are women), and fanfiction is totally invisible in it. That makes it a useful starting point for further work.

The Story of Finn

LullabyKnell

Chapter 1: BeeKay's Bunkroom

The only thing Stormtroopers own are stories.

At least, that's how it works in their base, in their bunkroom of messenger pilots. Maybe things work differently for other groups. Maybe they fall asleep in silence, not talking to each other, not even looking at each other. Maybe that's how things would have been for them too, if not for BK-1245.

BK-1245 is old, for a Stormtrooper, though how old is something that no one's dared to ask her. But they checked and there's not a single other BK Trooper left in the whole First Order, just her, lasting against all the life-expectancy statistics, and to ask why she's the only one left feels wrong somehow.

BK-1245 doesn't talk about her old squads, and she's scary when she wants to be.

Stormtroopers aren't meant to be inquisitive anyway, but there's something else keeping them from asking how she did it—how she's stayed alive so long for a First Order soldier—besides respect for a commanding officer and an education forbidding curiosity. It just doesn't feel right.

They think they know the answer already anyway. It's luck. It's sheer dumb luck for you to make it when the Trooper next to you, who you might have grown up next to since you were brought into the First Order, didn't. BK-1245 just has more luck than most, something she's commented more than a time or two.

Well, it's not just that. BK-1245 is also an incredible pilot and a flawless

250

officer. Her bunkroom is without disciplinary issue and there's no faster messenger in the whole First Order, so the First Order hasn't had a reason to dismiss her. She's considered one of their greatest successes by her commanding officer, a compliment that she takes with a nod and a blank face, as a good Trooper does.

That's what they do here, in their strategically placed base on an otherwise inhospitable rock, carry messages for more important people than them, data too important to be transmitted but not so important that it can't wait for hyperspace transport. Shipments of food, weapons, ship parts, everything necessary to the First Order imaginable, moves through their base.

It's a link in the chain that the higher-ups probably never think about—a stopover place that never stops moving, never sleeps.

Except that Troopers, for all that they're trained and conditioned for the utmost efficiency, still need sleep. It's a preset amount, and they're never allowed a minute more or less than their allotted period, but it's a time they've managed to make their own, thanks to BK-1245.

JN-1500 didn't know what to think when she first walked into her newly assigned bunkroom, and started preparing for her allotted dormancy period only for JM-2002 and JM-2003 to pen her in between them and march her to where the rest of the bunkroom was gathered. They sat her down in a large semicircle and then sat down on either side of her, looking towards their commanding officer expectantly and not paying her and her confusion any attention whatsoever.

BK-1245 was sitting in the middle of their circle, having removed her armor and helmet and changed into the plain black sleepwear that all of them wore, which didn't look much different from their underarmor wear. JN-1500's first thought was that BK-1245 was so *old*, all solid and thick with the beginnings of *lines* around her eyes.

And then that their commanding officer was . . . pretty. With her smooth dark skin and wide lips and black eyes and hair, BK-1245 is a splash of unexpected color among the monochrome First Order by her appearance alone.

JN-1500 will never forget that first night, because it marked a different kind of memory than the regular training-delivery-repeat. She remembers how BK-1245 looked around the room and the Troopers leaned forward eagerly, how BK-1245 locked eyes with JN-1500 for a moment and smiled, a shock of white teeth against her dark face that JN-1500 hadn't known what to make of then. And how BK-1245 started to speak, eyes on JN-1500 the whole time, and gave JN-1500 her first Second-Hand Story.

"Because we've got a new face with us tonight, I'm going to tell Maolo V Story," BK-1245 said, in a low and soothing tone that made it the most rich voice JN-1500 had ever heard. So different from barked orders and the monotone exchanges of First Order soldiers. "As a new pilot, I was shipping construction supplies to two new outposts on Maolo V . . ."

BK-1245's story lasted no more than fifteen minutes, but those fifteen minutes changed JN-1500's life forever. It wasn't a controversial story, though the higher-ups never liked any information to be spread around unnecessarily, or a story that would be told around the galaxy for generations to come, but it made JN-1500's heart act strangely all the same. Because it was . . . funny.

Funny.

A humorous anecdote about two outpost commanders constantly arguing and seemingly incapable of sharing supplies—though JN-1500 wondered why such silly men had been put in charge of anything—and that worked out happily for all parties in the end.

JN-1500 didn't know why she didn't report BK-1245's behavior, which was definitely against regulations and probably grounds for the reconditioning of their entire bunkroom. She reasoned to herself that BK-1245 was her commanding officer and it wasn't her place to attract attention or speak out, and that it had clearly been happening in this bunkroom without issue for quite a while.

They went to sleep then, twenty minutes into their allotted dormancy period, and JN-1500 spent the next twenty wondering why the story had been told. There seemed little point to such things, as they interrupted limited allotted dormancy periods and the information was completely unnecessary to JN-1500's ability to do her duties. There was no point to it at all.

JN-1500 fell asleep wondering if BK-1245 would do the same again the next night.

BK-1245 did.

And again the next night.

And again the night after that.

Every night, BK-1245 told them another story, sometimes two or three. She never went past thirty minutes of interrupted allotted dormancy period, but she made those thirty minutes count.

On the nights that BK-1245 wasn't present, off on a crucial mission that only their leader was deemed fit to handle, or was simply tired, another Trooper would take over and give their own stories. Most weren't nearly as good at telling stories as BK-1245, but JN-1500 listened intently all the same, because every Trooper had unique, interesting tales of their own to tell.

They were messengers, every one of them, selected for their piloting abilities and fast reflexes, showing superior skill in speed flights and evasive maneuvering. They traveled constantly, to many systems, to many other bases and outposts, and had collected many stories.

The ones that transferred from farther bases had been to systems that JN-1500 had never heard of before, would likely never go to, and they could give vivid descriptions of exotic planets. GC-0492, called Postcard after a joke a higher-up made after his first transfer of his total of three, was the best at telling those stories—Place Stories—of seas that never ended, of trees taller than Star Destroyers, and of cities carved into mountains that touched the clouds.

After a while, reporting what went on their bunkroom became unthinkable.

JN-1500 didn't notice any changes in herself, maybe more than a little intentionally. She went on missions, she delivered data, she did her job without any difficulties—got herself a nickname from her bunkmates, Double-O, or Doublo. Then she came home, removed her helmet and armor, sat herself down between JM-2002 and JM-2003, whom she learned were called Two and Three, and listened to her fellow messengers tell stories.

If she remembered how their activities would not be permitted by the First Order, she made sure not to.

If she noticed that no other base or bunkroom did what they did, she looked the other way.

If she paid more attention to her surroundings on missions, listened more closely to other people's conversations, and started looking for stories of her own, then . . . well, it didn't interfere with her ability to run messages. So it didn't matter.

There was no need to turn herself and all her bunkmates in for reconditioning. Not Postcard, with his delighted descriptions of colorful fish and beautiful birds. Not Two and Three, with their touchy jockeying and somewhat endearing annoyingness. Not BeeKay, who hooked them in with harmless stories and then put increasingly dangerous ones into their heads, and yet watched over them protectively and forcibly kept them in line and out of suspicion.

No need at all, Doublo tells herself.

The First Order already owns their lives.

The only thing Stormtroopers own are stories.

Doublo has many stories now. Second-Hand, Third-Hand, and Fourth-Hand Stories mostly, with some Further-Hands too—even a couple Far-Hands, though they're the same ones everyone has. She has a respectable number of First-Hands to her name, though she's never quite got the hang of telling them or other stories, and they're not very good.

She hasn't found what she's best at yet either. BeeKay is good at everything and has so many stories, though she specializes in Mission Stories best. Postcard (GC-0492), as stated, is good at Place Stories. Two (JM-2002) tends towards People Stories, and Three (JM-2003) likes Thing Stories best, and they both say that Doublo will find her sort eventually.

It takes feeling to tell a good story, and sometimes it takes a while to find the ones you really feel for, their bunkroom agrees. Sometimes it takes a while for the feeling to build.

Doublo's thought about it, and the thing is that she feels the Far-Hand Stories the best—the ones where nobody knows where they started—the ones that could be called legends or myths. BeeKay says they're real, but she's also warned Doublo that Far-Hand Stories only come once in a lifetime, in small bunches in short bursts after long, long waits.

But still, these are the ones that Doublo really feels. The ones filled with Death Stars and Old Empires and Skywalkers. The ones with smugglers riding Millennium Falcons and princesses commanding Rebellions and Jedi and Sith wielding the mystical Force.

Some Troopers don't like these ones—almost hate them—because they're far more dangerous than Postcard's scenery descriptions and BeeKay's mission anecdotes. Treason of a far more explicit kind than their other Story Circles. They don't want to hear them; they don't believe they're true, they don't want to listen to something that could get them killed, or they're just not comfortable with something that goes against everything the First Order taught them to oppose and destroy.

They're stories rarely told and rarely listened to. Some of Doublo's bunkmates will curl up in their bunks rather than listen, and mutter wondering why they're even told.

Doublo thinks they're told because they have to be, like all of BeeKay's stories and storytelling tradition, though she doesn't know why.

Either she'll die in the line of duty without ever knowing, like several of her bunkmates have already, as is her primary duty as a Stormtrooper of the First Order, or . . .

Or she'll find out one day.

There's been a strained feeling in the base for the last while when they first hear the news.

Not of Kylo Ren, not of Starkiller Base finishing construction and being turned towards the Republic, not of Luke Skywalker gone missing, not of the map to him that both the First Order and the Resistance are searching for—no, they know those things already. They make it their business to know those things, do the storyteller messengers of BeeKay's bunkroom, because it's all they have, really.

The news they hear is that of FN-2187.

He's a defector—a traitor to the First Order. He's not the first, nor will he be the last, and the First Order expects to retrieve him and end him quickly.

The higher-ups have more important things to worry about than the rumors running through the ranks. Stormtroopers aren't supposed to do things like gossip, and have learned to keep the named officers under the impression that they don't. To most of the higher-ups, Stormtroopers might as well be a part of the walls rather than anything sentient, much less alive.

Stormtroopers are everywhere and hear everything, and they often talk to each other, because the only thing that Stormtroopers own are stories.

So the story of FN-2187 spreads quickly. Postcard returns to their base with a Second-Hand Story, having been making a delivery to the higher-ups on the ship where FN-2187 was assigned when it happened.

Postcard is built as all Stormtroopers are: tall and stocky with muscle. He has pale skin, stubbles of blond over his scalp, and a squashed and scarred sort of face. He looks more like a brawler than a pilot who takes delight in describing fields of exotic flowers. Postcard's not as ancient as BeeKay, but he's definitely one of the senior Troopers in their bunkroom— older than Doublo, Two, and Three at the least—but he's almost jittery with excitement like a nervous Trooper just assigned when he comes in.

Three asked him if he just visited a really amazing new planet with flying oceans or something.

Postcard responded with a story like nothing they'd ever heard before.

FN-2187 went down to Jakku with frequent subjects of People Stories: Kylo Ren and Captain Phasma, on his first mission. For his first mission, they raided a settlement of Resistance Sympathizers for the map to Luke

Skywalker, the infamous religious fanatic and Rebel terrorist. Kylo Ren captured the Resistance's best pilot, then ordered the destruction of the settlement and all who lived there.

Except FN-2187, whose file is marked with officer potential but empathetic tendencies towards weak links, didn't fire a single shot. Not one. His blaster record has been checked again and again, but the result never changes. He never pulled his trigger.

Upon return to base, FN-2187 was marked for review and reconditioning by Captain Phasma, but never reported to his new assignment. Instead, he freed the Resistance pilot, stole a TIE Fighter, dealt severe damage to the Star Destroyer he was escaping from, was shot down over Jakku, and is either dead or missing on the planet's surface. Like the Resistance pilot and the BB-8 droid currently holding the map to Luke Skywalker.

This is . . . different. Defection Stories are those of Stormtroopers who are caught, then reviewed, reconditioned, or dismissed by the First Order. Defection Stories are those of Stormtroopers who malfunction like a droid with bad programming and run, only to be hunted down by the First Order and made examples, to die unable to survive on their own, or to just disappear entirely.

What FN-2187 did was . . . loud. Even when a Stormtrooper defies the First Order, they don't so *openly defy* the First Order. They defect quietly and hope to hell no one notices. But FN-2187 went out with a bang. Literally.

"Traitor," some Troopers growl, since they're all trained from birth to obey and reject the idea of doing anything else and to enforce obedience in everyone else.

Their bunkroom doesn't dare, though. It would be incredibly hypocritical, even if what they do isn't so explicit as what FN-2187 did. Doublo isn't sure that she could get that hateful vitriol into her voice, so like a good Stormtrooper, she doesn't say anything.

She's still not sure why BeeKay's bunkroom hasn't all been dismissed for spreading Resistance propaganda, but she's not going to be the one to reveal them. She's not going to damn her bunkmates and stop the only part of her life that she actually looks forward to.

"But why did he do it?" some others ask each other, confused and helpless. "But *why?*"

"Maybe he was a Resistance plant?" someone suggests, but that's quickly shot down as incorrect.

FN-2187 was a Stormtrooper, trained and raised, no different from any of them. He was taken from a place that many others were and educated through the exact same program. He ran the same procedures and took the same tests, was quick to obey and quicker to learn. Top of his training group in most if not all skills; he was a cadet who was going places, as far as Troopers can go, and his fellow cadets were probably jealous of him. Just given the way some of them apparently spit his designation and how he never got a nickname of any kind, though most Troopers do.

He had some behavioral problems, but was marked as officer potential nevertheless by Captain Phasma herself. And most Stormtroopers had at least a couple issues that needed to be fixed, that's what conditioning and reconditioning is for, even if some tried to pretend otherwise.

FN-2187 was just the same as all of them, without any prior signs of disobedience. Just another Trooper in the hallways, just another Trooper on the ground, just another Trooper on the training field, that was FN-2187.

Except . . . when FN-2187 was dropped into his first battle, he wouldn't pull the trigger.

He wouldn't shoot.

He wouldn't kill.

He didn't exactly *say* no, but . . .

He said no in the loudest way possible, by breaking Kylo Ren's personal prisoner free, stealing a TIE Fighter, shooting up a hanger bay, and breaking free of the First Order's orders. All that, without any sort of prior indication or obvious reasons; FN-2187 chose not to obey.

"But *why?*" the Stormtroopers whisper to each other, while the higher-ups ignore them in favor of searching somewhat desperately for more important things than rumors. "But *why* did he do it?"

Why *him?* Doublo hears them say without saying it.

*What makes **him** different? Why him and not . . . just for example . . . **me?***

Notes

Preface

1. This is actually why there's no *Twilight* story included in this volume. *Twilight* fandom seems to pride itself on writing very long stories: novel length—or longer.

2. Henry Jenkins, *Textual Poachers* (New York: Routledge, 1992), 36.

3. Today, or any day, on Tumblr: "*pulls up to the fanfic drive-thru window* uh yeah, I'll take a fake relationship with a side of mutual pining and thinking the other isn't interested, thanks." And the reply: "One of my favorites. Can you super-size it?"

4. This is just one way of insulting the female spectator; another might be implicit in Dorothy Parker's wry note, "Men never make passes at girls who wear glasses." Women aren't valued for how they see, but for how they look; sweatpants and glasses not welcome. Men have not been similarly insulted for binge-watching *Breaking Bad*.

5. And in fact, orgasms have always been seen as one of the potential—and dangerous—side effects of modern fictional storytelling; Thomas Laqueur goes so far as to theorize that masturbation as a modern concept (addictive, degenerate) develops at the same time, and in conjunction with, the rise of the novel—and of course, women have always been the great novel readers. See Thomas Laqueur, *Solitary Sex: A Cultural History of Masturbation* (New York: Zone Books, 2003), 269.

6. The dangers, especially to women, of novel reading have been well described; Ana Vogrincic summarizes many of them in "The Novel Reading Panic in 18th Century England: An Outline of an Early Moral Media Panic," *Medijska istraživanja* 14, no. 2 (2008): 103–24. See also Terry Lovell, *Consuming Fiction* (London: Verso, 1987).

7. Jane Austen, *Northanger Abbey* (Mineola, NY: Dover Thrift, 2000), 72.

8. Susan Torrey Barstow, "Hedda Is All of Us: Late-Victorian Women at the Matinee," *Victorian Studies* 43, no. 3 (2001): 391.

Introduction

1. Jacqueline Lichtenberg, Sondra Marshak, and Joan Winston, *Star Trek Lives!* (New York: Corgi, 1975), 221–22.

2. Seanan McGuire, "Seanan Loves Her Some Fanfic, Yes, She Does: On Transformative Works," Livejournal, http://seanan-mcguire.livejournal.com/431092.html

3. Camille Bacon-Smith, *Enterprising Women: Television Fandom and the Creation of Popular Myth* (Philadelphia: University of Pennsylvania Press, 1992), 48.

4. Bacon-Smith, *Enterprising Women*, 45.

5. Henry Jenkins, "Gender and Fan Studies (Round Five, Part One): Geoffrey Long and Catherine Tosenberger," Confessions of an Aca-Fan, June 28, 2007, http://henryjenkins.org/2007/06/gender_and_fan_studies_round_f_1.html

6. Anne Jamison, *Fic: Why Fanfiction Is Taking Over the World* (Dallas, TX: Smartpop Books, 2013), 35.

7. Lev Grossman, "The Boy Who Lived Forever," *Time*, July 7, 2011.

8. Lev Grossman, foreword to Jamison, *Fic*, xii.

9. Jamison, *Fic*, 28.

10. Jamison, *Fic*, 27.

11. In *ficathons* and *fests*, the challenge moderators solicit story requests from the community and either allow participants to pick from them or else match up writers with requests. A *Secret Santa* is a fest in which people request stories with particular characters or themes and an anonymous writer creates the story and gives it to the requestor as a gift, though there is often later a reveal of authorship. *Yuletide* is the largest and best known Secret Santa exchange; it is dedicated to rare fandoms, and typically about two thousand people play each year. A *Big Bang* challenge is characterized by two features: first, it is designed to solicit long stories—originally over fifty thousand words, but now any "long" length—and second, it pairs writers with artists/illustrators, so that the final story includes artwork or some kind of multimedia. A *porn battle* is designed to elicit the sexiest fanfic the writer is capable of; it is a challenge that celebrates dirty-mindedness. In a *bingo challenge*, participants get a bingo card of squares featuring different prompts, and wins by writing five stories to collect B-I-N-G-O.

12. Alan Sinfield, *Cultural Politics: Queer Reading* (Philadelphia: University of Pennsylvania Press, 1994), 4–5.

13. Henry Jenkins quoted in Amy Harmon, "In TV's Dull Summer Days, Plots Take Wing on the Net," *New York Times*, August 18, 1997.

14. Francesca Coppa, "Writing Bodies in Space: Media Fanfiction as Theatrical Performance," in Hellekson and Busse, *Fan Fiction Studies Reader*, 219.

15. Kristina Busse, "The Return of the Author: Ethos and Identity Politics," in *A Companion to Media Authorship*, ed. Jonathan Gray and Derek Johnson (Chicester: Wiley-Blackwell, 2013), 51.

16. Karen Hellekson and Kristina Busse, "Introduction: Work in Progress," in *Fan Fiction and Fan Communities in the Age of the Internet*, ed. Hellekson and Busse (Jefferson, NC: McFarland, 2006), 5.

17. Naomi Novik, interview by Annalee Newitz, "Naomi Novik Says Fanfiction Is Part of Literary History—and Reveals What's Next for Temeraire," io9, September 9, 2010, http://io9.com/5634183/naomi-novik-says-fanfic-is-part-of-literary-history--and-reveals-whats-next-for-temeraire

18. For more about fan engagement with social media tools, see Francesca Coppa, "Pop Culture, Fans, and Social Media," in the *Routledge Handbook of Social Media*, ed. Theresa Senft and Jeremy Hunsinger (New York: Routledge, 2014).

19. Mel Stanfill, "Kindle Worlds II: The End of Fandom as We Know It?," June 3, 2013, http://www.mclstanfill.com/kindle-worlds-ii-the-end-of-fandom-as-we-know-it/

20. Karen Hellekson and Kristina Busse, introduction to *The Fan Fiction Studies Reader*, ed. Hellekson and Busse (Iowa City: University of Iowa Press, 2014), 6–7.

21. For definitions of these and more, please consult Fanlore, the OTW's fan culture wiki at fanlore.org.

22. Arduinna, "Slash Fiction Is Like a Banquet," Fanlore, http://fanlore.org/wiki/Slash_Fiction_is_Like_a_Banquet

23. Karen Hellekson, "A Fannish Field of Value: Online Fan Gift Culture," *Cinema Journal* 48, no. 4 (2009). 113–18.

24. Cupidsbow, "How Fanfiction Keeps Us Poor," Livejournal, 2007.

25. DeKosnik's "Sugarhill moment" is a metaphor from hip-hop; in 1979, a manufactured group, the Sugarhill Gang, released "Rapper's Delight," which put hip-hop on the map before any of the more authentic inventors of the form. Abigail DeKosnik, "Should Fan Fiction Be Free?," *Cinema Journal* 48, no. 4 (2009): 119.

26. DeKosnik, "Should Fan Fiction Be Free?," 124.

27. Sunny Moraine, aka Sarah Wanenchak, "*Fifty Shades of Grey* and the Ethics of Fannish Prosumption," Cyborgology, June 6, 2012, https://thesocietypages.org/cyborgology/2012/06/06/fifty-shades-of-grey-and-the-ethics-of-fannish-prosumption/

28. Bethan Jones, "Fifty Shades of Exploitation: Fan Labor and *Fifty Shades of Grey*," *Transformative Works and Cultures* 15 (2014): 3.12, http://journal.transformativeworks.org/index.php/twc/article/view/501/422

29. Mary Ellen Curtin, aka Doctor Science, "The Color and Definition of Fanfiction," Obsidian Wings, August 22, 2012, http://obsidianwings.blogs.com/obsidian_wings/2012/08/the-definition-and-color-of-fanfiction.html

30. N. E. Lilly, "What Is Speculative Fiction?," Green Tentacles, March 2002, http://www.greententacles.com/articles/5/26/; see also the OED, which cites Heinlein as saying, in 1953, "The term 'speculative fiction' may be defined negatively as being fiction about things that have not happened."

31. Yahtzee, "Relatives & Relativity," Archive of Our Own, March 16, 2010.

32. As I have argued elsewhere, Sherlock Holmes was transmedia almost from the get-go, the stories being published with accompanying paratextual drawings by Sidney Paget, and plays and films soon to follow, and even enormous book fandoms like *Harry Potter* or *Lord of the Rings* grew exponentially when made into films. See Francesca Coppa, "Sherlock as Cyborg: Bridging Mind and Body," in *Sherlock and Transmedia Fandom: Essays on the BBC Series*, ed. Louisa Ellen Stein and Kristina Busse (Jefferson, NC: McFarland, 2012).

33. One of the things a beta reader—an editor who works with a writer on her fanfiction—is likely to do is to insist on a clear narrative point of view (POV). Fans argue about the merits of first- vs. third-person POV (and will apologize and justify themselves when they use second). A tight third-person POV is most typical and considered "best," and an omniscient POV is often disdained as incorrect; fans don't like to jump from the inside of one head to another, likely because it ruins the suspense of trying to figure out what another character is thinking.

34. For more about the ways in which fanfiction uses the bodies of actors, see my article "Writing Bodies in Space."

35. Interview with Rebecca Tushnet, "Fan Fiction vs. Copyright—Q&A with Rebecca Tushnet," July 20, 2012, http://reason.com/blog/2012/07/20/fan-fiction-vs-copyright-qa-with-rebecca

36. Livia Penn, "Two Really Good Reasons Why Kindle Worlds Is Bullshit," Dreamwidth, May 23, 2013, quoted in Rebecca Tushnet, "All of This Has Happened Before and Will Happen Again: Innovation in Copyright Licensing," *Berkeley Tech Law Journal* Vol. 28, 2014: 1481: note 128.

37. Rebecca Tushnet, "Remix/Mashup at Ohio State, Panel 1," March 13, 2009, http://tushnet.blogspot.com/2009/03/remixmashup-at-ohio-state-panel-1.html

38. Tushnet, "All of This Has Happened."

39. Jamison, *Fic*, 281–82.

40. John Scalzi quoted in Stanfill, "Kindle Worlds II."

41. In fact, women have had to confront these issues all across craftwork. Artist Nina Paley, who went from making digital animation (e.g., "Sita Sings the Blues") to analog objects (quilts), was dismayed to find that the selling price of quilts "seldom covers the cost of materials; quilters often prefer to give their quilts away." (Paley began to make ironic "statement" quilts of ten-thousand-dollar bills to comment on this notion of value.) http://blog.ninapaley.com/2013/06/01/bargain-ten-thousand-dollars/. Similarly, knitters on Etsy often have to remind potential customers to consider the time a project will take as well as the cost of materials before asking for something custom-made.

42. Viviana Zelizer, a pioneer of "economic sociology," specializes in theorizing the vexed places where intimate personal relations and economics meet. In "The Price and Value of Children: The Case of Children's Insurance," *American Journal of Sociology* 86, no. 5 (1981): 1036–56, she explores the late nineteenth-century emergence of the "economically 'worthless' but emotionally 'priceless' child"; in more recent books like *The Purchase of Intimacy* (Princeton, NJ: Princeton University Press, 2005), Zelizer negotiates between extreme positions—what she calls "hostile world" arguments (money and intimacy should never mix!) and "nothing but" arguments (all relationships are really economic exchanges underneath)—to explore more nuanced connections between intimacy and money.

The Communication's Officer's Tale

1. See *Saturday Night Live*'s sketch "Get a Life," in which most of the Trekkies are guys, or even the parody film *Galaxy Quest*, in which the key fans are male.

2. Pon farr appears in "Amok Time," genderswap in "Turnabout Intruder," alternate universes in "Mirror Mirror," time travel in "City on the Edge of Forever" (among others); "Assignment Earth" was a crossover with a proposed series of the same name; rapid aging appears in "The Deadly Years," sex pollen in "This Side of Paradise"; Kirk and Uhura were forced to kiss by aliens in "Plato's Stepchildren," and Kirk has amnesia for most of "The Paradise Syndrome."

3. It's an ongoing delight to me to see new fans on Tumblr and other new fannish meeting grounds marvel over GIFs of the original *Star Trek*: "Wait, so you mean that really *happened*??"

4. For instance, Jacqueline Lichtenberg's "Kraith" series became a large, shared alternative *Star Trek* universe in which Vulcan culture plays a much larger role.

5. The story, which warns, "BEWARE! NEW YORK JEWISH HUMOR AT WORK! YOU'RE GONNA BE SORRY!," is still notable for its projection of Jewish religion and culture into the world of Starfleet. Mindy Glazer, *Tales of Feldman*, print zine, 1981.

6. Jane Land, *Demeter*, 1987, preserved in the Archive of Our Own by the Open Doors project of the OTW.

7. Jenkins, *Textual Poachers*, 167.

8. *Star Trek*, "The Menagerie" (1966).

9. *Star Trek*'s first pilot featured a strong female character—Number One, the ship's first officer—who was replaced for the second *Star Trek* pilot: many subsequent female characters were disappointing to female fans looking for role models. Fans have also been disappointed in *Trek*'s heterosexism and lack of sexual diversity.

10. Though as I note earlier in this volume, it's only some kinds of sexuality that are shocking. Every eight o'clock cop show can start with a rape, but if Harry Potter turns out to be gay or Buffy and Faith have an orgasm then it's obscene.

The FBI Agent's Tale

1. For an interview with Paula Smith and a discussion of the Mary Sue, see "A Conversation with Paula Smith," interview by Cynthia W. Walker, *Transformative Works and Cultures* 6 (2001), doi:10.3983/twc2001.0243.

2. Paula Smith, "A Trekkie's Tale," *Menagerie* 2 (December 1973).

3. Bacon-Smith, *Enterprising Women*, 53.

4. Bacon-Smith, *Enterprising Women*, 53.

5. This has led to things like the "Mary Sue Litmus Test," where you can find out if your character qualifies. Questions include whether she has "unusual eye color (violet, amber, etc.)," an "unusual name," excels at everything, socializes with senior staff rather than her own peer group, etc.

6. Mulder was often tortured both in *X-Files* canon as well as in fanfiction. (There is an entire fanfic genre known as Muldertorture, but fans also enjoy comforting Mulder at length—often by pairing him with Dana Scully, Alex Krycek, or Walter Skinner.)

The Slayer's Tale

1. It was also Josiah Bartlet's recurring question on *The West Wing* (1999–2006).

2. The show, as creator Joss Whedon once noted, "lends itself to polymorphously perverse subtext." Milly Williamson, "*Buffy the Vampire Slayer*," in *The Essential Cult TV Reader*, ed. David Lavery (Lexington: University Press of Kentucky, 2010), 65. Popular pairings include Buffy/Angel, Buffy/Spike, Angel/Spike, Willow/Tara, Buffy/Giles, Willow/Oz, and Spike/Xander, as well as Buffy/Faith.

3. Buffy and Faith also switch bodies in the season 4 episode "Who Are You?" (2000) and proceed to bathe and have sex in the other's body—as if the pairing needed *more* subtext. "Who Are You?" is also the episode where it becomes apparent that Willow and Tara are having sex, and Faith is the first one to recognize it: here, too, she signifies desire. (Oh, and later, Faith spends time in a women's prison: that's pretty much lesbian fantasy bingo, isn't it?)

4. "Wolves at the Gate," *Buffy the Vampire Slayer Season Eight* (Dark Horse Comics), March–June 2008.

The Super Man's Tale

1. Fanlore, "Lois and Clark," http://fanlore.org/wiki/Lois_%26_Clark:_The_New_Adventures_of_Superman

2. Fanlore, "Lex Luthor," http://fanlore.org/wiki/Lex_Luthor_(Smallville)

3. There was always a gayest look of the episode.

4. Omar, Television Without Pity, http://www.televisionwithoutpity.com/show/smallville/hourglass-1/5/

5. No, really: *anything*. In Superman canon, Lex and Superman have a baby together. Also Superman was hypnotized into doing porn, and he adopted and disowned Jimmy Olsen and fought giant ants and destroyed planets by accident, and that's not even going into Bizarro Superman and Beppo the Super Monkey and stories featuring Red Kryptonite. Also Lex Luthor is president of the United States.

6. Basingstoke, "Five Things That Aren't True," Archive of Our Own, November 30, 2001.

7. "DVD Commentary! For the Challenge Thingy!," http://serrico.livejournal.com/396576.html

8. Pete Ross, Fanlore, http://fanlore.org/wiki/Pete_Ross_(Smallville)

9. Yahtzee, "Them Mean Ol', Low-Down, Lando Calrissian Blues," Archive of Our Own, January 8, 2010.

The Dwarf's Tale

1. In fact, Tolkien-inspired bands like Led Zeppelin were arguably the first "wizard rock"; listen to Robert Plant warble about "the darkest depths of Mordor," in "Ramble On," for instance, or "Misty Mountain Hop," or "The Battle of Evermore."

2. There has been similar friction between some old-school Sherlockians and fans of the recent Sherlock Holmes films or television series.

3. To be fair, many of the *LOTR* cast got matching tattoos at the conclusion of filming. If you don't want fans to slash you, possibly consider *not* getting matching tattoos.

4. "Lobelia321," private correspondence, February 13, 2014.

5. And into the afterlife, in fact. Tolkien tells us in his appendix that Legolas took Gimli with him to Valinor (the Undying Lands, Tolkien's version of Avalon or paradise). Tolkien adds, "If this is true, then it is strange indeed: that a Dwarf should be willing to leave Middle-earth for any love." As *LOTR* fan spatz mused, "Wow. Sometimes you just have to admit canon did all the work for you" (private correspondence, February 14, 2014).

The Pop Star's Tale

1. "Puppies in a Box" was a website formed by a number of early and influential popslash writers, including Helenish, Synchronik, Cecilia, Laura, Sinead, and Wax Jism. Fanlore notes that the site's eponymous metaphor reflected "the fannish feeling toward boybands: the boys in said bands were all cute, pick any one, any two, any group of them!"

2. Kristina Busse, "'I'm Jealous of the Fake Me,'" in *Framing Celebrity: New Directions in Celebrity Culture*, ed. Sue Holmes and Sean Redmond (New York: Routledge, 2006), 253.

3. In Sandy Keene's "Isle of View," Lance and Justin swap bodies; in Kittie's ". . . and a Treasure Chest, Too," the boys are fish; in Keene's meta-fic "As Lucid as Hell," hundreds of Lances and Justins and JCs and Joeys and Chrises live in a dorm and compare the stories they're in, while complaining about how slow their authors are.

4. Helenish's popslash can be found at her website helenish.talkoncorners.net.

5. You might well ask yourself where Lance got such a robot. Kaneko doesn't answer that question, but another writer, Linbot, wrote a companion story to supply the obvious answer: Lex Luthor, who directed Lance to buy from the Troica, a trio of sexbot makers who were the big bads of *Buffy* season 6. See Linbot, "Lance Knows a Guy," Archive of Our Own, April 27, 2002.

6. "Lance Bass Knows 'Tons' of Closeted Gay Celebrities, but Won't Out Them," *Huffington Post*, September 23, 2013, http://www.huffingtonpost.com/2013/09/23/lance-bass-closeted-gay-celebrities_n_3975351.html

The Spymaster's Tale

1. Kingsley Amis, *The James Bond Dossier* (London: Jonathan Cape, 1965), 38.

2. Amis, *The James Bond Dossier*, 54.

3. Lisa Funnell, "'I Know Where You Keep Your Gun': Daniel Craig as the Bond–Bond Girl Hybrid in *Casino Royale*," *Journal of Popular Culture* 44, no. 3 (2011): 456.

4. Funnell, "I Know Where You Keep Your Gun," 456.

5. See, among other works, Gail DeKosnik, "M Stands for Mother: James Bond

and Freudian Family Romance in *Casino Royale* and *Quantum of Solace*," in *The Cultures of James Bond*, ed. Christian Krug and Joachim Frank (Tricr: WVT, 2011).

The Wizard's Tales

1. Fanlore, "Harry Potter," http://fanlore.org/wiki/Harry_Potter

2. Fanlore, "Epilogue? What Epilogue?," http://fanlore.org/wiki/Epilogue%3F_What_Epilogue%3F

3. Rowling has since said that she regrets pairing Hermione and Ron and that they would, as Yahtzee suggests in her story, have needed relationship counseling.

4. Ika Willis, in her article "Keeping Promises to Queer Children: Making Space (for Mary Sue) at Hogwarts," in Hellekson and Busse, *Fan Fiction and Fan Communities*, argues that Harry/Snape slash is so powerful because it postulates an affair between the point-of-view character, Harry, the locus of "readerly/desiring subjectivity," and Snape, the text's defined "outsider" character.

5. Having Snape turn out to be Harry's father is another way that fans reread Snape's intense feelings for Harry; the genre of stories where this turns out to be true is called "Severitus."

6. *Star Trek* fans have explored the intimacy of the mind-meld with similar results.

7. "Ten Ways to Rewrite a Television Show," in Jenkins, *Textual Poachers*.

The Companions' Tale

1. Rory is actually living through the twentieth century for the second time, as he retains the memories of a duplicate version of himself called the Centurion who lived for nearly two thousand years while protecting an Amy who was in statis in something called the Pandorica. It's *Doctor Who*: things like this happen all the time.

The Detective's Tale

1. See Richard Ohmann, *Selling Culture* (London: Verso, 1996), 14.

2. Michele Tepper, "The Case of the Traveling Text Message." http://www.micheletepper.com/blog/2011/6/14/the-case-of-the-traveling-text-message.html

3. The question of how likely the current BBC versions of Sherlock and John are to come out and be openly gay—that is, for the pairing, nicknamed Johnlock, to become canon—has been divisive in *Sherlock* fandom. Abbreviated "TJLC" (The JohnLock Conspiracy), the issue has polarized fandom. Some fans believe that Sherlock/John is the "endgame" resolution of the show and that there is thus a conspiracy among the show's gay and gay-friendly makers to seduce mainstream viewers into watching a queer romance. Others fans read the show's queer subtext, which is extensive, as either winking at or, conversely, queerbaiting the show's audience.

The Demon Hunter's Tale

1. Or maybe, considering the two characters in question, they end up shaking hands and deciding to take in a baseball game, maybe eat a couple of hotdogs.

2. Lucy Gilliam, fan, fanfiction writer and founder of the Fanfic Symposium, one of the earliest online sites for fandom meta and criticism, wrote an essay called "The Ten Commandments of Crossovers," in 2001. The first commandment? "Thou Shalt Not Cross Sources Just Because It Would Be 'Neat.'" But fans do it anyway (or we wouldn't need to have a commandment prohibiting it).

3. Okay, maybe this isn't canon, strictly speaking, but the show has received numerous petitions to make the ship, known as "Sterek," canon in the show. Furthermore, the actors who play Stiles and Derek (Dylan O'Brien and Tyler Hoechlin) filmed a notorious segment urging fans to vote for *Teen Wolf* for the Teen Choice Awards in which they sat, arms and legs wrapped around each other, on a boat and said: "We're on a ship!—Pun intended!"

4. "Racebending Revenge," 2010, Archive of Our Own.

The Billionaire Superheroes' Tale

1. There is still a Bat-Family in many of the comics, though their tone has darkened consistently since Frank Miller's influential *The Dark Knight Returns* (1986) and there have been estrangements (Dick Grayson) and deaths (later Robins Jason Todd, Stephanie Brown, Damian Wayne) among them. Moreover, as my student Megan Falasco observed in her thesis, "A Downright Batty Family: Portrayal of Deviant Family Dynamics within the Batman Mythos," the very idea of "family" has come to be associated with the villains, including the Joker and his girlfriend, Harley Quinn. Falasco argues that the new grim Batman has to stay isolated to keep him from growing up: because if Batman grows up, the story ends.

2. In the recent Arkham Asylum videogames, the death of Bruce's parents is a recurring feature; you are forced to encounter their dead bodies again and again.

3. Andy Medhurst, "Batman, Deviance, and Camp," in *The Many Lives of the Batman*, ed. Roberta E. Pearson and William Urrichio (London: Routledge, 1991).

4. Not that that's stopped him in the comics, though the Batman is acknowledged to be a *terrifyingly bad* guardian.

5. As the playground jingle of my childhood ran, "Jingle Bells, Batman smells, Robin laid an egg. The Batmobile lost its wheel and the Joker ran away."

6. Quoted in Medhurst, "Batman, Deviance, and Camp," 151.

7. The person who is killed is usually a woman (wife, girlfriend, sister, or mother) and sometimes a child. Fans have a name for this too: *fridging*, or the deliberate victimization of a woman in order to generate manpain. Fridging—which gets its name from a comic book plot in which Green Lantern found his girlfriend dead in the refrigerator—dictates that the audience's sympathy be with the grieving male (who is important) and not with the victimized woman (who isn't), as in: "His girl-

friend's been raped, tortured, and murdered; how terrible for him" (when of course, how terrible for *her*).

8. Also that he's played by Tom Hiddleston, who currently owns much of media fandom along with Benedict Cumberbatch (see the chapter in this volume on *Sherlock*) and the guys from *Teen Wolf* (see the chapters on *Teen Wolf* and *Supernatural*).

The Stormtrooper's Tale

1. *Doctor Who*, while running in the UK since 1963, was picked up by American PBS stations in the mid-1970s, and became a cult in the United States among media fans around the same time as *Star Wars*.

2. I remember seeing posts from young Harry Potter fans insisting that participating in fandom was absolutely, positively something they were going to stop doing once they graduated from high school; does it need saying that many of those fans are still around? Fandom has a way of becoming a way of life; old-school fans abbreviate it as FIAWOL.

3. Jenkins, *Textual Poachers*, 31.

4. Ironically, and somewhat amusingly, at some point Lucasfilm, which despite the prohibitions on romance and erotica was still drowning in zines, had to beg fans to *stop* sending them. Lucasfilm's library of zines was returned to fans, where it became the basis of a circulating zine library first called the SW Zine Archive and then the Correlian Archive. In 1990, the library was expanded beyond *Star Wars* zines and so became known as the Fanzine Archive. The collection—thousands of zines—was later donated to the Special Collections Library at the University of Iowa.

5. Lucasfilm also forced fans to use Eyespot, an editing platform hosted online at starwars.org, and claimed ownership over all the results. Their goal was to control and monetize all remix by hosting it on the company's own site (and away from You-Tube); Lucasfilm paid to have all videos watched through and approved by human beings before they were made public. See Laurence Lessig, "Lucasfilm's Phantom Menace," *Washington Post*, July 12, 2007. Lessig complains, "The remixer is allowed to work, but the product of the work is not his." Lessig's presumptively male remixer aside, the deal Lucasfilm offered was even less attractive to women fans and vidders.

6. Anthony Lane, "The Surreal Achievements of the 2016 Oscars," *New Yorker*, February 29, 2016.

7. Peradi, "Have You Heard," Archive of Our Own, January 24, 2016.

8. Dimircharmer, "Tomorrow (There'll Be More of Us)," Archive of Our Own, January 5, 2016.

9. "The Story of Finn" was posted a mere six days earlier, on December 31, 2015.

Bibliography: For More On . . .

Fanfiction

Barenblat, Rachel. "Fan Fiction and Midrash: Making Meaning." *Transformative Works and Cultures* 17 (2014). http://dx.doi.org/10.3983/twc.2014.0596

Black, Rebecca. *Adolescents and Online Fan Fiction.* New York: Peter Lang, 2008.

Clerc, Susan. "Estrogen Brigades and 'Big Tits' Threads: Media Fandom On-line and Off." In *The Cybercultures Reader*, edited by Barbara Kennedy and David Bell, 216–29. New York: Routledge, 2000.

Coppa, Francesca. "Writing Bodies in Space: Media Fanfiction as Theatrical Performance." In *Fan Fiction and Fan Communities in the Age of the Internet*, edited by Kristina Busse and Karen Hellekson. 225–44. Jefferson, NC: McFarland, 2006.

Cuntz-Leng, Vera, and Jacqueline Meintzinger. "A Brief History of Fan Fiction in Germany." In "European Fans and European Fan Objects: Localization and Translation," edited by Anne Kustritz, special issue, *Transformative Works and Cultures* 19 (2015). http://dx.doi.org/10.3983/twc.2015.0630

DeKosnik, Abigail. "Should Fan Fiction Be Free?" *Cinema Journal* 48, no. 4 (2009). 118–24.

Driscoll, Catherine, and Melissa Gregg. "Convergence Culture and the Legacy of Feminist Cultural Studies." *Cultural Studies* 25, nos. 4–5 (2011): 566–84.

Farley, Shannon K. "Translation, Interpretation, Fan Fiction: A Continuum of Meaning Production." *Transformative Works and Cultures* 14 (2013). http://dx.doi.org/10.3983/twc.2013.0517

Green, Shoshanna, Cynthia Jenkins, and Henry Jenkins. "'Normal Female Interest in Men Bonking': Selections from the *Terra Nostra Underground* and *Strange Bedfellows*." In *Theorizing Fandom: Fans, Subculture, and Identity*, edited by Cheryl Harris and Alison Alexander, 9–38. Cresskill, NJ: Hampton Press, 1998.

Grossman, Lev. "The Boy Who Lived Forever." *Time*, July 7, 2011.

Hellekson, Karen, and Kristina Busse, eds. *Fan Fiction and Fan Communities in the Age of the Internet: New Essays.* Jefferson, NC: McFarland, 2006.

Hellekson, Karen, and Kristina Busse, eds. *The Fan Fiction Studies Reader*. Iowa City: University of Iowa Press, 2014.

Herzog, Alexandra. "'But This Is My Story and This Is How I Wanted to Write It': Author's Notes as a Fannish Claim to Power in Fan Fiction Writing." *Transformative Works and Cultures* 11 (2012). http://dx.doi.org/10.3983/twc.2012.0406

Jamison, Anne, ed. *Fic: Why Fanfiction Is Taking Over the World*. New York: BenBella Books, 2013.

Jenkins, Henry. *Textual Poachers: Television Fans and Participatory Culture*. New York: Routledge, 1992.

Jones, Bethan. "Fifty Shades of Exploitation: Fan Labor and *Fifty Shades of Grey*." In "Fandom and/as Labor," edited by Mel Stanfill and Megan Condis, special issue, *Transformative Works and Cultures* 15 (2014). http://dx.doi.org/10.3983/twc.2014.0501

Jones, Sara Gwenllian. "The Sex Lives of Cult Television Characters." *Screen* 43, no. 1 (2002): 79–90.

Kaplan, Deborah. "'Why Would Any Woman Want to Read Such Stories?' The Distinctions between Genre Romances and Slash Fiction." In *New Approaches to Popular Romance Fiction: Critical Essays*, edited by Sarah S. G. Frantz and Eric Selinger, 121–32. Jefferson, NC: McFarland, 2012.

LaChev, Anik. "Fan Fiction: A Genre and Its (Final?) Frontiers." In "Get a Life? Fan Cultures and Contemporary Television," edited by Lauri Mullens, special issue, *Spectator* 25 (2005): 83–94. http://cinema.usc.edu/

Parrish, Juli J. "Metaphors We Read By: People, Process, and Fan Fiction." *Transformative Works and Cultures* 14 (2013). http://dx.doi.org/10.3983/twc.2013.0486

Pugh, Sheenagh. *The Democratic Genre: Fan Fiction in a Literary Context*. Brigend, Wales: Seren, 2005.

Roh, David S. *Illegal Literature: Toward a Disruptive Creativity*. Minneapolis: University of Minnesota Press, 2015.

Russ, Joanna. "Pornography by Women, for Women, with Love." In *Magic Mommas, Trembling Sisters, Puritans and Perverts: Feminist Essays*, 79–99. Trumansburg, NY: Crossing Press, 1985.

Schawbach, Aaron. *Fan Fiction and Copyright: Outside Works and Intellectual Property Protection*. London: Ashgate, 2011.

Smith, Paula. "A Conversation with Paula Smith." Interview by Cynthia W. Walker. *Transformative Works and Cultures* 6 (2011). doi:10.3983/twc.2011.0243

Stein, Louisa Ellen, and Kristina Busse. "Limit Play: Fan Authorship between Source Text, Intertext, and Context." *Popular Communication* 7 (2009): 192–207. doi:10.1080/15405700903177545.

Turk, Tisha. "Metalepsis in Fan Vids and Fan Fiction." In *Metalepsis in Popular Culture*, edited by Karin Kukkonen and Sonja Klimek, 83–103. Berlin: Walter de Gruyter, 2011.

Tushnet, Rebecca. "Legal Fictions: Copyright, Fan Fiction, and a New Common Law." *Loyola of Los Angeles Entertainment Law Journal* 17 (1997): 641–86.

TWC Editor. Interview with Jo Graham, Melissa Scott, and Martha Wells. *Transformative Works and Cultures* 5 (2010). doi:10.3983/twc.2010.0239.

Van Steenhuyse, Veerle. "Wordplay, Mindplay: Fan Fiction and Postclassical Narratology." *Transformative Works and Cultures* 17 (2014). http://dx.doi.org/10.3983/twc.2014.0572

Waysdorf, Abby. "The Creation of Football Slash Fan Fiction." In "European Fans and European Fan Objects: Localization and Translation," edited by Anne Kustritz, special issue, *Transformative Works and Cultures* 19 (2015). http://dx.doi.org/10.3983/twc.2015.0588

Wilson, Anna. "The Role of Affect in Fan Fiction." In "The Classical Canon and/as Transformative Work," edited by Ika Willis, *Transformative Works and Cultures* 21 (2016). http://dx.doi.org/10.3983/twc.2016.0684

Crossovers

Booth, Paul. *Crossing Fandoms: SuperWhoLock and the Contemporary Fan Audience.* New York: Palgrave, 2016.

Flynn, Julie. "Dean, Mal and Snape Walk into a Bar: Lessons in Crossing Over." In *Writing and the Digital Generation: Essays on New Media Rhetoric*, edited by Heather Urbanski. 132–34. Jefferson, NC: McFarland, 2010.

Samutina, Natalia. "Fanfiction as World-Building: Transformative Reception in Crossover Writing." *Continuum* 2016: 433–50.

Femslash

Collier, Noelle R., Christine A. Lumadue, and H. Ray Wooten. "*Buffy the Vampire Slayer* and *Xena: Warrior Princess*: Reception of the Texts by a Sample of Lesbian Fans and Web Site Users." *Journal of Homosexuality* 56, no. 5 (2009): 575–609.

Hamming, Jeanne E. "Whatever Turns You On: Becoming-Lesbian and the Production of Desire in the Xenaverse." *Genders* 34 (2001). https://www.atria.nl/ezines/IAV_606661/IAV_606661_2010_51/g34_hamming.html

Hanmer, Rosalind. "Lesbian Subtext Talk: Experiences of the Internet Chat." *International Journal of Sociology and Social Policy* 23 (2003): 80–106.

Hanmer, Rosalind. *Understanding Lesbian Fandom: Xena: Warrior Princess Lesbian Internet Fans.* Saarbrücken: Lambert Academic Publishing, 2012.

Hanmer, Rosalind. "'Xenasubtexttalk': The Impact on the Lesbian Fan Community through Its Online Reading and Writing of Lesbian Fan Fiction in Relation to the Television Series *Xena Warrior Princess*." *Feminist Media Studies* 14, no. 4 (2014): 608–22.

Isaksson, Malin. "Pain as Pleasure: Tough Girls' Love in Fan Fiction." In *How Does It Feel? Making Sense of Pain*, edited by Hans T. Sternudd and Angela Tumini, 99–116. Oxford: Inter-Disciplinary Press, 2011.

Isaksson, Malin. "Buffy/Faith Adult Femslash: Queer Porn with a Plot." *Slayage* 7, no. 4 (2009). http://www.whedonstudies.tv/uploads/2/6/2/8/26288593/isaks-son_slayage_7.4.pdf

Jones, Sara Gwenllian. "Histories, Fictions, and *Xena: Warrior Princess*." *Television and New Media* 1 (2000): 403–18.

Jones, Sara Gwenllian. "Starring Lucy Lawless?" *Continuum* 14, no. 1 (2000): 9–22.

Jones, Sara Gwenllian. "The Sex Lives of Cult Television Characters." *Screen* 43, no. 1 (2002): 79–90.

Kapurch, Katie. "Rapunzel Loves Merida: Melodramatic Expressions of Lesbian Girlhood and Teen Romance in Tangled, Brave, and Femslash." *Journal of Lesbian Studies* 19, no. 4 (2015): 436–45.

Russo, Julie Levin. "Hairgate! TV's Coiffure Controversies and Lesbian Locks." *Camera Obscura* 22, no. 2 (2007). 166–72.

Russo, Julie Levin. "Hera Has Six Mommies (a Transmedia Love Story)." *FlowTV* 7, special issue (2007). http://www.flowjournal.org/2007/12/hera-has-six-mom-mies-a-transmedia-love-story/

Russo, Julie Levin. "Sex Detectives: Law & Order: SVU's Fans, Critics, and Characters Investigate Lesbian Desire." *Transformative Works and Cultures* 3 (2009). http://dx.doi.org/10.3983/twc.2009.0155

Russo, Julie Levin. "Textual Orientation: Female Fandom Online." In *Routledge Companion to Media and Gender*, edited by Cynthia Carter, Linda Steiner, and Lisa McLaughlin, 450–60. New York: Routledge, 2013.

Stanfill, Mel. "'They're Losers, but I Know Better': Intra-fandom Stereotyping and the Normalization of the Fan Subject." *Critical Studies in Media Communication* 30, no. 2 (2013): 117–34.

The Mary Sue

Aleo, Cindy. "On Writing—and Being—a Mary Sue." In *Fic: Why Fanfiction Is Taking Over the World*, edited by Anne Jamison, 207–11. New York: BenBella Books, 2013.

Beck, Julia, and Frauke Herrling. "Playing Sue." *Transformative Works and Cultures* 2 (2009). http://dx.doi.org/10.3983/twc.2009.0093

Busse, Kristina. "Beyond Mary Sue: Fan Representation and the Complex Negotiation of Gendered Identity." In *Seeing Fans: Representations of Fandom in Media and Popular Culture*, edited by Lucy Bennett and Paul Booth, 159–68. New York: Bloomsbury, 2016.

Chander, Anupam, and Madhavi Sunder. "Everyone's a Superhero: A Cultural Theory of 'Mary Sue' Fan Fiction as Fair Use." *California Law Review* 95, no. 2 (2007): 597–626.

Pflieger, Pat. "Too Good to Be True": 150 Years of Mary Sue." Presented at the American Culture Association conference, March 31, 1999, San Diego, CA. http://www.merrycoz.org/papers/MARYSUE.xhtml

Smith, Paula. "A Conversation with Paula Smith." Interview by Cynthia W. Walker. *Transformative Works and Cultures* 6 (2011). doi:10.3983/twc.2011.0243.

Popslash and Boy Bands

Busse, Kristina. "'Digital Get Down': Postmodern Boy Band Slash and the Queer Female Space." In *Eros.USA: Essays on the Culture and Literature of Desire*, edited by Cheryl Alexander Malcolm, and Jopi Nyman, 103–25. Gdansk: Wydawyictwo Uniwersytetu Gdanskiesgo, 2005.

Busse, Kristina. "'I'm Jealous of the Fake Me': Postmodern Subjectivity and Identity Construction in Boy Band Fan Fiction." In *Framing Celebrity: New Directions in Celebrity Culture*, edited by Su Holmes and Sean Redmond, 253–67. New York: Routledge, 2006.

Ehrenreich, Barbara, Elizabeth Hess, and Gloria Jacobs. "Beatlemania: Girls Just Want to Have Fun." In *The Adoring Audience*, edited by Lisa A. Lewis, 84–106. London: Routledge, 1992.

Jones, Bethan. "'I Will Throw You Off Your Ship and You Will Drown and Die': Death Threats, Intra-fandom Hate and the Performance of Fangirling." In *Seeing Fans: Representations of Fandom in Media and Popular Culture*, edited by Lucy Bennett and Paul Booth. 53–66. New York: Bloomsbury, 2016.

Pahati, Omar J. "Sexing Up the Boy Bands" AlternNet. April 9, 2002. http://www.alternet.org/story/12823/sexing_up_the_boy_bands

Piper, Melanie. "Real Body, Fake Person: Recontextualizing Celebrity Bodies in Fandom and Film." *Transformative Works and Cultures* 20 (2015). http://dx.doi.org/10.3983/twc.2015.0664

Thomas, Bronwen. "Fans Behaving Badly? Real Person Fic and the Blurring of the Boundaries between the Public and the Private." In *Real Lives, Celebrity Stories: Narratives of Ordinary and Extraordinary People across Media*, edited by Bronwen Thomas and Julia Round, 171–85. New York: Bloomsbury, 2014.

Wald, Gayle. "I Want It That Way: Teenybopper Music and the Girling of Boy Bands." *Genders* 35 (2002). http://www.genders.org/g35/g35_wald.html

Wilson, D. "Queer Bandom: A Research Journey in Eight Parts." *Transformative Works and Cultures* 11 (2012). doi:10.3983/twc.2012.0426

Race Issues

Gatson, Sarah N., and Robin Anne Reid. "Race and Ethnicity in Fandom." In "Race and Ethnicity in Fandom," edited by Robin Anne Reid and Sarah Gatson, special issue, *Transformative Works and Cultures* 8 (2012). doi:10.3983/twc.2012.0392

Pande, Rukmini. "Squee from the Margins: Racial/Cultural/Ethnic Identity in Global Media Fandom." In *Seeing Fans: Representations of Fandom in Media and Popular Culture*, edited by Lucy Bennett and Paul Booth, 209–20. New York: Bloomsbury, 2016.

Stanfill, Mel. "Doing Fandom, (Mis)doing Whiteness: Heteronormativity, Racialization, and the Discursive Construction of Fandom." In "Race and Ethnicity in Fandom," edited by Robin Anne Reid and Sarah Gatson, special issue, *Transformative Works and Cultures* 8 (2011). doi:10.3983/twc.2011.0256

Stanfill, Mel. "Straighten Up and Fly White: Whiteness, Heteronormativity, and the Representation of Happy Endings for Fans." In *Seeing Fans: Representations of Fandom in Media and Popular Culture*, edited by Lucy Bennett and Paul Booth, 187–96. New York: Bloomsbury, 2016.

TWC Editor. "Pattern Recognition: A Dialogue on Racism in Fan Communities." *Transformative Works and Cultures* 3 (2009). http://dx.doi.org/10.3983/twc.2009.0172

Wanzo, Rebecca. "African American Acafandom and Other Strangers: New Genealogies of Fan Studies." *Transformative Works and Cultures* 20 (2015). http://dx.doi.org/10.3983/twc.2015.0699

Warner, Kristen J. "ABC's *Scandal* and Black Women's Fandom." In *Cupcakes, Pinterest, and Lady Porn*, edited by Elana Levine, 32–50. Urbana: University of Illinois Press, 2015.

Batman / Marvel Comics Universe

Brooker, Will. *Batman Unmasked: Analyzing a Cultural Icon*. New York: Bloomsbury Academic, 2001.

Brooker, Will. *Hunting the Dark Knight: Twenty-First Century Batman*. London: I. B. Tauris, 2012.

Costello, Matthew J., ed. "Appropriating, Interpreting, and Transforming Comic Books." Special issue of *Transformative Works and Cultures* 13 (2013). http://journal.transformativeworks.org/index.php/twc/issue/view/11

Darowski, Joseph. *The Ages of Iron Man: Essays on the Armored Avenger in Changing Times*. Jefferson, NC: McFarland, 2015.

Fingeroth, Danny. *Superman on the Couch: What Superheroes Really Tell Us about Ourselves and Our Society*. New York: Bloomsbury Academic, 2004.

Leow, Hui Min Annabeth. "Subverting the Canon in Feminist Fan Fiction: 'Concession.'" *Transformative Works and Cultures* 7 (2011). doi:10.3983/twc.2011.0286

Pearson, Roberta E., and William Uricchio, eds. *The Many Lives of the Batman*. London: Routledge, 1991.

Wei, John. "Queer Encounters between Iron Man and Chinese Boys' Love Fandom." *Transformative Works and Cultures* 17 (2014). http://dx.doi.org/10.3983/twc.2014.0561

Weldon, Glen. *The Caped Crusade: Batman and the Rise of Nerd Culture*. New York: Simon and Schuster, 2016.

James Bond

DeKosnik, Abigail. "M Stands for Mother: James Bond and Freudian Family Romance in *Casino Royale* and *Quantum of Solace*." In *The Cultures of James Bond*, edited by Christian Krug and Joachim Frank, 145–57. Trier: WVT, 2011.

Eco, Umberto. "The Narrative Structure in Fleming." In *The James Bond Phenom-*

enon: A Critical Reader, edited by Christoph Lindner, 34–55. Manchester: Manchester University Press, 2009.

Funnel, Lisa. *For His Eyes Only: The Women of James Bond*. New York: Wallflower Press, 2015.

Funnel, Lisa. "'I Know Where You Keep Your Gun': Daniel Craig as the Bond–Bond Girl Hybrid in *Casino Royale*." *Journal of Popular Culture* 44, no. 3 (2011): 455–72.

Funnel, Lisa, ed. *The James Bond Phenomenon: A Critical Reader*. Manchester: Manchester University Press, 2003.

Hines, Claire. *Fan Phenomena: James Bond*. Bristol: Intellect, 2015.

Lindner, Christoph, ed. *Revisioning 007: James Bond and "Casino Royale."* New York: Wallflower Press, 2010.

McDougall, Sophia. "The Rape of James Bond." *New Statesman*, March 14, 2013. http://www.newstatesman.com/cultural-capital/2013/03/rape-james-bond

Buffy the Vampire Slayer

Bloustein, Geraldine. "Fans with a Lot at Stake: Serious Play and Mimetic Excess in *Buffy the Vampire Slayer*." *European Journal of Cultural Studies* 5 (2002): 427–49.

Hodges, Amanda L., and Laurel P. Richmond. "Taking a Bite out of *Buffy*: Carnivalesque Play and Resistance in Fan Fiction." *Transformative Works and Cultures* 7 (2011). doi:10.3983/twc.2011.0265

Kaveney, Roz, ed. *Reading the Vampire Slayer: An Unofficial Critical Companion to Buffy and Angel*. London: I. B. Tauris, 2002.

Roine, Hanna-Riikka. "What Is It That Fanfiction Opposes? The Shared and Communal Features of *Firefly/Serenity* Fanfiction." *Fafnir: Nordic Journal of Science Fiction and Fantasy Research* 1, no. 1 (2014): 31–45.

Slayage: The Online Journal of Buffy Studies. http://slayageonline.com/

Wilcox, Rhonda. *Why Buffy Matters: The Art of "Buffy the Vampire Slayer."* Oxford: Rowman and Littlefield, 2005.

Wilcox, Rhonda, and David Lavery, eds. *Fighting the Forces: What's at Stake in "Buffy the Vampire Slayer."* Oxford: Rowman and Littlefield, 2002.

Williamson, Milly. "*Buffy the Vampire Slayer*." In *The Essential Cult TV Reader*, edited by David Lavery, 60–67. Lexington: University Press of Kentucky, 2010.

Doctor Who

Booth, Paul, ed. *Fan Phenomena: "Doctor Who."* Bristol: Intellect, 2013.

Ellis, Sigrid, and Michael Damian Thomas, eds. *Queers Dig Time Lords: A Celebration of "Doctor Who" by the LGBTQ Fans Who Love It*. Des Moines, Iowa: Mad Norwegian Press, 2013.

Fogle, Krystal. "It's Bigger on the Inside: Fandom, Social Media, and *Doctor Who*." In *Television, Social Media, and Fan Culture*, edited by Alison F. Slade, Dedria

Givens-Carroll, and Amber J. Narro, 295–315. Lanham, MD: Lexington Books, 2015.

Hadas, Leora. "The Web Planet: How the Changing Internet Divided *Doctor Who* Fan Fiction Writers." *Transformative Works and Cultures* 3 (2009). http://dx.doi.org/10.3983/twc.2009.0129

Hills, Matt. *Triumph of a Time Lord: Regenerating "Doctor Who" in the Twenty-First Century*. London: I. B. Tauris, 2010.

Hoge, Charles William. "Whodology: Encountering *Doctor Who* Fan Fiction through the Portals of Play Studies and Ludology." In "Textual Echoes," edited by Cyber Echoes, special issue, *Transformative Works and Cultures* 8 (2011). doi:10.3983/twc.2011.0262

Johnston, Jessica Elizabeth. "Doctor Who–Themed Weddings and the Performance of Fandom." In "Performance and Performativity in Fandom," edited by Lucy Bennett and Paul J. Booth, *Transformative Works and Cultures* 18 (2015). http://dx.doi.org/10.3983/twc.2015.0637

Leitch, Gillian I., ed. *"Doctor Who" in Time and Space: Essays on Themes, Characters, History and Fandom, 1963—2012*. Jefferson, NC: McFarland, 2013.

Potter, Amanda. "Classical Monsters in New *Doctor Who* Fan Fiction." In "The Classical Canon and/as Transformative Work," edited by Ika Willis, special issue, *Transformative Works and Cultures* 21 (2016). http://dx.doi.org/10.3983/twc.2016.0676

Thomas, Lynne M., and Tara O'Shea, eds. *Chicks Dig Time Lords: A Celebration of "Doctor Who" by the Women Who Love It*. Des Moines, Iowa: Mad Norwegian Press, 2010.

Tulloch, John, and Henry Jenkins. *Science Fiction Audiences: Watching "Doctor Who" and "Star Trek."* New York: Routledge, 1995.

Sherlock Holmes

Kestner, Joseph A. "'Real' Men: Construction of Masculinity in the Sherlock Holmes Narratives." *Studies in the Literary Imagination* 29, no. 1 (Spring, 1996): 73–88.

McClellan, Ann. "A Case of Identity: Role Playing, Social Media, and BBC *Sherlock*." *Journal of Fandom Studies* 1, no. 2 (2013): 139–57.

McClellan, Ann. "Redefining Genderswap Fan Fiction: A *Sherlock* Case Study." *Transformative Works and Cultures* 17 (2014). http://dx.doi.org/10.3983/twc.2014.0553

Pearson, Roberta. "It's Always 1895: Sherlock Holmes in Cyberspace." In *The Fan Fiction Studies Reader*, edited by Karen Hellekson and Kristina Busse, 44–60. Iowa City: University of Iowa Press, 2014.

Petersen, Line Nybro. "Sherlock Fans Talk: Mediatized Talk on Tumblr." *Northern Lights: Film and Media Studies Yearbook* 12 (2014): 87–104.

Porter, Lynnette, ed. *Sherlock Holmes for the 21st Century: Essays on New Adaptations*. Jefferson, NC: McFarland, 2012.

Stein, Louisa Ellen, and Kristina Busse, eds. *"Sherlock" and Transmedia Fandom: Essays on the BBC Series.* Jefferson, NC: McFarland, 2012.

Lord of the Rings

Allington, Daniel. "'How Come Most People Don't See It?': Slashing *The Lord of the Rings.*" *Social Semiotics* 17, no. 1 (2007): 43–62.
Barker, Martin, and Ernest Mathijs, eds. *Watching "The Lord of the Rings": Tolkien's World Audiences.* New York: Peter Lang, 2007.
Booker, Susan. "Tales around the Internet Campfire: Fan Fiction in Tolkien's Universe." In *Tolkien on Film: Essays on Peter Jackson's "The Lord of the Rings,"* edited by Janet Brennan Croft, 259–82. Altadena, CA: Mythopoeic Press, 2005.
Bogstad, Janice M., ed. *Picturing Tolkien: Essays on Peter Jackson's "The Lord of the Rings" Film Trilogy.* Jefferson, NC: McFarland, 2011.
Isaacs, Neil D., and Rose A Zimbardo. *Understanding "The Lord of the Rings": The Best of Tolkien Criticism.* Boston: Houghton Mifflin, 2004.
Mathijs, Earnest, ed. *"Lord of the Rings": Popular Culture in Global Context.* New York: Wallflower Press, 2006.
McCormack, Una. "Finding Ourselves in the (Un)Mapped Lands: Women's Reparative Readings of *The Lord of the Rings.*" In *Perilous and Fair: Women in the Works and Life of J.R.R. Tolkien,* edited by Janet Brennan Croft and Leslie A. Donovan, 309–26. Altadena, CA: Mythopoeic Press, 2015.
Reid, Robin Anne. "Thrusts in the Dark: Slashers' Queer Practices." *Extrapolation* 15, no. 3 (2009): 463–83.
Shefrin, Elana. "*Lord of the Rings, Star Wars,* and Participatory Fandom: Mapping New Congruencies between the Internet and Media Entertainment Culture." *Critical Studies in Media Communication* 31, no. 3 (2004): 261–81.
Sturgis, Amy H. "Make Mine 'Movieverse': How the Tolkien Fan Fiction Community Learned to Stop Worrying and Love Peter Jackson." In *Tolkien on Film: Essays on Peter Jackson's "The Lord of the Rings",* edited by Janet Brennan Croft, 283–308. Altadena, CA: Mythopoeic Press, 2004.

Harry Potter

Anatol, Giselle Liza, ed. *Reading Harry Potter: Critical Essays.* Westport, CT: Praeger, 2003.
Blake, Andrew. *The Irresistible Rise of Harry Potter.* London: Verso, 2002.
Cuntz-Leng, Vera. "Twinship, Incest, and Twincest in the Harry Potter Universe." *Transformative Works and Cultures* 17 (2014). http://dx.doi.org/10.3983/twc.2014.0576
Green, Lelia, and Carmen Guinery. "Harry Potter and the Fan Fiction Phenomenon." *M/C Journal* 7, no. 5 (2004). http://journal.media-culture.org.au/0411/14-green.php

Gupta, Suman. *Rereading Harry Potter*. New York: Palgrave, 2003.

Hampton, Darlene Rose. "Bound Princes and Monogamy Warnings: *Harry Potter*, Slash, and Queer Performance in LiveJournal Communities." In "Performance and Performativity in Fandom," edited by Lucy Bennett and Paul J. Booth, *Transformative Works and Cultures* 18 (2015). http://dx.doi.org/10.3983/twc.2015.0609

Horáková, Erin. "Britpicking as Cultural Policing in Fanfiction." In *Play, Performance, and Identity: How Institutions Structure Ludic Spaces*, ed. Matt Omasta and Drew Chappell, 128–41. New York: Routledge, 2015.

Jenkins, Henry, and Sangita Shrevtova, eds. "Transformative Works and Fan Activism." Special issue of *Transformative Works and Cultures* 10 (2014). http://journal.transformativeworks.org/index.php/twc/issue/view/12

Ingram-Waters, Mary. "Writing the Pregnant Man." *Transformative Works and Cultures* 20 (2015). http://dx.doi.org/10.3983/twc.2015.0651

Kustritz, Anne. "Domesticating Hermione: The Emergence of Genre and Community from WIKTT's Feminist Romance Debates." *Feminist Media Studies:* 15 (3): 444–59. (2014).

Mendlesohn, Farah. "Crowning the King: Harry Potter and the Construction of Authority." In *The Ivory Tower and Harry Potter*, edited by Lana A. Whited, 159–81. Columbia: University of Missouri Press, 2002.

Millman, Joyce. "To Sir, with Love: How Fan Fiction Transformed Professor Snape from a Greasy Grit to a Byronic Hero . . . Who's Really, Really into S/M." In *Mapping the World of Harry Potter: Science Fiction and Fantasy Writers Explore the Best Selling Fantasy Series of All Time*, edited by Mercedes Lackey and Leah Wilson, 39–52. Dallas, TX: BenBella Books, 2006.

Rémi, Cornelia. *Harry Potter Bibliography*. June 9, 2008. http://www.eulenfeder.de/hpliteratur.html

Tandy, Heidi. "How Harry Potter Fanfic Changed the World (or at Least the Internet)." In *Fic: Why Fanfiction Is Taking Over the World*, edited by Anne Jamison, 165–74. New York: BenBella Books, 2013.

Thomas, Bronwen. "Update Soon!" Harry Potter Fanfiction and Narrative as a Participatory Process." In *New Narratives: Stories and Storytelling in the Digital Age*, edited by Ruth Page and Bronwen Thomas, 205–19. Lincoln: University of Nebraska Press, 2011.

Tosenberger, Catherine. "Homosexuality at the Online Hogwarts: Harry Potter Slash Fanfiction." *Children's Literature* 36 (2008): 185–207.

Tosenberger, Catherine. "'O My God, the Fanfiction!' Dumbledore's Outing and the Online Harry Potter Fandom." *Children's Literature Association Quarterly* 33, no. 2 (2008): 200–206.

Tresca, Don. "Spellbound: An Analysis of Adult-Oriented *Harry Potter* Fanfiction." In *Fan CULTure: Essays on Participatory Fandom in the 21st Century*, edited by Kristen M. Barton and Jonathan Malcolm Lampley, 36–44. Jefferson, NC: McFarland, 2014.

Whited, Lana A., ed. *The Ivory Tower and Harry Potter*. Columbia: University of Missouri Press, 2002.

Willis, Ika. "Keeping Promises to Queer Children: Making Space (for Mary Sue) at Hogwarts." In *Fan Fiction and Fan Communities in the Age of the Internet: New Essays*, edited by Karen Hellekson and Kristina Busse, 153–70. Jefferson, NC: McFarland, 2006.

Star Trek

Bacon-Smith, Camille. *Enterprising Women: Television Fandom and the Creation of Popular Myth.* Philadelphia: University of Pennsylvania Press, 1992.

Bernardi, Daniel, and Michael Green. "Star Trek." Oxford Bibliographies, 2011. http://www.oxfordbibliographies.com/view/document/obo-9780199791286/obo-9780199791286-0138.xml

Coppa, Francesca. "Women, Star Trek, and the Early Development of Fannish Vidding." *Transformative Works and Cultures* 1 (2008). http://journal.transformativeworks.org/index.php/twc/article/view/44

Geraghty, Lincoln. "Reading on the Frontier: A *Star Trek* Bibliography." *Extrapolation* 43, no. 3 (2002): 288–315.

Lamb, Patricia Frazer, and Diane Veith. "Romantic Myth, Transcendence, and *Star Trek* Zines." In *Erotic Universe: Sexuality and Fantastic Literature*, edited by Donald Palumbo, 236–55. Westport, CT: Greenwood Press, 1986.

Lichtenberg, Jacqueline, Sondra Marshak, and Joan Winston. *Star Trek Lives!* New York: Corgi, 1975.

Pearson, Roberta, and Maire Messinger Davies, eds. *"Star Trek" and American Television.* Berkeley: University of California Press, 2015.

Reagin, Nancy. *"Star Trek" and History.* New York: Wiley, 2013.

Tulloch, John, and Henry Jenkins. *Science Fiction Audiences: Watching "Doctor Who" and "Star Trek."* New York: Routledge, 1995.

Verba, Joan Marie. *Boldly Writing: A Trekker Fan and Zine History, 1967–1987.* 2nd ed. Minnetonka, MN: FTL Publications, 2003.

Woledge, Elizabeth. "Decoding Desire: From Kirk and Spock to K/S." *Social Semiotics* 15, no. 2 (2005): 235–50.

Star Wars

Brooker, Will. *Using the Force: Creativity, Community and "Star Wars" Fans.* New York: Continuum, 2002.

Gunnels, Jen. "A Jedi Like My Father before Me": Social Identity and the New York Comic Con." *Transformative Works and Cultures* 3 (2009). http://dx.doi.org/10.3983/twc.2009.0161

Jenkins, Henry. "Quentin Tarantino's Star Wars? Digital Cinema, Media Convergence, and Participatory Culture." In *Rethinking Media Change: The Aesthetics of Transition*, edited by Henry Jenkins and David Thorburn, 281–312. Cambridge, MA: MIT Press, 2003.

Jenkins, Henry. "*Star Wars* and the Fracas over Fan Films." Interview by John Borland. CNet, May 2, 2005. http://news.cnet.com/Star-Wars-and-the-fracas-over-fan-films/2100-1008_3-5690595.html

Kapell, Matthew Wilhelm, and John Shelton Lawrence. *Finding the Force of the "Star Wars" Franchise: Fans, Merchandise, and Critics*. New York: Peter Lang, 2006.

Kustritz, Anne. "Painful Pleasures: Sacrifice, Consent, and the Resignification of BDSM Symbolism in *The Story of O* and *The Story of Obi*." *Transformative Works and Cultures* 1 (2008). http://journal.transformativeworks.org/index.php/twc/article/view/31

Murray, Simone. "'Celebrating the Story the Way It Is': Cultural Studies, Corporate Media, and the Contested Utility of Fandom." *Continuum* 18, no. 1 (2004): 7–25.

Phillips, Forrest. "The Butcher, the Baker, the Lightsaber Maker." In "Material Fan Culture," edited by Bob Rehak, special issue, *Transformative Works and Cultures* 16 (2014). http://dx.doi.org/10.3983/twc.2014.0498

Proctor, William. "Holy Crap, More *Star Wars*! More *Star Wars*? What If They're Crap? Disney, Lucasfilm, and *Star Wars* Online Fandom in the 21st Century." *Participations* 10, no. 1 (2013): 198–224.

Wille, Joshua. "Fan Edits and the Legacy of *The Phantom Edit*." *Transformative Works and Cultures* 17 (2014). http://dx.doi.org/10.3983/twc.2014.0575

Superman and *Smallville*

Barker, Cory, Chris Ryan, and Myc Wiatrowski, eds. *Mapping "Smallville": Critical Essays on the Series and Its Characters*. Jefferson, NC: McFarland, 2014.

Darowski, Joseph J. *The Ages of Superman: Essays on the Man of Steel in Changing Times*. Jefferson, NC: McFarland, 2012.

Geraghty, Lincoln, ed. *The "Smallville" Chronicles: Critical Essays on the Television Series*. Lanham, MD: Scarecrow Press, 2011.

Jones, Gerald. *Men of Tomorrow: Geeks, Gangsters, and the Birth of the Comic Book*. New York: Basic Books, 2005.

Kohnen, M. "The Adventures of a Repressed Farm Boy and the Billionaire Who Loved Him: Queer Spectatorship in *Smallville* Fandom." In *Teen Television: Essays on Programming and Fandom*, edited by Sharon Marie Ross and Louisa Stein, 207–23. Jefferson, NC: McFarland, 2008.

Meyer, Michaela D. E. "Slashing *Smallville*: The Interplay of Text, Audience, and Production on Viewer Interpretations of Homoeroticism." *Sexuality and Culture* 17 (2013): 476–93.

Stein, Louisa. "They Cavort, You Decide: Transgenericism, Queerness, and Fan Interpretation in Teen TV." *Spectator* 2005: 11–22.

Weldon, Glen. *Superman: The Unauthorized Biography*. New York: Wiley, 2013.

Yeffeth, Glenn. *The Man from Krypton*. Dallas, TX: BenBella, 2006.

Supernatural / *Teen Wolf*

Graham, Anissa M. "A New Kind of Pandering: *Supernatural* and the World of Fanfiction." In *Fan CULTure: Essays on Participatory Fandom in the 21st Century*, edited by Kristen M. Barton and Jonathan Malcolm Lampley, 131–45. Jefferson, NC: McFarland, 2013.

Larsen, Katherine, and Lynn S. Zubernis. *Fangasm: Supernatural Fangirls.* Iowa City: University of Iowa Press, 2013.

Schmidt, Lisa. "Monstrous Melodrama: Expanding the Scope of Melodramatic Identification to Interpret Negative Fan Responses to *Supernatural.*" *Transformative Works and Cultures* 4 (2010). http://dx.doi.org/10.3983/twc.2010.0152

Tosenberger, Catherine. "'The Epic Love Story of Sam and Dean': *Supernatural*, Queer Readings, and the Romance of Incestuous Fan Fiction." *Transformative Works and Cultures* 1 (2008). doi:10.3983/twc.2008.0030.

Tosenberger, Catherine, ed. "Saving People, Hunting Things." Special issue on *Supernatural*, *Transformative Works and Cultures* 4 (2010). http://journal.transformativeworks.org/index.php/twc/issue/view/5

Zubernis, Lynn, and Katherine Larsen. *Fandom at the Crossroads: Celebration, Shame, and Fan/Producer Relationships.* Newcastle: Cambridge Scholars, 2012.

Zubernis, Lynn, and Katherine Larsen, eds. *Fan Phenomena: "Supernatural."* Bristol: Intellect, 2014.

The X-Files

Backstein, Karen. "Flexing Those Anthropological Muscles: X-Files Cult TV, and the Representation of Race and Ethnicity." In *Cult Television*, edited by Sara Gwenllian Jones and Roberta E. Pearson, 115–46. Minneapolis: University of Minnesota Press, 2004.

Bury, Rhiannon. *Cyberspaces of Their Own: Female Fandoms Online.* New York: Peter Lang, 2005.

Johnson, Catherine. "Quality/Cult Television: The X-Files and Television History." In *The Contemporary Television Series*, edited by Michael Hammon and Lucy Mazdon, 57–72. Edinburgh: Edinburgh University Press, 2005.

Jones, Bethan. "The Fandom Is Out There: Social Media and *The X-Files* Online." In *Fan CULTure: Essays on Participatory Fandom in the 21st Century*, edited by Kristen M. Barton and Jonathan Malcolm Lampley, 92–105. Jefferson, NC: McFarland, 2013.

Koven, Mikel J. "The X-Files." In *The Essential Cult TV Reader.* Lexington: University Press of Kentucky, 2010: 337–44.

Lavery, David, Angela Hague, and Marla Cartwright, eds. *Deny All Knowledge: Reading "The X-Files."* Syracuse, NY: Syracuse University Press, 1996.

Scodari, Christine, and Jenna L. Felder. "Creating a Pocket Universe: 'Shippers,' Fan Fiction, and *The X-Files* Online." *Communication Studies* 51 (2000): 238–58.

Wills, Emily Regan. "'Fannish Discourse Communities and the Construction of Gender in *The X-Files.*" *Transformative Works and Cultures* 14 (2013). doi:10.3983/twc.2013.0410.

Wooley, Christine A. "Visible Fandom: Reading *The X-Files* through X-Philes." *Journal of Film and Video*, December 1, 2001.

Yang, Sharon R. *"The X-Files" and Literature: Unweaving the Story, Unraveling the Lie to Find the Truth.* Newcastle: Cambridge Scholars, 2007.

Contributor Bios

AlchemyAlice has written in a variety of fandoms including MCU, *Supernatural, Inception, X-Men*, James Bond, and others. She likes writing quiet stories where nothing happens and very loud stories where too many things happen. Her checkered real-life career has included being at turns a web designer, graphic designer, archivist, and teaching assistant. She holds a doctorate in nineteenth-century British literature and lives in NYC, where she works at a law firm and is writing an alternate history novel about robots.

astolat is a popular fanfiction writer and vidder in a wide variety of fandoms and also a major contributor to fannish infrastructure. She is the founder of Yuletide, an annual rare-fandoms fanfiction challenge, the Vividcon vidding convention, and the Archive of Our Own. She is also a bestselling and award-winning fantasy novelist whose works have spawned fandoms of their own.

Brancher has written in *Watchmen, Sherlock Holmes,* and other fandoms; her participation in fan communities dates back to alt.startrek.creative. erotica.moderated in the late 1990s. A journalist in her real life, she tends to appear and disappear in fandom like the sun on a cloudy day.

busaikko is a fan writer, vidder, podfic recorder, and wiki contributor for many fandoms, including Harry Potter, *Stargate: Atlantis, Nobuta wo Produce, Youkai Ningen Bem,* and *Haikyuu!!* Her Remus/Sirius Shoebox Project vid "So Sirius" is a fandom classic. She lives in Japan.

Francesca Coppa is Professor of English at Muhlenberg College and a founding member of the Organization for Transformative Works, a non-profit established by fans to provide access to and to preserve the history of fanworks and culture. She is writing a book about fan vidding and is a passionate advocate for fair use.

Glockgal is a well-known Canadian fan artist who has created work in numerous fandoms including DC comics, Harry Potter, and *Avatar: The Last Airbender*. She is one of the moderators of the Yuletart annual art challenge and is known in fandom for her advocacy of feminist issues and racial representation.

Kaneko is an Australian fanwriter who has written in several fandoms, including popslash, *due South*, *The Breakfast Club*, *Generation Kill*, and *Stargate: Atlantis*. She is currently working on an original fantasy novel. You can find more of her work at the Archive of Our Own.

kaydee falls is a fanfiction writer and vidder in far too many fandoms, including *X-Men*, MCU, *Doctor Who/Torchwood*, and Harry Potter. She works in the theater and is based in New York City.

Koi, also known as Koimistress, was a fan writer in *Smallville*; previously, under the name Jane Mortimer, she wrote fan stories in *The X-Files* and *Highlander*, as well as essays on fanfiction in general ("The Advantages of Fan Fiction As An Art Form"). She published four novels professionally before discovering the world of fanfiction and was at once intoxicated by the possibilities. She's also a screenwriter and producer who has written for a number of television shows and enjoys creating canon as well as playing with it. She is based in L.A.

LullabyKnell is a fanfiction writer and fan artist in fandoms like *Star Wars*, Marvel, *Lord of the Rings* and Harry Potter; she is also in various anime fandoms. LullabyKnell posts art and fic snippets on Tumblr. She is 19 and lives in Canada.

Mollyamory has been in online fandom since *Highlander* was a big thing, and has written fiction and vidded in fandoms like *The Sentinel*, popslash, *Stargate: Atlantis*, *Supernatural*, and *Smallville*. She has also been an archivist, list admin, and community moderator. She games a lot and lives in Boston.

Pares, aka kormantic, fell off a cliff and into the ocean that was the X-files fandom in the heady days of 1997. Since then, she has written in many fandoms, contributed original work to several anthologies of short fiction, and helped edit a series of Choose Your Own Adventure Books for grown-ups [www.chooseomatic.com/online-previews/]. Should you visit her page at Archive of Our Own, you are encouraged to skip ahead to her ridiculous romantic comedies and to stick around for Yuletide. She lives in Seattle in the heart of a volcano.

Rheanna has written in numerous fandoms from *Angel* to *X-Men*. She's written het, gen, and slash though she thinks of herself as a gen girl at heart.

Jennet Smith has been, at times, an avid fanfiction reader, a dabbling fanfiction writer, a medievalist, a computer programmer, a veterinarian, and a geneticist. She currently writes about the science of dogs. She is a New England ex-pat who hopes to return home soon.

Speranza is a fan writer, vidder, community mod, and archivist. Her *Stargate: Atlantis* story "Written by the Victors" was one of the ten "classics" selected for Vulture.com's "Fanfiction Syllabus," and her *MCU* story "4 Minute Window" was recently recced on the Empire Film Podcast. Read an interview with her at thesecurioustimes.com.

Suitesamba discovered fanfiction through her children—she wrote some kid-friendly "what if" Star Wars fic for them and then wondered if other fans were doing something similar (they were!) She has degrees in Journalism and Spanish-language literature and now owns her own technical company. A prolific writer and reccer in Harry Potter fandom, she participates in many communities and fic-festivals. Her real life friends are a bit puzzled, but that's how things roll.

Yahtzee is a celebrated author in many, many fandoms and is also a best-selling novelist outside of fandom. She is probably best known for her stories in *Buffy the Vampire Slayer* and *X-Men*. Her AU Buffyverse novel *Phoenix Burning* is among the most frequently recced stories in fandom.

Printed and bound by CPI Group (UK) Ltd, Croydon, CR0 4YY

09/06/2025

14685645-0004